The Path to AGI

Artificial General Intelligence: Past, Present, and Future

John K. Thompson

Technics Publications
SEDONA, ARIZONA

TECHNICS PUBLICATIONS
TECHNOLOGY / LEADERSHIP

115 Linda Vista, Sedona, AZ 86336 USA

https://www.TechnicsPub.com

Edited by Sadie Hoberman
Cover design by Lorena Molinari

First Printing 2025

ISBN, print ed.	9781634627016 (paperback)
ISBN, print ed.	9781634627184 (hardcover)
ISBN, Kindle ed.	9781634627023
ISBN, PDF ed.	9781634627030

Life is fantastic. We live in a world of wonder and change. One of life's great joys is finding a partner who loves you, supports you, and shares the journey with you. My professional and personal journey has been anything but linear. Over the past 30 years, Jennifer has been there each and every day. I have taken risky jobs, communicated professional positions that were not mainstream, and undertaken projects that most people said were impossible. Jennifer has always been there to discuss, collaborate, question, and improve what I have put forward. She is brilliant. Thank you, Jennifer. This book is a product of an idea that you put forward so many years ago. I would have never written a book without your encouragement, love, and support. You are amazing. Thank you for all that you have created, shared, provided, and given me and our family.

Acknowledgments

I want to thank Joseph Pistrui, Joe Ray, Gary D. Carter, Pablo Cebro, Nicola Morini Bianzino, Zak Thompson, Kate Thompson, Dominick Shakeshaft, and Joann Vanderpoel.

No problem can be solved from the same level of consciousness that created it.

Albert Einstein

Contents

Introduction

This book, like all the books that I write, is meant to be a long-term reference guide. The books I write are meant to be read, put back on the shelf, and then periodically referred to over time to gain knowledge, perspective, perhaps a deeper understanding, and to align your views with the direction of travel of the topic and technology of interest.

This book focuses on the long-term evolutionary path of Artificial Intelligence (AI). That path is taking us from where we are today, leveraging and building Artificial Specific Intelligence (ASI), toward and to Artificial General Intelligence (AGI). Some people refer to AGI as Super Intelligence. I do not like that label. This book will refer to a higher level of non-human intelligence as AGI.

ASI helps us forecast how many people will buy a product at a specific price, supported by a type of marketing campaign, when the products are distributed in selected sales channels. Also, ASI helps us generate text, images, videos, code, and more based on simple prompts written in our natural language. And ASI is beginning to help us predict why people do what they do. ASI is used every day and it is surfaced through the three eras of AI—Foundational AI, Generative AI and Causal AI. Our world is becoming suffused with systems that are augmented with ASI functionality and capabilities.

As a field of technology, we have developed a substantial body of technology, tools, techniques, methodologies, approaches, and more in the broader field of AI over the last 70 years. The advances and advancements have been impressive, continuous, and very useful to society. To date, AI has been a technological success. AI has been a business success. Also, AI has been a success for humanity.

Most of the people in the world have heard about AI. This is mostly thanks to the GenAI wave that has washed over the world since 2022. While most people have heard of AI, they really do not understand much, if anything, about AI. This lack of knowledge presents an opportunity for those less interested in real technological progress and more interested in chicanery to have an opening to mislead people about where we are in achieving AGI on a widespread basis.

This book covers the real, practical, pragmatic journey needed to achieve AGI. AGI is not here now. AGI will not be here in the next three to five years. AGI won't be here in the lifetime of anyone reading this book. AGI is hard. AGI is a long way from where we are today. If you really want to know how we will arrive at AGI and when, then you will enjoy this book.

Let's start our discussion of the path or journey to AGI. Thank you for buying this book and joining me in this dialog. I very much appreciate your interest, engagement, and support.

Best,

John

CHAPTER 1

Data and the Foundations of the Four Eras of AI

For me, it feels slightly uncomfortable to say, but it is true; predicting what will happen is now the *easy* part.

When I started working in the field of data and analytics in 1988, the concept of consistently, confidently, and accurately predicting the detailed actions, activities, and outcomes related to people, systems, processes, and more were considered nearly impossible by the majority of technologists. Certainly, it was considered creepy, improbable, and nearly impossible to believe by the majority of people who were non-technologists (i.e., most of the world's population).

Most analytics professionals, and there were comparatively few of us in the late 1980s, felt that predicting what will happen was a fool's errand. To do so was a waste of time and something akin to a parlor trick.

The predominant mindset was that we, as technologists, were better off focusing on technology problems. Technology challenges include building a database for transactional processing, setting up a word processing center based on the new Wang word processing system, or connecting computer networks that actually worked, rather than working on data-oriented problems like those in analytics and prediction.

I recall working on computer networking problems for a significant amount of time from 1985 to 1987. What drudgery that was! In one instance, after 18 hours of plugging away at a networking problem, the system began to work. I still remember feeling completely exhausted and rather bored with it all. I did not feel joy in seeing that system come to life.

After thinking more about this specific instance, one of the ancillary factors that contributed to the intense feeling of dissatisfaction was that when I came to work the next day, I was not greeted with congratulations and accolades, which I expected. Instead, I was actually reprimanded. Why? Because my manager and his manager told me that I should have stayed even later to explain what I had done to one of my co-workers once the system was operational.

My main takeaway? Two levels of management had no idea what I had done, or how challenging it was, or where we stood on the evolutionary curve of technology. What did I learn from this experience?

Never propose, build, or support technology for managers or a company where the technology you are building is not core to the organizational mission.

Do not undertake the challenge to build technology for managers and companies that cannot and do not care to understand the complexity of the tasks to be undertaken. Doing so will likely be rewarded with indifference, indignation, or worse. At the time, I worked for a large international bank. No one cared about networking, telecommunications, data, or analytics. I was wasting my time, and eventually, two very kind executives told me as much, and I went on to a career in analytics.

I was, and still am, very good at diagnosing and fixing technology problems. Still, those early days of torturing nascent computer networks to connect and communicate were particularly soul-crushing for me. I really did not enjoy that type of work. There was no creativity or intelligence.

As we progress through our dialog of the Four Eras of AI on or way to discovering The Path to AGI, we will examine the role of core elements that are foundational to the construction, operation, and success of each era or area of AI and to the overall landscape of AI. In our discussion of the foundational concepts and technologies of AI, let's start with data.

What do we want? Data! When do we want it? Now!

Data—A prerequisite for analytics and all Four Eras of AI

Data is core and key to everything that we have done historically in the areas of business intelligence, analytics, advanced analytics, simulation, optimization, and AI. Data is the primary enabler of what we are doing today, and it will be core to what we will do in the future. Data is at the core of AI. It is one of the primary keys to success in all Four Eras of AI and, ultimately, the Path to AGI. Much has been written about data strategy, data engineering, and data management. Although these disciplines are foundational to obtaining, managing, and leveraging data effectively and efficiently, they are not the focus of this book. If you want to read about data management, I suggest you take a look at the book Fundamentals of Data Engineering: Plan and Build Robust Data Systems *by Joe Reis and Matt Housley.*[1]

---

[1] Fundamentals of Data Engineering: Plan and Build Robust Data Systems, 1st Edition by Joe Reis, Matt Housley, https://www.amazon.com/Fundamentals-Data-Engineering-Robust-Systems/dp/1098108302.

In relation to data, there are three core topics that I want to address.

Executive focus and awareness in relation to data

The first topic is the mindset common among business executives and senior managers. I have worked in companies in the US, Canada, Western Europe, Mexico, Brazil, Argentina, the Middle East, Australia, Singapore, and Japan. In all those countries and geographic areas, non-technical C-level executives (i.e., CEOs, COOs, CFOs, CROs, etc.) view data as a technological construct and issue. This is a myopic, short-sighted, and will limit the competitive advantage of any company led by the men and women who hold these views.

To determine if the leaders of these firms or any firm are data luddites, you only need to ask them. If they are data laggards, in most cases, they will proudly exclaim that data holds no interest for them, data is a technology issue and they have no time for thinking about such simple things as data. Find a new job in data science, AI, or advanced analytics if you hear the leaders talking about data in a way that it is not a strategic asset to be priced, proactively managed, and leveraged.

Most executive teams who inhabit the C-Suite will spend significant time and effort discussing the physical, financial, and operational planning of building a new factory, a distribution network, or a campus for a corporate headquarters. They will spend days, weeks, months, and in some cases, years planning for the requisite purchases and execution of these initiatives. They *should* take care and responsibility when considering and undertaking those projects. Still, those same teams will delegate, without much thought, the design, planning, and budgeting for the corporate data environment. Sometimes, it is delegated to the VP of IT to plan, build, and manage the data environment. In my opinion, this type of delegation borders on being irresponsible and illustrates a lack of understanding of where competitive advantage can be gained and where it can be sourced from.

> *Understanding, funding, planning, building, and operating the corporate data environment is a crucial element of the strategic success of any company.*

If this statement sounds dramatic to you, I am aware of that fact, but it is true. Corporate directors and officers need to spend more time planning for and funding the data ecosystems of the companies they are entrusted to manage and grow.

Data in corporate environments has only increased in value as AI technology has evolved and grown. With the advent and widespread use of Generative AI, *ALL* company data can be actively used and managed to provide value to every function of the company and to stakeholders and shareholders.

To be clear, up to about 2022, technologists and analytics professionals were routinely using about 10% of the data available to them. In 2024, analytics professionals and AI practitioners are leveraging 100% or more of the available data. This is because synthetic data enables us to derive new data and extend our data environments beyond naturally occurring data. We will talk about synthetic data as we develop our views and dialog around data.

Non-technical executives who are not actively investing in ways to proactively use all their data internally and are not considering how to license their data externally, are shirking their fiduciary duties and should be reprimanded for their lack of vision and engagement.

Let's now discuss how the majority of corporate data ecosystems are designed and managed.

Data strategy or what data to find, store, and keep

There is an entire industry of software, technology, and professional services vendors that build and maintain technologies that they want to sell to develop and manage corporate data ecosystems. Those vendors have much to offer and you should purchase what is needed to build and maintain your data environment. Also, there are industry analysts, pundits, and gurus who will tell you what they think you should be doing with your data environment, and it is good to listen to what they have to say. In my opinion, and it is an informed opinion, the following paragraph lays out all you need to know about your data strategy in relation to your success in building, operating, and growing the value of your analytic and AI systems.

> *You and your team should collect and manage every piece and source of data that you can—internal data, external data, open-source data, paid-for data, syndicated data, data from the US federal government, data from US State governments, data from all foreign governments, data from far-flung state and local governing bodies, survey data, transactional data, data from sensors, weather data, satellite data, geophysical data, logistics and shipping data, pricing data, stock market data, demographic data, biometric data, genetic data, psychological data, network performance data, financial and technology analysts commentary, all of it. Any data you can collect that is tangentially related to your business operations, employees, customers, partners, and more is worth collecting.*

And don't collect it just once, collect it each and every time a new piece of data is generated and collect it over time. If you and your team can see the value in the data, you should have a copy of it, store it, secure it, and build metadata that describes the data.

To restate and reiterate what I believe to be the basis of your data strategy and data operations—collect and keep data about EVERYTHING.

You should spend no time structuring or integrating the data. Collect all the data and store it in the form in which you find it. Label the data, describe the data, and keep it for all of time. Of course, you are not simply collecting or hoarding data. You are collecting data related to your current and future business interests.

For example, can you derive the price of what your competitors charge for products that are substitutes for your offerings? You should spend the time and energy to reverse engineer those price points for every competitive product and store those computed price points. You should collect and accurately compute every data element you can, store it, and keep it in perpetuity. If the data, real or computed, has a positive or negative impact on your business, you should collect or compute it.

Data retention and use policies

I hear the chorus of cries relating to data retention and use policies. Yes, of course, you will have to learn about data retention policies, and you will have to, more than likely, change the current data retention and usage policies of the firm. Policies are like roadmaps—they change. Change the relevant policies to state that you will be collecting and keeping data in such a manner. Policies need to reflect the known and planned operations of the business.

Policies need to communicate that a company complies with all of the relevant regulations. Policies should be clear, simple, and easy to read and understand. If you and your organization are collecting all data that is relevant today and you plan to collect and use all data that will be relevant in the future, say so. If there are use cases where you and the firms will use data that cannot be elucidated in detail, say so.

If, in writing the policies and reviewing operations, you find that you and the company are doing things that you shouldn't be doing, stop executing those activities. Document your findings and curtail the activities that are out of step with the current laws, regulations, and relevant policies.

Communicate the organizational view of data collection, data use, data privacy, consumer protection, data sharing, and more—be open, be clear, be transparent.

Communicate the use cases where you use the data today and the areas where you intend to use the data in the future. Plan to update the policies as you learn more about the data that will be collected, how that data will be retained, and how you intend to use that data. There is nothing wrong with doing this. This is what transparency, regular reviews, and change look like.

Consumers may or may not agree with what you are doing, and that is alright and to be expected. Customers, consumers, partners, and others will opt out. That is fine and should be planned for.

In the past, many companies were leery of being entirely transparent for many reasons, but one of those reasons was that their data operations and environments did not enable them to act on the expressed wishes of individuals and companies in relation to the data held documenting activities about customers, individuals, and partners. Still, with General

Data Protection Regulation (GDPR)[2] and the many other laws in effect, every company must honor the wishes of the companies and people they possess and leverage data from. If an individual wants to be forgotten, that instruction and direction must be honored.

Companies need to be transparent. Many of the laws and regulations that are in effect now and that will come into effect in the near future are related to ensuring that companies are transparent about activities that they are engaged in across all operational areas, including data operations and use cases that are in use today and those that can be reasonably anticipated in the near and far future.

From here forward, it is a new world in relation to data. Collect it, store it, manage it, react to demands from the market, and most of all, use data as a source of competitive advantage.

Managing data warehouse, data lakehouse, and operational data store data

The third and final general point related to data that I want to make is this: we have wasted an enormous amount of time and effort structuring data in ways that we *think* that people *might* want to review or use that data. What a colossal waste of time, and I should know, because I have spent decades designing, planning, executing, and directing this type of work.

About two decades ago, I was despondent that, from my perspective, much, if not all, of the work I had done was for naught. All that time structuring,

---

[2] GDPR defined, Council of the European Union, https://www.consilium.europa.eu/en/policies/data-protection/data-protection-regulation/#:~:text=The%20EU%20general%20data%20protection,may%20be%20processed%20and%20transferred. Cited December 19, 2023.

indexing, and aggregating data to ensure that end users could quickly access the right metrics and key performance indicators was a waste. Then I realized that it was not for nothing, that I was part of the movement of advancing the state of the art, and that I was moving the world forward to a more effective and efficient place in analyzing and understanding the world through data. I realized that we were on a journey and that all of the work that we had executed was needed to arrive at the new state of the art.

One of the most important epiphanies that came to me was the only time that we should be putting effort into refining and structuring data is when we are building a detailed and well-defined analytical or AI-based application that business professionals will use to achieve a defined business objective.

In previous eras, starting in the 1980s, we would build data warehouses where all the data was validated, structured, and indexed in a very specific way to ensure that when an exceedingly well-defined query was asked, the system would quickly produce an answer that was always 100% correct and delivered to the requestor in less than a second.

We worked diligently to gather and structure the data for an excruciatingly small number of queries or requirements. It may have taken months, if not years, to build the data backend to support this small number of users and to satisfy their limited requirements and specific interests. We built many systems for Consumer Packaged Goods (CPG) companies that examined how products were manufactured, priced, distributed, and sold. Still, if you asked the system how a specific distribution channel performed, the system did not have the right information structured correctly to answer that question. That is, if a slightly different query was asked, either the system would slow to a crawl, produce an unsatisfactory answer, or just error out. Clearly, the effort was not worth the result.

We moved on from that approach to the reasonably current approach, where we spent less time structuring and validating data and more time collecting data. This was a step in the right direction, but we continued to build brittle systems optimized to answer a very small number of exceedingly well-defined queries.

The approach that works well is to collect all the data you can get your hands on and then store it, label it, and describe it. Define applications that will drive significant value. Structure and integrate all the data related to that business and operational area for that specific application and operational area. Build AI-based applications that produce probabilistic results and analytical systems that produce deterministic results. Combine those outputs to provide business insights in real time, at the right time, for the right people, on an on-demand basis without needing support from the analytics team. That is a winning and cost-effective approach.

We have defined the overall data-related foundational views and concepts. Now, let's move on to talking about the data itself.

How not to request and obtain data

In the late 1980s and the early 1990s, analytics professionals had difficulty finding, understanding, accessing, obtaining, buying, collecting, integrating, and managing data.

In those days, most requests for data were from a singular internal system. Most requests sounded like this: We need the data related to a product line shipped from all factories in the United Kingdom (UK) for the calendar year of 1989. Once we have obtained and reviewed the data related to shipments of the specific product in the UK, we will ask for all the data relating to all products shipped in the UK. Then, we would ask for all the marketing data relating to all the marketing campaigns launched and managed in the UK for all of 1989. Then, we would ask for all the pricing data related to products shipped to the grocery store channel in the UK in 1989, and then we would ask for all the data about products returned from all grocery stores in the UK in 1989. You get the picture.

When we started the process, we were attempting to improve our understanding of the products that were manufactured and shipped, and we moved out from there, continually requesting more and more data until we reached the natural end of the data ecosystem. This way of operating meant that we rarely, if ever, got to the natural end of the data ecosystem.

To be fair to the people in IT who were providing data to the analytics team, we must have seemed to be exceedingly annoying, and, in the beginning, they told us as much. We were, and still are, always asking for more data. We were not very efficient in our requests. Ultimately, we either ran out of time or funding, or the IT department would simply stop providing data to us. In a macro sense, there are elements of this data dynamic that have not changed in the intervening decades.

In 1988, I worked with a very talented IT professional. During the project, as I continually expanded the data requests, he would develop the code, obtain the data, and make the extracts available to me. He was the first to kindly explain that I should start with the end in mind rather than finding my way aimlessly toward gathering all the data needed for the broader understanding of the process, products, or ecosystem I was trying to understand. He showed me a better way, and I am grateful for his guidance.

Over the past 35 years, not much has changed in the process of obtaining the data needed for analytics and AI. For example, recently, at my direction and guidance, one of my project teams was asking a team in the Information Technology (IT) department to dump all the data from a database underlying an internal system and provide the extract to our advanced analytics team. The response continually came back as, "Tell us exactly what records you want, and we will provide them." I had to meet with the VP of IT and explain that we had asked for exactly what we wanted. We wanted *all* the data. The VP of IT asked me why we would want all the data. I had to explain further that we wanted to analyze and predict an aspect of our operations and that we needed all the data in the system to do so. She looked at me with complete puzzlement.

We had to meet with the Chief Data Officer to discuss the request. Finally, we obtained the data and could move on, but I have seen this in IT departments and IT leadership many times. The IT mindset is not based on governance, data protection, or risk management. Mostly, it is based on the view of work avoidance. The IT staff simply does not want to provide the data.

I have described a process that is iterative and grows in scope. By the time you have obtained, loaded, cleaned, structured, integrated, and examined the data, you then realize that you need an additional set of data to get to where you need to be analytically. So, you request the new data, and you realize that the new data you will request will not align with the existing data you have, and you need an update of the previously requested data along with the new data that you just realized that you now need.

In addition, each time you expand the request to include all the data you need, all the previous related requests need to be executed again to update all the data elements.

Requesting data once is a recipe for frustration for everyone involved.

What should you do?

My approach, and it has been very successful, is to explain to the IT team, the analytics team, the business sponsors, and the executives involved that if the analytics team requests data, we should treat that request, and every request, as an on-going requirement an extension of all the requests that came before. An ongoing requirement will need to be executed every time the data being provided is updated. I always tell my analytics teams that if you request data once, you will request it on an ongoing, repeated, and scheduled basis. In that case, every request should be set up on an automated, routine schedule in a unified workflow that is executed each time the requested data is required.

No set of data or data elements are static, or at least very few data elements or data sets are static. Most data lives in the context of time or the context of a larger set of data, process, company, or country. The majority of data grows with time and context. Keep this in mind when thinking about the data you will need.

Let's move on to discuss the lifecycle of data and what the update or refresh cycle of data means to the process of obtaining data for analytics purposes.

The update cycle of data

All data has a natural update cycle. Some data is updated each time a transaction is executed. Other data is updated every millisecond, hourly, daily, weekly, monthly, quarterly, semiannually, annually, or maybe even longer time frames.

In most cases, the analytics team needs the data to be refreshed or updated after an update cycle. In most cases, real-time data is not required for analytics. In the majority of cases, the analytics team needs to look at when an update to the data makes the overall data set more useful and valuable to the end users and hence, the analytic results should be updated. The update cycle of the source data should drive when an extract is scheduled and updated data is delivered to the analytics team on an automated basis.

To be clear, automating the data acquisition process is a good start, and doing so removes many obstacles to building analytical applications, but the data should also be stored in a form and environment that is accessible and usable by all analytics professionals, or at least the data catalog describing the data should be accessible.

This approach to data achieves multiple goals:

- The work of providing the data is automated. No one has to manually pull/provide data.
- Once the data pull and provisioning process is automated, it is standardized.
- The data for analytics grows over time and accumulates in value.
- The data is available all the time to the analytics team.
- New data is integrated easily.
- The integrated ensemble of data provides the basis for new and novel analytics.
- When data is ready to use and easily accessible, more analytics will be requested and built.

As an example of the benefit of implementing the process outlined, when we implemented this process at a large multinational company, we found that most of the end users would come to the advanced analytics team with their requests, and not just requests for forecasting, simulation, and optimization. That is, their requests included the areas of advanced analytics and AI—they came to this group for every request for data, information, and insights. We asked them why they came to us and not to the teams that were supposed to support the end users with reporting, business intelligence, and other routine requests for data and information. We found out that we turned requests around in about 24 to 48 hours. The other teams took days or maybe weeks to produce the requested insights. We could do this because all the data was updated each hour, and the data was already integrated. We just had to develop the answers and provide them to the requestor. Building your data analytical data environment in this manner just makes sense.

Up to this point in our discussion of data, we have been focusing on and discussing data in general. We have been discussing the strategic, foundational, and operational considerations that apply to all data. Let's start by breaking down our discussion of data to examine the different types of data that we will use in our analytical and AI work.

With the advent and use of Generative AI, we need to talk about the types of data. We will not get down into technical details of the size of integers and whether data is floating point notation or other low-level data considerations.

We really just need to discern between two main types of data—structured data which is numbers of all types, and unstructured data, which is language of all types. Simple, but necessary given the change that the world has experienced since 2023 with the widespread use of Generative AI.

Structured data

Structured data is data used in computing since the invention of counting and record keeping. Structured data is the cornerstone of all computing—manual or electronic. It doesn't matter if you are using an abacus or a computer, you are using structured data.

Structured data is referred to as tabular, numerical, or numeric data. Structured data is often stored in databases and spreadsheets and displayed in dashboards and a wide range of data visualizations. When we learn about arithmetic and math in elementary or primary school, we generally learn using structured data.

Structured data has been the focus of the vast majority of science and computing. Most systems built by civilizations and companies up to this point have been focused on counting and record keeping and have been based on structured data. Archeologists have found evidence of humans using structured data for over 20,000 years.

Figure 1: This tablet has an account in Sumerian cuneiform describing the receipt of oxen. [3]

We use structured data in a ubiquitous manner. It may seem to many that structured data is the only data. Data comes in many forms. Structured data

---

[3] BBC online, Tim Harford, How the world's first accountants counted on cuneiform, Published 12 June 2017, https://www.bbc.com/news/business-39870485, Cited December 18, 2023.

is all around us and pervades almost every aspect of daily life. As such, it is a critical element of daily operations and how we conduct exchanges and transactions, but structured data is only part of our world.

Unstructured data

Unstructured data is language, video, images, and audio and does not include structured data. Unstructured data is text for the most part, but we should also include images, video, and graphics in the definition of unstructured data. Let's focus mainly on text as the basis of the majority of our initial discussion of unstructured data. Once we master working with text data, the other forms of unstructured data are much easier to understand and work with. To be clear, unstructured data can and does include numbers, either as numeric characters or in written language, but in unstructured data, the numbers are a descriptive part of the body. They are not the majority of the content.

In the commercial world of analytics, unstructured data has been largely ignored until very recently.

In the commercial teams I have managed, we started working with language models in 2020. We were trying to understand language in relation to applications in the biopharmaceutical industry. Our focus was early models like Bidirectional Encoder Representations from Transformers (BERT)[4] and A Robustly Optimized BERT Pretraining Approach (RoBERTa).[5]

[4] Wikipedia, BERT, https://en.wikipedia.org/wiki/BERT_(language_model), Cited December 19, 2023.

[5] Arxiv, RoBERTa, RoBERTa: A Robustly Optimized BERT Pretraining Approach, https://arxiv.org/abs/1907.11692, Cited December 19, 2023.

We found these language models very useful and quite good at determining sentiment, organizing new articles, and providing an early alert to signals that we might be interested in knowing.

The impetus for our work was that a competitor had leapfrogged ahead of our company and the market in general, by announcing a new innovation that surprised most firms with the timing of the announcement. The innovation was widely expected, and that it had come to the commercial market was not surprising. Still, the announcement and innovation timing was at least a year earlier than most informed industry participants had expected and projected. The executives were unaware of the other firm's progress—never underestimate the motivating power of embarrassment.

The inquiry came to my group in a rather ambiguous request. The request was something along the lines of, can we understand the state of the market of all our competitors and the progress each of them is making in each project they are actively undertaking and have made in the last calendar year? We asked a number of clarifying questions and began to work. Once I had replied that we probably could do it, the request became a directive to work on the project.

In the areas of forecasting and predicting performance of operational areas, we were well versed in using a wide range of models on structured data to predict how well our operations would miss, meet, or exceed performance targets. We had been executing this type of work for decades, but working with language models and text files was a relatively new area for us.

Initially, we used both BERT and RoBERTa models. We selected BERT for this project. We gathered a wide range of public and private sources of unstructured relevant information. We built an application that tracked multiple companies and all their relevant projects from information in news releases, public filings, information we had in our competitive intelligence systems, information we could buy, information from the

Federal Drug Administration (FDA) and the Security and Exchange Commission (SEC), and more. After about six months, we delivered version 1 of the application to the competitive intelligence team. The application was successful, and we learned a lot about collecting, cleaning, integrating, and analyzing unstructured information.

Personally, I found it challenging to assign some of the more experienced staff work with these new models. It took a significant amount of time and effort to convince the senior staff that this new area was worth their time and energy to learn and engage in. It was much easier to ask the younger staff members to work on language models with text. The younger staff members were curious, interested and jumped at the chance to do work in this area. If you are interested in the topic of the dynamics of building and managing a high-performance analytics team, including whom to assign work to, I suggest you read my 2nd book, Building Analytics Teams.[6]

Let's talk about internal data.

Internal data

Internal data is data in the internal systems that supports the daily, weekly, quarterly, and annual processes that keep companies moving forward. Internal data is data that companies own and manage on a daily basis.

Internal data is data related to the operational areas of a company and resides in systems that support the running of those functional areas: finance, manufacturing, supply chain, pricing, marketing, discounting,

---

[6] Thompson, John K., Building Analytics Teams, Packt - https://www.amazon.com/Building-Analytics-Teams-intelligence-improvement/dp/1800203160/ref=cm_cr_arp_d_product_top?ie=UTF8, Cited December 19, 2023.

design, advertising, outsourcing, product development, product management, compliance, innovation, competitive intelligence, sustainability management, human resources, external talent management, legal, and more.

In a previous example, I was careful to only talk about data related to products, such as shipments, marketing programs, returns, and pricing. Most analytics professionals and IT staff limit their thinking to a small number of systems and data sources. This mindset has held analytics back and limited the value derived from data and analytics.

For analytics of all types, especially AI, to be as valuable as it can be, we need all the data related to a phenomenon that we are attempting to analyze and understand. Without all the related data, we cannot accurately make predictions.

Not to get too technical in data management, but it is worth noting that beyond access, you and your team should obtain and maintain a copy of all the data you require and need for current and future analytics. I can hear the IT managers and executives howling that making and maintaining copies of data sets, databases, and files is wasteful. It may cost money to do so, but it is worth the cost/investment.

Those copies and repositories are a source of competitive advantage and future revenue. When the AI team is running applications that pass over the data millions if not billions of times a minute, a source system running a core operational area will run slowly if not completely crash due to the additional workload put on them by the analytics and AI applications.

Believe me, the IT team will be happy that the analytics team has its own data and systems. The key is to ensure that you have the budget to fund the building and maintenance of those environments.

External data—Literally all the data in the world

External data is data that is either outside the company on the public internet or has been created and maintained by another organization for free and unfettered access, open-source access, commercial fee-based access, or some other form of hybrid access. We have access to a wealth of data in a wide range of formats and commercial forms, and much of that data is available at a cost that we can afford if the value is there for our predictive models or systems.

When I am talking about external data, I mean ALL data. All data from federal, state, and local governments, all not-for-profit organizations, all for-profit organizations, and all data relating to human activities, such as farming, construction, airline schedules, famines, rainfall, building types, roads, weather, satellite launches, births, deaths, the occurrence and incidence of mental health in the global population and all subpopulations, hospital admissions, genomic information, knowledge of the respiratory system, knowledge of the composition of blood, the Earth's orbital patterns since the beginning of time and the predicted orbital patterns into the knowable future, incidents of shoplifting, immigration, the distance of all stars from Earth, miles driven by all cars, ocean temperature, number of mobile telephones in use at any one time, snowfall, carbon sequestration, number of active church attendees, social policies related to equity, size of lithium deposits on Earth and in celestial bodies. The list could go on and on and fill thousands of pages of this book or any other book.

The list is not infinite. We know all the things we know about and the areas where we might propose data for phenomena we want to understand. It is quite a long list, and it may seem infinite, but given the universe of known data, the list is, ultimately, finite.

I am making a point that listing all the data sources to be considered and used can be illustrative but not very useful in a practical sense. The point to take away from this portion of our discussion is that ALL data in the world is of interest to us and all data can now be used in a practical, efficient, and effective way to make models which predict, simulate, optimize, and generate new content for us that is highly accurate, relevant, and useful for all applications and use cases.

Data makes models possible. "Good data makes models interesting."[7]

Do not limit your thinking about the types of data to be used or how to combine data into new hybrid data sets. When you really start thinking about what data can be integrated into a new training data set, the list becomes infinite. There is no end to the new data that can be created from the existing data sets of naturally occurring data.

For all practical purposes, data is infinite. Data becomes infinite when you think about combining internal and external sources. When you integrate data, you create new data. New data can be created from any combination of data sources at the macro and micro senses. If you are interested in data in general, please consider buying and reading my third book, Data for All.[8]

External naturally-occurring data is a great starting point for building powerful models. Combining internally generated data with external data is like rocket fuel for models. Still, we face increasing limitations from governments, including regulators, legislators, watchdog groups, policy-making organizations, and more. These limitations are a good thing. As an

---

[7] Joseph Pistrui, LinkedIn, https://www.linkedin.com/feed/update/urn:li:activity:7143579626127114240/, Comment made on December 21, 2023. Cited December 22, 2023.

[8] Thompson, John K, Data for All, Manning, 2023 - https://www.amazon.com/Data-All-John-K-Thompson/dp/1633438775.

analytics thought leader, innovator, and practitioner, why would I advocate or support limitations on data use?

Decades ago, when starting in the analytics field, I would bristle at the idea that limitations would be put on our use of data. I would argue that the people who would limit the use of data and analytics had no idea of what they were trying to constrain. The industry was small, and for the most part, analytics professionals were interested in understanding the performance of companies, processes, factories, sales, marketing, and similar activities. There was little interest in nefarious uses of data and analytics.

Today, the analytics industry is global, widespread, and ubiquitous. Data is everywhere, and the tools to examine, model, and predict all sorts of actions and activities are very powerful. We need regulations and limitations on what can be done with naturally occurring data. These frameworks, guidelines, policies, and laws are very good things, and we need more policies and regulations, and we need them as soon as they can be practically drafted and passed into law.

Regulation is one avenue to protect the rights of individuals and I support developing more laws, policies, and regulations directly relating to naturally occurring data.

Technology and innovation provide other paths to protection. Synthetic data is an innovation growing quickly and provides powerful protection for naturally occurring data. Synthetic data can be generated from scratch and has no connection to naturally occurring data. As such, synthetic data provides a way to have all the data we need to design, develop, and train almost any model we can conceive without impinging on any individual's rights.

Synthetic data

The world of naturally occurring data is no longer a roadblock to our projects, our progress, and to the requirement for new and different data. If we don't have access to data we can afford or are limited by regulation or law to obtaining and leveraging naturally occurring data, we can create our own data through Synthetic Data Generation (SDG). Synthetic data can and does have all the characteristics of natural data, but it is not connected to any real person, activity, company, or operation.

SDG can start with no data other than describing the data we want and need. For this to be the case, we must understand the data we want to create. We need to describe the data distribution within each data element (i.e., columns and rows of numbers) and define all the relationships between the data elements. These definitions are not hard to define, but detail-oriented work needs to be done to derive a dataset that is descriptive of the real world but devoid of any actual connection to the real world. Again, we are only limited by our imagination and detailed understanding of the data we want to generate.

SDG can start with sample data as well. Starting with sample data is a great way to get your project moving in the right direction. Through techniques like differential privacy,[9] the data generated has no connection to the naturally occurring data that was used as a sample. The only practical roadblock we have encountered in generating synthetic data from a sample of naturally occurring data is proving to the more conservative project team members that reverse engineering a connection from the synthetic data to the naturally occurring sample data is impossible. This is not a technical problem. It is a problem of knowledge and understanding, which, as we all

---

[9] Differential Privacy, IEEE Digital Privacy, https://digitalprivacy.ieee.org/publications/topics/what-is-differential-privacy.

know, will lessen over time and completely disappear in the foreseeable future.

Beyond removing the roadblock of being unable to obtain the representative data we need to begin our projects, SDG holds a very real benefit for the widespread development of analytics and AI applications. That benefit is the ability to counter bias.

Synthetic data can be of any form and distribution we want or need. Let's say you are working with a data set with historical bias by not having a representative number of women in the naturally occurring data set. Not a problem. You can go back in time if you are using a past historical window, analyze what the correct proportion of women would be in the relevant general population or subpopulation, analyze the relevant characteristics of the women that should be in the dataset, and generate the new data, integrate the new data into the historical data set. You have a new dataset that addresses the historical bias of not enough women in the analysis. This is an awesome new and practical way to address bias in data.

The new and very real limitation of this approach is that people have difficulty agreeing on what is fair and what is representative. One person's basis for bias is another person's view of fairness and/or the representative way the world should be. That is a debate that cannot be addressed in data.

One way that you could address the issue is to gather all the participants together, have each person or group define what they think is fair and generate all the data that addresses each scenario, execute the analysis including each set of data in a simulation and then run an optimization analysis to determine which scenario generates the greatest good. It is not that hard to do, but it takes time, effort, patience, and resources.

Another benefit of synthetic data is creating derivative data. As noted, naturally occurring data can be integrated in nearly unlimited ways to create new data. We are creating new data by simply integrating naturally occurring data, but that data still has its roots in naturally occurring data. If we take the original data or the newly integrated data and create synthetic derivative data, we now have new data that has no connection to the real or natural world. And we can create as much synthetic data as we want. Hence, there is no limit to the amount of tailored and specific data that we can create and use without limitation.

We can create synthetic data for any application, problem, operation, or anything real or imagined. Real or natural data and synthetic data can be combined in any way you can conceive.

In summary, if you are in the business of delivering business value through data, analytics, and AI (and we all are in that business), this section has described how you should set up your data strategy and ecosystem. You are not collecting data for a project. Well, you are, but the bigger point is that you are missing an opportunity if you only look at data acquisition as a project-based task. You should be looking at data acquisition as a process of accumulating a strategic asset. Data acquisition is a strategic opportunity to drive value. Do not miss it.

Why all this data?

Why are we interested in such a wide range of diverse data? All models leverage data. All models are trained on data. All models generate scores, predictions, content, and more from data. We have learned that models built with a relevant ensemble of diverse data perform better than those trained on a more narrow and shallow data set.

Generative AI has proven that we can build models that produce results and align with what we expect from human behavior. To be clear, GenAI is not Artificial General Intelligence (AGI). In my opinion, it is nowhere near AGI. Still, GenAI results and outputs do appear to be in line with many operations that, until the past couple of years, have only been the purview of human activity. GenAI emphatically puts a fine point on the premise that large amounts of diverse data makes a significant improvement in the abilities of models to serve wider and wider sets of activities and purposes.

In my opinion, GenAI is most definitely a general-purpose technology. General-purpose technologies are technologies that can affect the entire global economy. Archetypal examples of general-purpose technologies are the steam engine, electricity, the automobile, the computer, and the Internet.[10] GenAI has changed how nearly everyone views technology, education, commercial offerings, application development, writing code, customer service, operational efficiency, and many more areas.

Models and applications should approximate how humans make decisions.

Humans make decisions in split seconds leveraging a wide range of data that comes to us from our internal state and from our five senses. Most of us do not think about the fact that we use a plethora of data to make nearly every decision, but we do.

Let's discuss how each of us feels when our bodies signal that we might be hungry. When you realize that you are hungry, something that we all do multiple times each day, the sensation comes to us from our gastrointestinal system. The first thing I check when I realize that sensation is to see if I have

[10] Wikipedia, General Purpose Technology defined, https://en.wikipedia.org/wiki/General-purpose_technology, Cited December 20, 2023.

been drinking enough water. Am I really hungry, or am I just experiencing the first signs of dehydration? I then begin to check outside my body. What time is it? Is it close to a traditionally agreed-upon mealtime? If I am outside my home, am I close to a restaurant I might want to visit? Are there leftovers I might want to eat if I am in my house? What am I hungry for? And the questions and the internal and external data leveraged continue until I eat or drink.

Checking all these internal and external data sources takes seconds, and most of us take the process for granted without examination. But for models to serve people in a way that those models are accepted and trusted as part of our daily lives, models have to have access to all the data that we have access to, and maybe even more. Hence, models need to be trained on a wide range of relevant data to supply humans with results, predictions, and outputs that we trust and use as part of our daily lives at home and work. When processes seem natural to us, we find those processes easier to understand, adopt, and assimilate into our daily lives.

A wide range of diverse data is a prerequisite for all models to operate so that they are seen as relevant, useful, trusted, and adopted by most people in the world.

I have noted this fact a few times in our discussion, but I want to be overt about the role multiple sources of integrated data play in the effectiveness and efficiency of models of all types. Many people think that GenAI is some sort of unknowable magic, which is far from the truth.

One of the breakthroughs of GenAI is the development of the ability to train very large models on the breadth and depth of all human knowledge and activity relatively quickly and easily. GenAI is the innovation that makes ingesting and using all the electronic data in the world practical for training all models. It is not the size of the models, although that is a critical fact, that makes GenAI so useful and impactful in such an impressive range of applications and areas. The efficient and effective use of data of all types and data sources from all areas of human endeavor makes GenAI so powerful and useful. Leveraging data from all the available sources *is* the magic.

For years, I have been saying that using data from many sources is the key to the ubiquitous development, deployment, and adoption of models on a society-wide basis. I have been absolutely correct in that assertion, but I had little to no idea that it would come from using unstructured data. But when you stop and think about it, it has to be this way. If we are to leverage all data, we would have to include unstructured data. In hindsight, it seems obvious and logical, but don't many radical innovations seem that way in retrospect?

I believe that for any models to approximate how humans obtain, analyze, assess, and act, those models need access to all the data that any human would leverage in making a similar decision.

Models probably, actually, need more data than people do when making decisions that are aligned with how humans make decisions. For models to even begin to approximate human-level capabilities, or AGI, access to a large and diverse amount of data will be required. We are many years away from this being the case.

Change is the constant

Let's move back to the late 1980s. Even if we could collect the data, our computers were small, slow, and not well networked to other computers, and most computers were not connected to the outside world. At this point, the internet was still a US governmental project at the Defense Advanced Research Projects Agency (DARPA).[11]

I remember feeling joy and excitement when I finally convinced my manager to allow me to buy a new IBM Personal Computer (PC) with this wildly expensive new enhancement, a permanent hard drive. No more flipping floppy discs back and forth and hoping that you did not completely fill or overflow the memory in your PC before you got everything loaded needed to run your workload.

When looking back, given all of the technology, data, and conceptual roadblocks, it is not hard to see why most people didn't see the value in taking the next steps toward predicting what would happen, but that was 38 years ago.

All the elements of predictive systems: technology, math, data, connectivity, system ubiquity, system size, memory size and usage, performance, and numerous other factors have grown, evolved, integrated, and changed in ways that not many could have imagined or predicted.

Since beginning in the analytics and AI field, I have built and implemented analytical applications in 21 industries globally. I have personally built and led teams who have implemented over 100 advanced analytics and AI

---

[11] DARPA. Wikipedia, https://en.wikipedia.org/wiki/DARPA. Also see - https://www.darpa.mil/ Cited November 24, 2023.

systems. We have proven that we can build systems that predict nearly anything you can imagine.

Now, we predict all kinds of action, activities, and metrics without a second thought. And what is even more mind-boggling is that the business professionals we work with accept and use these predictions without an in-depth debate or real discussion.

Predicting the *what* of the future is now commonplace and, in many cases, expected and demanded.

Post-determinism and probability

We have reached the era of probability. We have moved past a world ruled by determinism, at least with AI.

Remember your statistics classes in undergraduate school? If you understood what the professors were yarning on and on about, this new world would make perfect sense. This is a difficult point for most people to grasp and understand. For the majority of history, computing systems and applications were built in a deterministic manner. Arithmetic and processes were always the same. With a determined set of inputs, the outputs were always the same; 1+1 always equals 2.

AI has never been this way. Up to now, we have treated the outputs of models this way. In many cases, the results were close and reliable enough that we never really had to explain the difference between determinism and probability, but now we do.

The advent of and widespread use of GenAI has cracked this issue wide open. In 2023, we built and deployed the world's largest, private, secure

GenAI environment. We have hundreds of thousands of people using the system. Given the size of the population of people using the system, a subset of those users is going to experiment and begin to ask questions. Questions like: "I put in the same prompt multiple times and the answer or response is slightly different each time. Why is that?" This is because the model powering the system is a probabilistic model. It is predicting what is the right answer. It is not computing the right answer from a predetermined set of codes or rules. It reviews the input, compares that input to the relevant subset of all the weights in the billions of nodes in the model, and predicts the answer that matches the highest probability of being the correct or expected answer. Variations will happen. That is a hard lesson for a subset of the user population, especially for non-technical executives.

But this is where we are in our evolution of systems, applications, solutions, and AI. There is no going back. From here forward, we will always have a mix of deterministic and probabilistic systems. And the majority of systems built and deployed in the future will be probability-based.

Welcome to the post-deterministic world.

Summary

We are off on our journey. We have discussed and described the data foundations of AI. You now have a basic understanding of the data available to us, what we can do with that data and what the basic shape of the future looks like from the data perspective. Why do I spend so much time talking about data? Data is the foundation of everything we will discuss from here forward, and I wanted you to have a solid understanding before we jump into the Four Eras of AI and ultimately into The Path of AGI.

Let's move on in our discussion on Foundational AI (FAI).

CHAPTER 2

The History of Foundational AI

The term Artificial Intelligence (AI) was coined at the now famous Dartmouth Summer Research Project on AI in 1956. The initial meeting was organized by John McCarthy, then an associate professor of mathematics at Dartmouth. In his proposal, he stated that the conference was "to proceed based on the conjecture that every aspect of learning or any other feature of intelligence can, in principle, be so precisely described that a machine can be made to simulate it."[12]

One of the primary reasons for the proposal of the two-month summer workshop was that the organizers had been calling for proposals to develop a new type of computer system to illustrate and demonstrate practical applications of intelligence. Most of the submissions were focused on prototypes of automata, systems that were implementations of automating existing processes.

In the 1950s, automata were widely viewed as a simple automation of process steps, predominately by rule-based systems. Most of the systems were implemented on electro-mechanical systems that were not computer-

---

[12] Dartmouth College website, Artificial Intelligence Coined at Dartmouth, https://home.dartmouth.edu/about/artificial-intelligence-ai-coined-dartmouth, Cited on December 23, 2023.

based. The organizers of the summer project felt that there was much to learn from bringing together a set of leading thinkers to focus on the questions of leveraging computers and building a new type of intelligence. John McCarthy referred to the developing area of focus, or topic as Artificial Intelligence (AI).

The organizers of the summer project and other leading researchers offered their thoughts and views on where the field of automata could go next and what the promise of intelligent systems was in the journal, Automata Studies. (AM-34).[13] The consensus of the 13 authors was that not only was automation possible, but systems could learn in an incremental and automated manner, and those systems could interact with the physical world to change outcomes. In 1956, these were radically new ideas. Claude Shannon,[14] one of the primary organizers, offered this objective for the workshop, "Often in discussing mechanized intelligence, we think of machines performing the most advanced human thought activities—proving theorems, writing music, or playing chess."[15]

The workshop was held, but it did not live up to McCarthy's expectations. He was disappointed that most of the participants only came for a few days and only a small number were in attendance for the entire six weeks. His

[13] Automata Studies. (AM-34), C. E. Shannon, J. McCarthy, W. R. ASHBY, J. T. CULBERTSON, M. D. DAVIS, S. C. KLEENE, K. DE LEEUW, D. M. MAC KAY, J. MC CARTHY, M. L. MINSKY, E. F. MOORE, C. E. SHANNON, N. SHAPIRO, A. M. UTTLEY, J. VON NEUMANN, Series: Annals of Mathematics Studies, 1956, Princeton University Press, Pages: 285, https://www.jstor.org/stable/j.ctt1bgzb3s, Cited December 24, 2023.

[14] Encyclopedia Britannica Online, Claude Shannon, Biography, https://www.britannica.com/biography/Claude-Shannon, Cited December 24, 2023.

[15] J. McCarthy, A PROPOSAL FOR THE DARTMOUTH SUMMER RESEARCH PROJECT ON ARTIFICIAL INTELLIGENCE, http://jmc.stanford.edu/articles/dartmouth/dartmouth.pdf, Cited on December 24, 2023.

assessment was, "Anybody who was there was pretty stubborn about pursuing the ideas that he had before he came, nor was there, as far as I could see, any real exchange of ideas. People came for different periods. The idea was that everyone would agree to come for six weeks, and the people came for periods ranging from two days to the whole six weeks, so not everybody was there at once. It was a great disappointment to me because it really meant that we couldn't have regular meetings."[16]

The initial disappointment for McCarthy was real, but the lasting impact of the underlying principles that were set forth and codified to guide the meeting are still being felt today.

Marvin Minsky wrote the following in his research section of the initial proposal, "It is not difficult to design a machine which exhibits the following type of learning. The machine is provided with input and output channels and an internal means of providing varied output responses to inputs so that the machine may be 'trained' by a 'trial and error' process to acquire one of a range of input-output functions. Such a machine, when placed in an appropriate environment and given a criterion of 'success' or 'failure' can be trained to exhibit 'goal-seeking' behavior."

Unless the machine can develop a way of abstracting sensory material, it can progress through a complicated environment only through painfully slow steps. Generally, it will not reach a high level of behavior.

Now, let the criterion of success be not merely the appearance of a desired activity pattern at the output channel of the machine, but rather the performance of a given manipulation in a given environment. Then, in certain ways, the motor situation appears to be a dual of the sensory situation, and progress can be reasonably fast only if the machine is equally

---

[16] Ibid, Claude Shannon's section on his research focus for the summer project., Cited on December 24, 2023.

capable of assembling an ensemble of "motor abstractions" relating its output activity to changes in the environment. Such "motor abstractions" can be valuable only if they relate to changes in the environment, which can be detected by the machine as changes in the sensory situation, i.e., if they are related, through the structure of the environment, to the sensory abstractions that the machine is using.[17]

What collective authors wrote in 1956 outlines the primary objectives of nearly all AI systems since. In short, this is the design brief for the entire industry involved in designing research programs and developing AI technologies, systems, and software for the past 69 years.

In my opinion, the elements that make Minsky's description of a learning system so prescient is that he includes not only learning but learning at high-performance rates. He includes the ability of the system to interact with the external world or other systems to drive practical and actual changes.

Nathaniel (Nat) Rochester[18] extended the learning concept to include the machine having intuition or adding randomness to the operations to ensure that the machine or programming did not "follow this set of rules slavishly and to exhibit no originality or common sense".[19]

---

[17] Jørgen Veisdal, The Birthplace of AI, The 1956 Dartmouth Workshop, Cantor's Paradise, Sep 12, 2019, https://www.cantorsparadise.com/the-birthplace-of-ai-9ab7d4e5fb00, Cited December 24, 2023.

[18] Nathaniel Rochester, https://en.wikipedia.org/wiki/Nathaniel_Rochester_(computer_scientist), Cited on December 24, 2023.

[19] J. McCarthy, A PROPOSAL FOR THE DARTMOUTH SUMMER RESEARCH PROJECT ON ARTIFICIAL INTELLIGENCE,

Shannon added the ability of machines or programming to build over time to learn and to progress from the simple to the abstract and complex to build ensembles of learning components. His description was, "I am proposing here to start at the simple and when the environment is neither hostile (merely indifferent) nor complex, and to work up through a series of easy stages in the direction of these advanced activities."[20]

To add to the already immense value ensconced in the original proposal for the summer project, Rochester added a process whereby intelligent systems could operate. The following steps were offered…thus the solution of a problem which one already understands is done as follows:

1. The environment provides data from which certain abstractions are formed.
2. The abstractions together with certain internal habits or drives provide:
    2.1. A definition of a problem in terms of desired condition to be achieved in the future, a goal.
    2.2. A suggested action to solve the problem.
    2.3. Stimulation to arouse in the brain the engine which corresponds to this situation.
3. Then the engine operates to predict what this environmental situation and the proposed reaction will lead to.

---

http://jmc.stanford.edu/articles/dartmouth/dartmouth.pdf, Cited on December 24, 2023. Marvin Minsky's section on his research focus for the summer project., Cited on December 24, 2023.

[20] J. McCarthy, A PROPOSAL FOR THE DARTMOUTH SUMMER RESEARCH PROJECT ON ARTIFICIAL INTELLIGENCE, http://jmc.stanford.edu/articles/dartmouth/dartmouth.pdf, Cited on December 24, 2023. Nathaniel Rochester's section on his research focus for the summer project, Page 7., Cited on December 24, 2023.

4. If the prediction corresponds to the goal the individual proceeds to act as indicated.[21]

These elements of system design, or this type of foundational framework, had not been proposed in previous outlines, documents, and or designs for computer-based systems.

This is the much-recounted origin story of AI. Now we know where the process started for what has become the modern AI industry and field of research and study. We know what the founding members had in mind. We know what they conceived of as an area of innovation when they started the AI journey. This is the genesis of AI as we know it, define it, and work to further the field. Now, we can understand why the underlying tenants are in place and who postulated those foundational principles.

The blueprint for all Four Eras of AI

Even if the physical meeting did not meet McCarthy's expectations, the outcomes, thoughts, and guiding principles were radically innovative and groundbreaking and have changed the world in immeasurable and innumerable ways. McCarthy's ambition and goals for the workshop set the direction for the participants to elucidate what AI could be. When you read the proposal for the Dartmouth Summer Project, as a practitioner of AI today or even as an AI enthusiast, you see and recognize the blueprint of

---

[21] J. McCarthy, A PROPOSAL FOR THE DARTMOUTH SUMMER RESEARCH PROJECT ON ARTIFICIAL INTELLIGENCE,
http://jmc.stanford.edu/articles/dartmouth/dartmouth.pdf, Cited on December 24, 2023. Claude Shannon's section on his research focus for the summer project, Page 5., Cited on December 25, 2023.

the nascent AI field in 1956, where we have evolved into, and where we have arrived today.

Machine Learning (ML) has been being discussed by luminaries like Alan Turing[22] since the early 1940s. Still, the conversations and concepts took a turn and gained a new focus with discussions around and convening at the Dartmouth event. Regarding AI, the proposal for the Dartmouth Summer Project is the US Constitution or the Magna Carta of AI. This document formally described what the AI industry has aspired to be and to become for the past six decades.

In my opinion, even if the meeting had not happened, the proposal to hold the meeting contains most of the foundational concepts that are the basis of what we think of as Foundational AI today, and hence, the conceptual and design foundations of all Four Eras of AI.

2026 marks the 70th anniversary of the 1956 meeting. The journey has not been a straight line, and the progress has not been smooth. In several cases, significant commentators, observers, and even some innovators have pronounced AI dead, but the AI industry has expired and been reborn multiple times. Let's examine the process and progress of the past nearly seven decades.

Are we on the road to nowhere?

The evolution of AI has not been linear, smooth, or consistently moving in a direction that is easily discernable as being positive progress for the field of AI, society, companies, governments and/or individuals. Depending on

[22] Copeland, B.J. "Alan Turing". Encyclopedia Britannica, 3 Dec. 2023, https://www.britannica.com/biography/Alan-Turing., Accessed 27 December 2023.

the sources of information and the timelines you read or believe in, we are in the fifth resurgence of AI.

A few years ago, in the period from 2016 to 2018, several notable people kept talking about the next "AI Winter".[23] Those Cassandras[24] postulated that the industry was getting ahead of itself (again) with the marketing messages being communicated and promoted and that the technologies that we had at hand would not be able to deliver the described value.

Companies like IBM certainly did not help the industry with their breathless pronouncements of the abilities of their Watson[25] system, mainly in the healthcare domain. Still, the overall AI industry weathered the criticism and continued to move forward, and like the AI industry as a whole has done with AI in general, IBM has revised and released Watson numerous times.

Watson can be seen as a microcosm of the AI industry. It never really dies. It just gets repackaged, rebranded, and rereleased.

[23] Ellen Glover, "What Is AI Winter? AI winter is coming — here's how to recognize the signs of an AI decline", Updated by Brennan Whitfield, Apr 21, 2023, BuiltIn Online, https://builtin.com/artificial-intelligence/ai-winter, Cited on December 27, 2023.

[24] Britannica, The Editors of Encyclopedia. "Cassandra". Encyclopedia Britannica, 7 Sep. 2023, https://www.britannica.com/topic/Cassandra-Greek-mythology. Accessed 27 December 2023.

[25] Wikipedia, The Contributors to Wikipedia, IBM Watson, https://en.wikipedia.org/wiki/IBM_Watson, Cited on December 27, 2023.

And, here we find ourselves again, in 2025, there are numerous commentators, Goldman Sachs[26] primary among them, calling out the folly of the newest branch of AI, Generative AI[27] (GenAI), as being full of hype and lacking the ability to generate a return on investment. I find paying attention to the many self-serving reports, articles, and posts challenging. So, for the most part, I don't pay attention to them, but to be illustrative, let's look quickly at Goldman Sachs' (GS) vacillating positions on the value of GenAI.

In April 2023, the Goldman Sachs Research team published an article titled "Generative AI could raise global GDP by 7%".[28] The report stated, "Breakthroughs in generative artificial intelligence have the potential to bring about sweeping changes to the global economy. As tools using advances in natural language processing work their way into businesses and society, they could drive a 7% (or almost $7 trillion) increase in global GDP and lift productivity growth by 1.5 percentage points over a 10-year period."[29] Quite a striking statement and projection by the research team at GS.

In July 2024, the GS team had this to say about GenAI, "The promise of generative AI technology to transform companies, industries, and societies is leading tech giants and beyond to spend an estimated ~$1tn on capex in coming years, including significant investments in data centers, chips, other

---

[26] Wikipedia, The Contributors to Wikipedia, Goldman Sachs, https://en.wikipedia.org/wiki/Goldman_Sachs, Cited on July 27, 2024.

[27] Gartner Glossary, Generative AI Defined, https://www.gartner.com/en/information-technology/glossary/generative-ai, Cited July 27, 2024.

[28] Joseph Briggs, Goldman Sachs Research Staff, Generative AI could raise global GDP by 7%, April 5, 2023, https://www.goldmansachs.com/intelligence/pages/generative-ai-could-raise-global-gdp-by-7-percent.html, Cited July 27, 2024.

[29] Ibid., Cited July 27, 2024., Cited July 27, 2024.

AI infrastructure, and the power grid. But this spending has little to show for it so far. Whether this large spend will ever pay off in terms of AI benefits and returns, and the implications for economies, companies, and markets if it does—or if it doesn't."[30]

I have never found the sideline commentary useful in my AI journey. I am a believer in data, analytics, and AI. Let those on the sideline say what they will. After all, it is their job to observe and offer commentary. I would rather listen to technologists and practitioners in the field, build technology, and deliver measurable results for businesses and organizations worldwide.

If you need to read commentary and projections from pundits, I recommend reading the research and narrative from McKinsey. The McKinsey research team seems to focus on what is happening in the market and what actual companies are doing with AI. I much prefer their analyses and narratives to the many others on offer.

Let's continue our discussion and examine what has occurred in the AI industry since the early 1960s.

The first heyday of AI

The years after the Dartmouth Summer Project when discussing, describing, and observing AI advancements were, to most people, simply

---

[30] Joseph Briggs, Goldman Sachs Research Staff, GenAI: too much spend, too little benefit?, June 27, 2024, https://www.goldmansachs.com/intelligence/pages/gen-ai-too-much-spend-too-little-benefit.html, Cited July 27, 2024.

"astonishing."[31] Computers were solving algebra word problems, proving theorems in geometry, and learning to speak English. Few, at the time, would have believed that such "intelligent" behavior by machines was possible at all.[32] Researchers expressed an intense optimism in private and in print, predicting that a fully intelligent machine would be built in less than 20 years.[33] Government agencies like DARPA poured money into the new field.[34] Artificial Intelligence laboratories were set up at a number of British and US universities in the late 1950s and early 1960s.[35] The optimism for the field was intense and the possibilities seemed limitless.

As an interesting side note, most people do not realize that nearly all early-stage innovations in computing from the 1940s up to the 1980s were first built in hardware and then evolved into a combination of general-purpose hardware driven and operated by software. Most early-stage neural network research involved building and using custom, purpose-built hardware.[36]

---

31 Russell, Stuart J.; Norvig, Peter (2003), Artificial Intelligence: A Modern Approach (2nd ed.), Upper Saddle River, New Jersey: Prentice Hall, ISBN 0-13-790395-2, Cited on December 26, 2023.

32 Crevier, Daniel (1993). AI: The Tumultuous Search for Artificial Intelligence. New York, NY: Basic Books. ISBN 0-465-02997-3, Cited on December 26, 2023.

33 McCorduck, Pamela (2004), Machines Who Think (2nd ed.), Natick, MA: A. K. Peters, Ltd., ISBN 978-1-56881-205-2, OCLC 52197627, Cited on December 26, 2023.

34 Moravec, Hans (1988), Mind Children, Harvard University Press, ISBN 978-0-674-57618-6, OCLC 245755104, Cited on December 26, 2023.

35 Copeland, J (Ed.) (2004). The Essential Turing: the ideas that gave birth to the computer age. Oxford: Clarendon Press. ISBN 0-19-825079-7, Cited on December 26, 2023.

36 Olazaran Rodriguez, Jose Miguel. A historical sociology of neural network research. PhD Dissertation. University of Edinburgh, 1991. See especially Chapters 2 and 3. Cited on December 26, 2023.

Databases share a similar lineage. Early-stage databases from Britton-Lee[37] and Teradata[38] were combinations of unique hardware and proprietary, custom-built software. Interestingly, in 2025, one of the predictions that seems quite popular is that in the next year or two, neural networks will be burned into hardware to increase the speed and efficiency of operations. Once again, we have come full circle in our innovation journey.

The initial optimism for AI and anticipation of what AI could and would deliver did not last. Academics, researchers, and commercial organizations made pronouncements and predictions that were too grandiose and too ambitious. In Life Magazine[39] in 1970, Marvin Minsky was quoted as saying, "In from three to eight years we will have a machine with the general intelligence of an average human being."[40] In 1970, I listened to these predictions with amazement and wonder, but I had no idea that my future would be focused on AI.

By the mid-1970s, funding had begun to be reduced and, in some cases, completely disappeared. The benefits and possibilities of AI were oversold and overblown; hubris had replaced progress.

---

[37] Wikipedia, The Contributors to Wikipedia, Britton Lee, Inc., https://en.wikipedia.org/wiki/Britton_Lee,_Inc., Cited on December 27, 2023.

[38] Wikipedia, The Contributors to Wikipedia, Teradata, https://en.wikipedia.org/wiki/Teradata., Cited on December 27, 2023.

[39] Britannica, The Editors of Encyclopedia. "Life". Encyclopedia Britannica, 14 Dec. 2022, https://www.britannica.com/topic/Life-magazine. Accessed 27 December 2023.

[40] Minsky strongly believes he was misquoted. See McCorduck 2004, pp. 272–274, Crevier 1993, p. 96 and Darrach 1970., Cited on December 26, 2023.

The first AI Winter

By 1975, most US- and European-based governmental funding programs for undirected AI had been pared back or shut down. The overselling and zealous claims led people in government positions and the general population to believe that AI could not and would not deliver on its promises. And, for the most part, they were correct in that belief.

In contrast, the Japanese government continued to fund general AI programs that were unrestricted or undirected. Much of the work of the late 1970s and early 1980s related to expert systems originated in Japan.

The AI winter was not solely caused by over-excited pronouncements. There were real limitations that curtailed AI ambitions, development, and progress. Some of the well-known and documented constraints were a lack of computing processing power (at the desktop and server levels), computer memory, disk drives of small size, and high-speed networking. Beyond the limitations of the hardware of the era, other roadblocks remained and were significant. Data management software was in the early stages of development and not up to the challenges of accessing, moving, integrating, and making the new, integrated data sets available in a timely manner.

Early algorithms had reached the end of their ability to continue to scale up and address more data and larger problem sets. New conceptual approaches had yet to be invented, let alone codified into code, and these new approaches were certainly not near being ready to address the data and computing challenges of the day.

One of the early approaches to machine learning was based on a simple search paradigm. Search is still a valuable approach and tool used widely today, but the ability for software of the 1960s and 1970s to iteratively search for the optimal solution sequentially through all the possible combinations limited this approach from the start. Search, at this time, would only be pragmatically possible on challenges that involved low dimensional data, smaller amounts of data, and where the overall problem being addressed embodied a limited number of scenarios to be evaluated. Also, when considering the issue of the combinatorial explosion,[41] the performance of early AI systems was less than satisfactory even for research applications. Also, one of the foundational issues underlying the first wave of widespread AI failure was the inability to obtain, integrate, and leverage large amounts of diverse data.

The combination of slow and constrained hardware, coupled with the further needs and requirements in the development of algorithms and software and the inability to obtain, integrate, and access large amounts of data, doomed the AI efforts of the 1960s to the 1980s, and when you add in a splash of overexcited hype, you end up with widespread disillusionment. With those factors as the industry context, AI moved to the back burner of research and commercial development. Still, as with all ideas whose time will eventually come, AI did not completely recede from the picture. AI believers continued their journey to develop more capable technologies, mostly in software at this point.

AI is back....for now...

Given the overreach of AI in the previous development phase, a natural reaction would be to refocus and limit the areas of research and development, which is exactly what researchers, developers, government funding sources, and commercial organizations did. The result of this redirection of effort was expert systems. "An expert system is a program

---

[41] Wikipedia, The Contributors to Wikipedia, Combinatorial Explosion, https://en.wikipedia.org/wiki/Combinatorial_explosion., Cited on December 27, 2023.

that answers questions or solves problems about a specific domain of knowledge, using logical rules that are derived from the knowledge of experts."[42]

Expert systems were well received across all industries, globally, and by private organizations and government groups that provided funding for such early-stage innovation projects. Expert systems were easy to understand and simple to build, delivered exactly what was expected, and, in the beginning, delivered impressive performance on a predictable basis.

The power of expert systems came from the expert knowledge contained in the rules built into the environment. Manually building rules into a system provided predictability, measurable accuracy, and transparency that was needed to prove that the AI system did work, but there were limitations to the expert systems approach. "AI researchers were beginning to suspect—reluctantly, for it violated the scientific canon of parsimony—that intelligence might very well be based on the ability to use large amounts of diverse knowledge in different ways…"[43]

When developing novel approaches to nearly any vexing problem, there is a balancing act between adhering to the underlying scientific foundations and balancing the needs of the real world. The research-oriented view held by academics and scientists was that the smallest amount of data should be used to create knowledge or intelligence. This view was a hindrance to the AI field. It is clear that given the constrained world that those innovators were operating within, smaller data was better for their short-term goals but posed a real block to the development of further advancements in the AI

---

[42] History of artificial intelligence, https://en.wikipedia.org/wiki/History_of_artificial_intelligence, Cited on December 26, 2023.

[43] McCorduck, Pamela (2004), Machines Who Think (2nd ed.), Natick, MA: A. K. Peters, Ltd., ISBN 978-1-56881-205-2, OCLC 52197627, Cited on December 26, 2023.

field. We now know that vast amounts of diverse data are needed to enable AI.

As noted, expert systems delivered on the areas where previous AI systems had failed. Expert systems were seen as a viable alternative to machine learning approaches, but the design and architecture of the systems themselves would constrain the early success of expert systems. Expert systems were, and are, laborious to build. The performance of expert systems slows dramatically as the number of rules grows, and in many cases, conflicting rules come into play.

In addition to these drawbacks, expert systems are brittle, meaning that they do not generalize beyond the rules that systems administrators or owners explicitly build, and they are hard to maintain and take a significant amount of manual administration to keep them accurate and up to date.

In the current world of AI, expert systems are no longer considered AI systems. Expert systems that rely on manually built rules, or even rules built by another AI model, are not learning systems. For a system to be an AI system, it must learn from data, not from human experts building rules or directing other systems or models to build rules. Expert systems, like those built in the area of Systems Dynamics[44] are useful, but they are not AI.

With the early success of expert systems and related software and projects, funding organizations started to allocate money to fund AI research once more. The funding started flowing in the mid-1980s, and the money was directed toward research and academic work on advancing neural networks.

---

[44] Wikipedia, The Contributors to Wikipedia, Systems Dynamics, https://en.wikipedia.org/wiki/System_dynamics., Cited on December 29, 2023.

As with most technically advanced ideas and innovations, one of the foundational developments that has taken AI and neural networks to the next level, backpropagation, has many fathers and a long history of evolution and application.

The first reference to the mathematics that underlies backpropagation can be traced back to "an efficient application of the Leibniz chain rule in 1673."[45] Backpropagation was initially referred to as "the reverse mode of automatic differentiation" or "reverse accumulation" by the Seppo Linnainmaa in 1970.[46] The term "back-propagating error correction" was introduced in 1962 by Frank Rosenblatt.[47] As you can see, numerous people have had a hand in the development of backpropagation as a mathematical approach, and even more, people come into the story when we start to discuss backpropagation in relation to the development of neural networks.

---

[45] Leibniz, Gottfried Wilhelm Freiherr von (1920). The Early Mathematical Manuscripts of Leibniz: Translated from the Latin Texts Published by Carl Immanuel Gerhardt with Critical and Historical Notes (Leibniz published the chain rule in a 1676 memoir). Open court publishing Company. ISBN 9780598818461, Cited on December 28, 2023.

[46] Linnainmaa, Seppo (1970). The representation of the cumulative rounding error of an algorithm as a Taylor expansion of the local rounding errors (Masters) (in Finnish). University of Helsinki. pp. 6–7., Cited on December 28, 2023.

[47] Rosenblatt, Frank (1962). Principles of Neurodynamics: Perceptrons and the Theory of Brain Mechanisms Cornell Aeronautical Laboratory. Report no. VG-1196-G-8 Report (Cornell Aeronautical Laboratory). Spartan. pp. Page XIII Table of contents, Page 292 "13.3 Back-Propagating Error Correction Procedures", Page 301 "figure 39 BACK-PROPAGATING ERROR-CORRECTION EXPERIMENTS". Cited on December 28, 2023.

Most people involved in the AI field today are well aware of Geoffrey Hinton[48], Yann LeCun[49], and Yashua Bengio[50], and many believe that the trio invented backpropagation. To Mr. Hinton's credit, when asked if he did invent the approach or even have the idea to apply the concept to neural networks, he replied that, "David E. Rumelhart[51] came up with the basic idea of backpropagation, so it's his invention".[52]

Backpropagation in relation to neural networks can be discussed or defined in the following manner. Strictly speaking, "the term backpropagation refers only to the algorithm for computing the gradient, not how the gradient is used; but the term is often used loosely to refer to the entire learning algorithm—including how the gradient is used, such as by stochastic gradient descent."[53]

As noted, the term is colloquially used to describe the process of computing "the gradient of a loss function with respect to the weights of the network

---

48 Geoffery E. Hinton's Homepage at the University of Toronto, https://www.cs.toronto.edu/~hinton/, Cited on December 28, 2023.

49 The Contributors of Wikipedia, Yann LeCun, https://en.wikipedia.org/wiki/Yann_LeCun, Cited on December 28, 2023.

50 Yoshua Bengio's Homepage, https://yoshuabengio.org/, Cited on December 28, 2023.

51 The Contributors of Wikipedia, David E. Rumelhart, https://en.wikipedia.org/wiki/David_Rumelhart, Cited on December 28, 2023.

52 Google search, "Did Geoffrey Hinton invent backpropagation?", https://www.google.com/search?q=when+was+backpropagation+invented&rlz=1C1RXQR_enUS1041US1041&oq=invention+of+backprop&gs_lcrp=EgZjaHJvbWUqDQgCEAAYhgMYgAQYigUyBggAEEUYOTIICAEQABgWGB4yDQgCEAAYhgMYgAQYigUyDQgDEAAYhgMYgAQYigXSAQkxNjMwNmowajeoAgCwAgA&sourceid=chrome&ie=UTF-8, Cited on December 28, 2023.

53 The Contributors of Wikipedia, Backpropagation, https://en.wikipedia.org/wiki/Backpropagation, Cited on December 28, 2023.

for a single input-output example, and does so efficiently, computing the gradient one layer at a time, iterating backward from the last layer to avoid redundant calculations of intermediate terms in the chain rule; this can be derived through dynamic programming, gradient descent, or variants such as stochastic gradient descent, are commonly used."[54]

Research into neural networks was ongoing, and as a result, neural networks were improving and showing small gains in research and laboratory settings. Still, progress started to accelerate when backpropagation began to be widely incorporated as an approach to refine and improve the accuracy and efficiency of learning in neural networks.

The progress of expert systems and the discovery of the value of backpropagation to the viability and ultimate value to be gained from neural networks was not enough to prove to the broader economic market that AI was ready for prime time and for widespread commercialization and the second AI Winter set in.

...And AI is gone again, the second AI Winter takes hold

The macroeconomic conditions in the US in the mid to late 1980s were challenging for funding early-stage research, and AI was not immune to this downturn.

One of the first indications of a change in the AI market was the sudden collapse of demand for specialized AI hardware. Thinking Machines, Cray, nCUBE, Kendall Square Research, MasPar, and Meiko Scientific were all companies that developed and sold hardware-based high-performance

[54] Ibid., Cited on December 28, 2023.

computing systems specifically for AI workloads.[55] Most of them were founded in the early 1980s, and the majority of the firms went bankrupt by the mid-1990s. The era of specialized hardware for AI and other analytic workloads had ended. Of course, there would be specialized hardware for targeted and tailored workloads, but the hardware segment for AI processing was defunct and would not return for roughly another 40 years.

Other drivers of the loss of confidence in AI in general were:

- As noted, even the most successful expert systems proved too expensive to maintain, they were difficult to update, they could not learn, and they were described as being "brittle."[56]

- DARPA had decided that AI was not "the next wave" and directed funds away from the field.[57]

- Japan's Fifth Generation Project goals had not been met. Indeed, some of them, like "carry on a casual conversation" had not been met by 2010.[58]

- Over 300 AI companies had shut down or been acquired by the end of 1993, effectively ending the second summer of AI. In 1994, HP Newquist stated that, "The immediate future of artificial

---

[55] The Contributors of Wikipedia, Thinking Machines Corporation, https://en.wikipedia.org/wiki/Thinking_Machines_Corporation, Cited on December 28, 2023.

[56] McCorduck, Pamela (2004), Machines Who Think (2nd ed.), Natick, MA: A. K. Peters, Ltd., ISBN 978-1-56881-205-2, OCLC 52197627, p 435., Cited on December 28, 2023.

[57] Ibid., pp. 430–431., Cited on December 28, 2023.

[58] Ibid., p. 441, McCorduck writes "Two and a half decades later, we can see that the Japanese didn't quite meet all of those ambitious goals.", p 441., Cited on December 28, 2023.

> intelligence—in its commercial form—seems to rest in part on the continued success of neural networks."[59]

Going into the second AI winter, it was clear to most in the field that the last technology standing was neural networks. Neural works were the best bet in the field of AI. Researchers and academics knew this fact and continued focusing on neural networks, but the commercial market and governmental funding moved on to other areas.

My entrance to the AI market

This is the point at which I joined the industry. I graduated from undergraduate school in 1983 and started building computer systems for five years for corporate environments. In 1988, I was finishing my MBA when I joined Metaphor Computer Systems and worked with Jay McGrath, Bill Schmarzo, Laura Reeves, Paul Kautza, Ralph Kimball, David Liddle, and Don Massaro.

I was a junior staff member living in Chicago. Jay McGrath asked me to move to London. I worked on the accounts of Pillsbury, Anheuser-Busch, Coors, Coca-Cola, Cadbury-Schweppes, Miles Labs, and others. I worked mainly on databases and advanced analytics. All the systems I built at Metaphor for Consumer Packaged Goods (CPG) clients were considered implementations of advanced analytics, leveraging and integrating multiple data sources overlaid with a touch of expert systems.

[59] Newquist, HP (1994), The Brain Makers: Genius, Ego, And Greed in the Quest For Machines That Think, New York: Macmillan/SAMS, ISBN 978-0-9885937-1-8, OCLC 313139906., Cited on December 28, 2023.

I had a burgeoning interest in AI, but there were no open-source software or commercial offerings that I could access and use to build applications. I left Metaphor and joined IBM in 1991 before IBM bought Metaphor. At IBM, I worked in the CPG industry vertical market team, where I continued to focus on advanced analytical systems for CPG companies on a global basis. I had a chance to work with Snow Brands (Japan), South African Brewers (SAB), Brahma (Brazil), and other leading companies.

I had made it known internally at IBM that I wanted to include AI in the systems I was designing and building, and subsequently, I was asked to travel to Rochester, Minnesota, to test and work with a new product that was referred to as the IBM Neural Network Utility[60] (NNU v1). I sat alone in a windowless room and tested the NNU for a couple of days. I was not impressed. I could build a small, three-level neural network, train it on data that I created, and see that the network was learning from the data, but I could not apply the software or the resulting neural networks to real-world problems for my clients. I found the software to be slow, limiting, and frustrating, but that early exposure set me on a path where I wanted to do more with software that could be programmed to learn from data of all types.

I wanted to work with AI systems. I wanted to work with databases, business intelligence, analytics, advanced analytics, and AI. I did not, and do not, see the delineation between data and analytics. Most people in the field either focus on data or analytics. I never understood that demarcation. I see those two elements as part of one consideration set.

---

60 Khoshgoftaar, T. M., and Szabo, R. M. (1996). Using neural networks to predict software faults during testing. IEEE Transactions on Reliability, 45(3), 456-462. https://ieeexplore.ieee.org/document/537016/similar#similar, Cited on December 30, 2023.

You need data and analytics, not one or the other.

My early experiences in building analytical applications for business users made it clear to me that the end users, who were senior managers and executives, did not care what I put into the applications from a technology perspective. All they wanted were accurate, reliable, timely, and auditable results that they could rely on to make better and faster business decisions. They wanted the solutions, applications, models, and data to help derive a competitive advantage in the market.

At the core, what many of them wanted, but they did not know it by this description, was the ability to explain their decision logic, processes, data, relevant business contextual factors, and the required timing or temporal dimensions to someone like me, specifically me. Then, they wanted me to build a model they could use and understand to predict the future or simulate various scenarios they might see as plausible. And if they were visionary, they wanted all that, plus an optimization engine that would tell them what the optimal choice is or was given the time, macro-economic environment, and the microenvironment internal to their company, relevant geographic areas, and the specific time period of interest. Which is, in reality, what most businesspeople still want today.

After nearly 40 years of being involved in the process of building leading-edge analytics applications, I still find AI and its possibilities fascinating. I am not surprised that neural networks have delivered so much and can deliver so much more than we currently know. Let's move back to discussing the evolution of FAI and the role of neural networks in that growth and evolution.

Neural networks continued to be the primary focus of corporate and academic research. The software improved by adding innovations like backpropagation, recurrent processing, convolutional architectures, and more. Corporations like IBM proposed ensemble approaches to solving real-world problems. Companies, like and including IBM, built systems that were combinations of expert systems, neural networks, fast search, and other approaches or technologies that could work in tandem to produce better answers in an acceptable time frame.

AI is back....to stay this time...with a few wobbles

By the late 1990s, researchers and technology companies were ready to ply the market with their newest offerings.

- On May 11, 1997, IBM‘s Deep Blue, the precursor to IBM's Watson, became the first computer chess-playing system to beat a reigning world chess champion, Garry Kasparov.[61]

- In 2005, a Stanford robot won the DARPA Grand Challenge by driving autonomously for 131 miles on a previously unseen desert trail.[62]

- In 2007, a team from Carnegie Mellon University won the DARPA Urban Challenge by autonomously navigating 55 miles in a city environment.[63]

---

[61] McCorduck, Pamela (2004), Machines Who Think (2nd ed.), Natick, MA: A. K. Peters, Ltd., ISBN 978-1-56881-205-2, OCLC 52197627, Cited on December 30, 2023.

[62] "DARPA Grand Challenge—home page". Archived from the original on 31 October 2007. Cited on December 30, 2023.

[63] "Welcome". Archived from the original on 5 March 2014. Retrieved 25 October 2011.

- In 2011, on the US television program Jeopardy!, IBM's Watson defeated the two previous champions, Brad Rutter and Ken Jennings, by a significant margin.[64]

The business, general media, and general public were sufficiently wowed. The widespread sentiment began to turn towards a view that perhaps AI was real this time. Interest from commercial organizations increased steadily and funding began to return to the AI sector.

Coming out of the second AI winter, it was and is clear that neural networks were and are the front runners in how AI would move forward.

The trio in Toronto (LeCun, Bengio, and Hinton) were making impressive progress in research and development of neural networks that could learn rapidly, scale up in size, ingest and leverage larger and larger amounts of data, and it was becoming clear that the innovations being tested showed great promise in enabling neural networks to be applied to real-world problems across a wide range of industries and use cases.

The successes that were being realized by leading firms were gaining attention, and the credibility of AI was being built.

An AI Autumn

Beginning around 2010, and for the next ten years, AI systems would demonstrate uneven promise and results. In 2016, IBM announced the

64 Markoff, John (16 February 2011). "On 'Jeopardy!' Watson Win Is All but Trivial". The New York Times., Cited December 30, 2023.

promise of Watson Health.[65] In 2017, articles began to appear in a wide range of media outlets, piercing the claims that Watson Health could understand cancer cases and offer accurate and reliable diagnostic support to medical professionals.[66]

It seemed to many that we were always on the edge of tipping back into the next AI winter. I never believed that it would be as bad as that or that the market would lapse back into AI failing to deliver. Of course, AI failed to deliver on the lofty marketing promises of IBM and a handful of other technology companies. Still, no technology could deliver on the set of claims set out by the marketing departments of those firms.

In 2017, McKinsey[67] started tracking the progress of AI annually in their "The state of AI in…".[68] The annual survey and report is a mainstay of observers and pundits who track and discuss the current and future state of the AI industry.

---

[65] IBM, 29 Nov, 2016, 11:27 ET, IBM Unveils Watson-Powered Imaging Solutions for Healthcare Providers, https://www.prnewswire.com/news-releases/ibm-unveils-watson-powered-imaging-solutions-for-healthcare-providers-300369727.html, Cited December 30, 2023.

[66] Casey Ross, Ike Swetlitz, Sept. 5, 2017, STAT, IBM pitched its Watson supercomputer as a revolution in cancer care. It's nowhere close., https://www.statnews.com/2017/09/05/watson-ibm-cancer/, Cited on December 30, 2023.

[67] McKinsey & Company, History of our firm, https://www.mckinsey.com/about-us/overview/history-of-our-firm, Cited on December 31, 2023.

[68] Quantum Black by McKinsey & Company, The state of AI in 2023: Generative AI's breakout year, https://www.mckinsey.com/~/media/mckinsey/business%20functions/quantumblack/our%20insights/the%20state%20of%20ai%20in%202023%20generative%20ais%20breakout%20year/the-state-of-ai-in-2023-generative-ais-breakout-year_vf.pdf, Cited on December 31 2023.

From 2017 to 2023, McKinsey's "The state of AI reports" said that the steady progress in the belief in the transformative power of AI in leading commercial organizations, the incremental and increasing adoption of AI on a global basis, and the ability of AI to provide leaders in a wide range of industries and geographic markets with the ability to maintain and increase their overall and general competitiveness in diverse industries and markets.

The 2022 edition of the McKinsey report starts with the following paragraph, "Adoption has more than doubled since 2017, though the proportion of organizations using AI has plateaued between 50 and 60 percent for the past few years. A set of companies seeing the highest financial returns from AI continue to pull ahead of competitors. The results show these leaders making larger investments in AI, engaging in increasingly advanced practices known to enable scale and faster AI development, and showing signs of faring better in the tight market for AI talent. On talent, for the first time, we looked closely at AI hiring and upskilling. The data show that there is significant room to improve diversity on AI teams, and, consistent with other studies, diverse teams correlate with outstanding performance."[69]

In our discussion of FAI, we are now current. We have traversed AI history from 1956 to 2023. We have discussed how FAI has evolved over the past six decades. Let's move on to discussing what FAI is today.

---

[69] Quantum Black by McKinsey & Company, The state of AI in 2022—and a half decade in review, https://www.mckinsey.com/capabilities/quantumblack/our-insights/the-state-of-ai-in-2022-and-a-half-decade-in-review, Cited on December 31 2023.

Enter Foundational AI

I found reading the original monographs, white papers, and proposals from the 1950s interesting and intriguing. I would have loved to read Alan Turing's original thoughts on machine learning from the 1940s, but Turing did not publish a paper on his earliest thinking of machine learning.

"Turing gave quite possibly the earliest public lecture (London, 1947) to mention computer intelligence, saying, "What we want is a machine that can learn from experience," and that the "possibility of letting the machine alter its own instructions provides the mechanism for this." Turing did not publish this paper, and many of his ideas were later reinvented by others."[70] What a loss that is for us and for all of history.

Terms used in the 1950s were neuron nets, nerve nets, brain models, abstractions, automata, automatons, and more. FAI has always been described as being based on, or a replica of, the human brain. To understand an innovation or new development, people are always searching for metaphors, descriptions, and models that enable them to connect the new to the known.

At the heart of FAI are neural networks. The most powerful and well-known neural networks are in the human brain; hence, the language of FAI is a mirror of neurobiology.[71]

---

[70] Copeland, B.J. "Alan Turing". Encyclopedia Britannica, https://www.britannica.com/technology/artificial-intelligence/Is-artificial-general-intelligence-AGI-possible, Cited on December 31 2023.

[71] Arbib, M. A. (Ed.). (2003). The handbook of brain theory and neural networks. MIT press., https://mitpress.mit.edu/9780262511025/the-handbook-of-brain-theory-and-neural-networks/ , Cited on December 25, 2023.

I am glad that the term nerve net did not stick; that term creeps me out. I get visions of Frankenstein when I think of a nerve net, but that is just me.

Let's formally define the neural networks in AI systems and models. "Neural networks are mathematical models that use learning algorithms inspired by the brain to store information. Since neural networks are used in machines, they are collectively called an 'artificial neural network.' Nowadays, the term machine learning is often used in this field and is the scientific discipline that is concerned with the design and development of algorithms that allow computers to learn, based on data..."[72]

A new term has been introduced in our discussion, and I do not want to miss the opportunity to define it and discuss the evolution and importance of models. Let's define the term *model* in the context of AI. "In the context of AI and ML, a model is a mathematical representation of a problem. It is used to describe how the problem can be solved and how data can be used to make predictions or decisions."[73]

A model can be very simple. A linear regression model is one of the easiest to write and understand.

A model can be very complex, an example shown in Figure 3.

Terminology is important. When talking about AI, models, training data, and more, you want to be correct and accurate in expressing your thoughts and ideas.

---

[72] N.L.W. Keijsers, Neural Networks, Definition and History, Encyclopedia of Movement Disorders, 2010, Science Direct, https://www.sciencedirect.com/topics/neuroscience/neural-network, Cited on December 25, 2023.

[73] Abdullah Sajjad, Quora, https://www.quora.com/What-does-model-mean-in-the-context-of-AI-and-ML-in-simple-terms, Cited on December 25, 2023.

$$y = \alpha + \beta x$$

Figure 2: A linear regression model.[74]

Recently, I have seen and encountered an increasing and significant number of people who want to be involved in the AI industry. 2023 was a breakout year for AI, that is for certain. I hear people saying (and writing) things like this, "A model is created by training an algorithm on a set of data." Actually, that is not true or accurate. A model is a model whether it has been trained on data or not.

Let's walk through how to talk about models and data. A model is an algorithm. As noted above, the model can be simple or incredibly complex. A trained model is an algorithm or set of algorithms that has been trained on a set of data. A fine-tuned model is a trained model with its training set extended or refined with additional data. This taxonomy is rather simple and relatively easy to grasp.

---

[74] Google, Simple Linear Regression,
https://www.google.com/search?q=simple+linear+regression+model&sca_esv=593593980
&rlz=1C1RXQR_enUS1041US1041&biw=1372&bih=728&sxsrf=AM9HkKnx15aQkUxF
UjCubGyYWyqsOf-
qNg%3A1703515176925&ei=KJSJZf2NOLmGptQPyMyviA4&oq=simple+linear&gs_lp=
Egxnd3Mtd2l6LXNlcnAiDXNpbXBsZSBsaW5lYXIqAggAMgoQABiABBgUGIcCMgUQ
ABiABDIKEAAYgAQYFBiHAjIFEAAYgAQyBRAAGIAEMgUQABiABDIFEAAYgAQy
BRAAGIAEMgUQABiABDIFEAAYgARIpmFQ4glYqVFwAHgCkAEAmAFjoAG4GaoB
AjQwuAEByAEA-
AEBwgIEEAAYR8ICBxAjGLACGCfCAggQABiABBiiBMICBRAhGKABwgIFECEYnwX
CAgsQABiABBiKBRiRAsICBxAAGIAEGArCAhMQABiABBiKBRiRAhixAxhGGPkBwg
IqEAAYgAQYigUYkQIYsQMYRhj5ARiXBRiMBRjdBBhGGPQDGPUDGPYD2AEBwgI
LEAAYgAQYsQMYgwHCAg0QLhiABBjHARjRAxgKwgIOEC4YgAQYxwEY0QMY1AL
CAg4QLhiABBixAxjHARjRA8ICCBAAGIAEGLEDwgIOEAAYgAQYigUYsQMYgwHC
AgsQLhiABBjHARjRA8ICCxAuGIAEGMcBGK8BwgIOEC4YgAQYxwEYrwEYjgXCAgg
QLhiABBjUAuIDBBgAIEGIBgGQBgi6BgYIARABGBM&sclient=gws-wiz-serp#ip=1,
Cited on December 25, 2023.

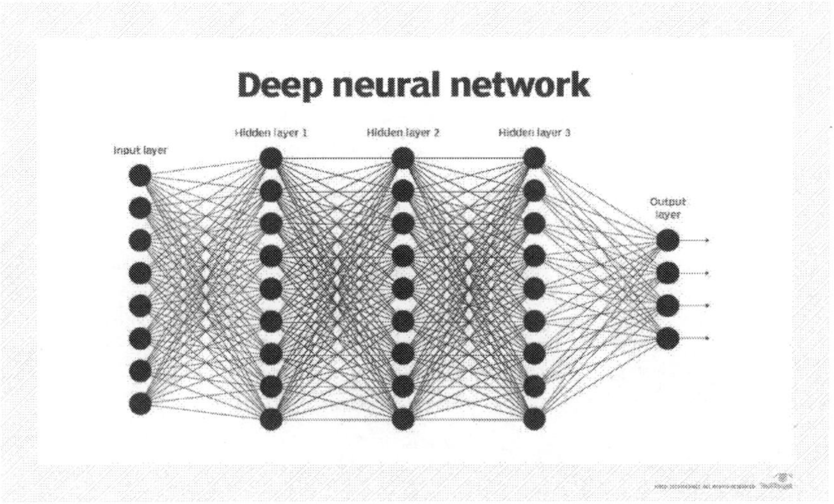

Figure 3: A deep neural network model.[75]

As this book is for executive and senior management staff in non-technical operational business functions, we will not delve deeply into FAI's variants and variations. Still, it is good for you to know and be aware of all the different major areas of FAI.

There are many overly complex diagrams and illustrations that depict the taxonomy of FAI. You are free to use any illustrations that meet your view of the FAI landscape. I like the illustration below (Figure 4) mainly for its simplicity.

Let's discuss the primary elements of FAI. Again, this is an overview of these areas and concepts meant for senior managers and executives. If you are seeking a detailed technical review of each of these areas, many other books approach those topics in a technical and in-depth manner.

---

[75] Kinza Yasar, Tech Target, Neural Network Defined, https://www.techtarget.com/searchenterpriseai/definition/neural-network, Cited on December 25, 2023.

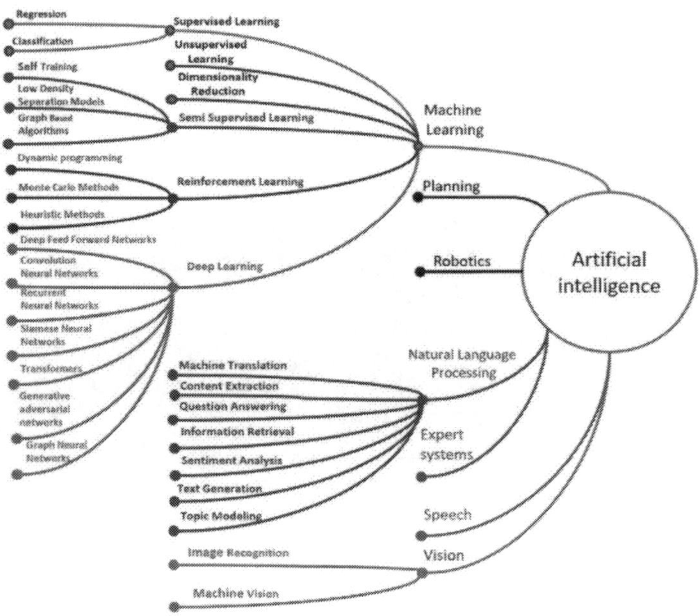

Figure 4: Elements of Foundational AI (FAI). This chart is representative and not to be considered exhaustive.[76]

Machine learning

Machine Learning (ML) is the densest branch and the most developed area in FAI. Machine Learning is a discipline in FAI concerned with the implementation of computer software that can learn autonomously.[77] "Machine Learning is a subfield of artificial intelligence, which is broadly

---

[76] Mukhamediev RI, Popova Y, Kuchin Y, Zaitseva E, Kalimoldayev A, Symagulov A, Levashenko V, Abdoldina F, Gopejenko V, Yakunin K, et al. Review of Artificial Intelligence and Machine Learning Technologies: Classification, Restrictions, Opportunities and Challenges. Mathematics. 2022; 10(15):2552. https://doi.org/10.3390/math10152552, Cited on December 30, 2023.

[77] Hosch, W. L. (2023, December 22). machine learning. Encyclopedia Britannica. https://www.britannica.com/technology/machine-learning, Cited on December 31, 2023.

defined as the capability of a machine to imitate intelligent human behavior. Artificial intelligence systems are used to perform complex tasks in a way that is similar to how humans solve problems."[78]

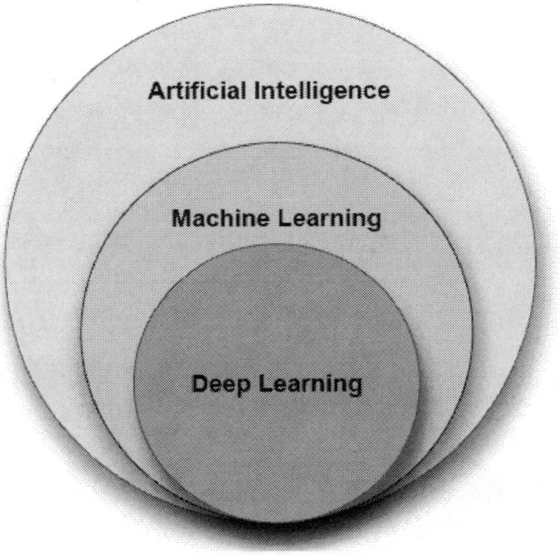

Figure 5: AI, ML, Deep Learning Taxonomy.[79]

Over the past ten to 15 years, the majority of the work undertaken and completed in FAI was in the areas of Machine Learning.

---

[78] Sara Brown, Apr 21, 2021, MIT Sloan Management School, Ideas Made to Matter, Machine Learning, explained, https://mitsloan.mit.edu/ideas-made-to-matter/machine-learning-explained#:~:text=Machine%20learning%20is%20a%20subfield%20of%20artificial%20intelligence%2C%20which%20is,to%20how%20humans%20solve%20problems. Cited December 31, 2023.

[79] Kumar Abhishek, 10 May 2022, Introduction to artificial intelligence, https://www.red-gate.com/simple-talk/development/data-science-development/introduction-to-artificial-intelligence/, Cited December 31, 2023.

Of the 100+ applications that my teams have been responsible for designing, building, and implementing, over 90% of those applications have been in the area of Machine Learning and/or Deep Learning (DL).

ML and DL FAI forms are relatively easy to design and build with a high-performing data science team. The required data is plentiful and easy to access, and most of the data is from internal or open-source repositories. The required software can be accessed as open-source software or proprietary software is available at a reasonable cost. So, in essence, ML and DL applications can be built quickly and at a reasonable cost.

One of the primary drawbacks of leveraging these techniques and approaches is the lack of explainability and the inability to understand how decisions inside the models are being formulated. Hence, we are prohibited from using these techniques in most highly regulated markets and industries like pharmaceuticals and finance. Still, in unregulated markets, we are free to leverage these approaches without constraint.

A consideration that needs to be taken into account is implied above. These approaches are reasonably easy to leverage if you have a high-performing data science team. A broader set of analysts are learning these techniques, and we are training more and more data scientists, but we still have a skills gap and need more professional data scientists.

The efficiency and effectiveness of ML and DL projects rely heavily on the skills and talents of data scientists. Simply having access to data is not enough. The art of understanding the data required to analyze and predict business factors and outcomes is a rare skill.

Deep learning

To differentiate between ML and DL, let's define Deep Learning.

"Deep learning networks are neural networks with many layers. The layered network can process extensive amounts of data and determine the "weight" of each link in the network. For example, in an image recognition system, some layers of the neural network might detect individual features of a face, like eyes, nose, or mouth. In contrast, another layer could tell whether those features appear in a way that indicates a face. The more layers you have, the more potential you have for doing complex things well."[80]

For clarity, Deep Learning models *are* neural network models and, as such, are modeled on the way the human brain works and powers many machine learning use cases, like autonomous vehicles, chatbots, and medical diagnostics.

The Deep Learning architecture has enabled the majority of the breakthroughs that we have experienced in FAI and all of those we have seen in Generative AI (GenAI), the second pillar of AI. Of course, we will discuss GenAI extensively in the second section of this book.

Reinforcement learning

"Reinforcement Learning (RL) is a subset of machine learning that allows an AI-driven system to learn through trial and error using feedback from its actions. This feedback is either negative or positive, signaled as punishment or reward with the aim of maximizing the reward function. RL

---

[80] Sara Brown, Apr 21, 2021, MIT Sloan Management School, Ideas Made to Matter, Machine Learning, explained, https://mitsloan.mit.edu/ideas-made-to-matter/machine-learning-explained#:~:text=Machine%20learning%20is%20a%20subfield%20of%20artificial%20intelligence%2C%20which%20is,to%20how%20humans%20solve%20problems. Cited December 31, 2023.

learns from its mistakes and offers artificial intelligence that mimics natural intelligence."[81]

Supervised learning

Supervised learning is a type of ML algorithm that leverages a known dataset, called the training dataset, to make predictions. The term "supervised" refers to the presence of a guide that directs the learning process. In most supervised learning processes or projects, the supervisor is the labeled training data set from which the learning algorithm learns to make predictions. The training data consists of input-output pairs, where the input is a known data point, and the output is a predetermined label or target value. The goal of supervised learning is to find an algorithmic function that, given the input data, can predict the output with high accuracy for unseen data.[82]

"Supervised learning can be broadly categorized into two types:

- Classification: In classification tasks, the output variable is a category, such as "spam" or "not spam" in email filtering, or "malignant" or "benign" in tumor diagnosis. The model aims to assign the input features to one of the predefined classes.

- Regression: In regression tasks, the output variable is a continuous value, such as the price of a house or the temperature tomorrow.

[81] Ruth Brooks, University of York, What is reinforcement learning?, https://online.york.ac.uk/what-is-reinforcement-learning/, Cited December 31, 2023.

[82] DeepAI, Supervised Learning Defined, https://deepai.org/machine-learning-glossary-and-terms/supervised-learning, Cited January 1, 2024.

The model aims to predict a numerical value based on the input features."[83]

Semi-supervised learning

"Semi-supervised learning is a broad category of machine learning techniques that utilizes both labeled and unlabeled data; in this way, as the name suggests, it is a hybrid technique between supervised and unsupervised learning."[84]

"In a generic semi-supervised algorithm, given a dataset of labeled and unlabeled data, examples are handled one of two different ways:

- Labeled data points are handled as in traditional supervised learning; predictions are made, loss is calculated, and network weights are updated by gradient descent.
- Unlabeled data points are used to help the model make more consistent and confident predictions. Whether by an added unsupervised loss term or by pseudo-labels, unlabeled examples are used to build upon the progress of labeled examples."[85]

---

[83] Ibid., Cited January 1, 2024.

[84] Avi Bewtra, July 1, 2022, V7 Labs, The Ultimate Guide to Semi-Supervised Learning, https://www.v7labs.com/blog/semi-supervised-learning-guide#:~:text=we've%20covered%3A-,Semi%2Dsupervised%20learning%20is%20a%20broad%20category%20of%20machine%20learning,of%20the%20larger%20data%20distribution, Cited on January 1, 2024.

[85] Ibid., Cited on January 1, 2024.

Unsupervised learning

"Unsupervised learning in artificial intelligence is a type of machine learning that learns from data without human supervision. Unlike supervised learning, unsupervised machine learning models are given unlabeled data and allowed to discover patterns and insights without any explicit guidance or instruction."[86]

The three primary types of unsupervised learning approaches are clustering, association rules, and dimensionality reduction.

Clustering

Clustering is a technique for examining unlabeled data and organizing the data into clusters based on measurable similarities or differences. Clustering is broadly used in a wide range of use cases including customer segmentation, purchasing behavior, fraud detection, and churn analysis. Clustering algorithms sort data into naturally occurring groups by finding similar or dissimilar groupings in uncategorized/unlabeled data.

The multiple types of unsupervised learning algorithms employed in clustering processes include - exclusive, overlapping, hierarchical, and probabilistic.

---

[86] Google Cloud, What is unsupervised learning?, https://cloud.google.com/discover/what-is-unsupervised-learning#:~:text=Unsupervised%20learning%20in%20artificial%20intelligence,any%20explicit%20guidance%20or%20instruction, Cited on January 1, 2024.

Association

Association rule mining is a rule-based approach to reveal useful relationships between data elements. Unsupervised learning algorithms search the input data for naturally occurring associations or rules to discover definable correlations and the different connections between data elements in the data set.

Association is most commonly used to analyze transactional datasets to represent how often certain items are found in the data together. The discovered patterns could signify purchasing patterns, product or service usage patterns, or affinities that illustrate or highlight previously unknown relationships.

Dimensionality reduction

"Dimensionality reduction is an unsupervised learning technique that reduces the number of features, or dimensions, in a dataset. Dimensionality reduction extracts important features from the dataset, reducing the number of irrelevant or random features present. This method uses Principal Component Analysis (PCA)[87] and Singular Value Decomposition (SVD)[88] algorithms to reduce the number of data inputs without compromising the integrity of the properties in the original data."[89]

---

[87] Casey Cheng, Feb 3, 2022, Towards Data Science, Principal Component Analysis (PCA) Explained Visually with Zero Math, https://towardsdatascience.com/principal-component-analysis-pca-explained-visually-with-zero-math-1cbf392b9e7d, Cited January 1, 2024.

[88] Gregory Gunderson, December 10, 2018, Singular Value Decomposition as Simply as Possible, https://gregorygundersen.com/blog/2018/12/10/svd/, Cited January 1, 2024.

[89] ibid., Cited January 1, 2024.

The main difference between supervised and unsupervised learning is the type of input data used. Unlike unsupervised machine learning algorithms, supervised learning relies on labeled training data to determine whether pattern recognition within a dataset is accurate.

The goals of supervised learning models are also predetermined, meaning that the type of output of a model is already known before the algorithms are applied. In other words, the input is mapped to the output based on the training data.

Natural language processing

"Natural Language Processing (NLP) is a branch of artificial intelligence that focuses on the interaction between computers and humans through natural language. The objective is to program computers to process and analyze large amounts of natural language data. NLP involves enabling machines to understand, interpret, and produce human language in a way that is both valuable and meaningful."[90]

As a field, NLP has been an area of great interest and importance, but it has not historically been at the forefront of the commercial marketplace for AI. Teams that I have managed have been working with NLP models since 2019.

The first NLP model that performed at a level where we felt we could build applications was BERT or Bidirectional Encoder Representations from

---

[90] Matt Crabtree, October 2023, Data Camp, What is Natural Language Processing (NLP)? A Comprehensive Guide for Beginners, https://www.datacamp.com/blog/what-is-natural-language-processing, Cited January 1, 2024.

Transformers. BERT is a language model based on the transformer architecture. It was introduced in October 2018 by researchers at Google.[91]

In 2020, we built an application that monitored a competitive field of companies. We used BERT to analyze US governmental filings, press releases, news stories, company pronouncements, and announcements. We were able to monitor and understand all the relevant activities, actions, product developments, and more at a very detailed level for each company, product, and project that we were interested in. This was the first application that proved to me that NLP was ready for commercial use.

After our success with BERT, we worked with an extension of the BERT model referred to as RoBERTa: A Robustly Optimized BERT Pretraining Approach.[92] We found the results slightly better than BERT, but not dramatically so.

Also, we worked with Natural Language Generation (NLG)[93] software to ingest financial statements, database content, and regulatory support materials to test and determine if NLG software could generate content that would save us time and effort in writing a range of required internal and external documents. We found that, in 2020, the software was good enough

---

91 The Contributors of Wikipedia, BERT (language model), https://en.wikipedia.org/wiki/BERT_(language_model)#:~:text=It%20was%20introduced%20in%20October,analyzing%20and%20improving%20the%20model.%22, Cited January 1, 2024.

92 Yinhan Liu, Myle Ott, Naman Goyal, Jingfei Du, Mandar Joshi, Danqi Chen, Omer Levy, Mike Lewis, Luke Zettlemoyer, Veselin Stoyanov, July 26, 2019, RoBERTa: A Robustly Optimized BERT Pretraining Approach, arXiv:1907.11692v1, https://doi.org/10.48550/arXiv.1907.11692, Cited January 1, 2024.

93 Ellen Glover, updated by Matthew Urwin, May 19, 2023, Builtin, What Is Natural Language Generation?, https://builtin.com/artificial-intelligence/what-is-natural-language-generation, Cited January 1, 2024.

for first drafts of financial statements, but the accuracy and style were not good enough for a wide range of required documents.

Of course, the world has changed dramatically in 2023, and Generative AI (GenAI) is widely used today and will be even more so as GenAI models grow, improve, and proliferate. We will deeply examine GenAI in the next section of this book.

Summary

FAI is a fascinating area of computer science that brings in ideas and concepts from neurobiology, psychology, mathematics, anthropology, and more. The idea of reproducing elements of human intelligence in machines has enticed leading thinkers for millions of years.

In this chapter, we have examined the evolution of FAI from the 1950s to today. It is clear that FAI has ebbed and flowed over those nearly 70 years, and we can deduce from what has transpired in the past ten years and the incredible acceleration that we have experienced in the past two years, that FAI is here to stay. FAI will be part of the human condition forever.

This fact creates a great deal of consternation, hand-wringing, and doom saying among people. In the summer of 2018, the Pew Research Center[94] asked 979 technology pioneers, innovators, developers, business and policy leaders, researchers, and activists to answer the following question, "As emerging algorithm-driven artificial intelligence (AI) continues to spread,

---

[94] Pew Research Center, https://www.pewresearch.org/, Cited January 1, 2024.

will people be better off than they are today?[95] The multiplicity of responses reflects the range of optimism, trepidation, sadness, fear, uncertainty, doubt, and all the other warnings and emotions associated with one of the greatest developments of all time.

The bottom line is that FAI is a great achievement, many great achievements, and it has taken a significant amount of human effort from some of the smartest people who have ever lived to reach this point. There is no going back. It is our responsibility and duty to move FAI forward in a way that is a net positive for all of humanity from this point forward.

Let's move on in our discussion of Foundational AI and talk about the impact this technology has had and will have on the world.

---

95 JANNA ANDERSON AND LEE RAINIE, December 10, 2018, Pew Research Center, Artificial Intelligence and the Future of Humans, https://www.pewresearch.org/internet/2018/12/10/artificial-intelligence-and-the-future-of-humans/, Cited January 1, 2024.

CHAPTER 3

The Impact of Foundational AI

Foundational AI has been and is one of the most impactful technologies ever developed. However, when you ask people about what they consider to be the technology that has changed the world the most, very few knowledgeable individuals or research organizations cite Foundational AI. I reviewed several lists written after 2023, comprising technologies considered the most impactful from an economic perspective, and only one list included FAI.

In June 2024, I spoke with a senior executive in a leading global firm. After we spoke for nearly an hour, he remarked, "There are so many AI experts, I can't tell one from the other, or if they really know anything about AI."[96] This conversation indicates two facts. The first is that people outside of technology, from entry-level personnel to senior executives, know little to nothing about Foundational AI, or AI in general. Second, many of these same people act as if they *know about AI because they either mistakenly think that they do or are afraid of being seen as out of the loop or clueless about a technology* critical to shaping the future of work and society.

[96] John K Thompson, Personal Conversation, Cited on August 17, 2024.

This indicates that governments, companies, and society have not done enough to train our youth, adults, and seniors in the areas of Science, Technology, Engineering, and Math (STEM). We need to do more at all educational levels and companies need to do more, too, but that is a topic for another day and possibly a complete book.

Let's look at the impact FAI has had, continues to have, and will have on our world. We will examine FAI's impact from a number of perspectives. Let's start with the broad economic impact.

Economic impact

From the viewpoint of the overall economic impact on the global economy, the macroeconomic view is that AI has been, and will continue to be, a force multiplier and will result in faster growth across all industries and all countries. That is an impressive assertion. Very few technologies have this kind of impact forecasted on a global basis. And the expected impact of AI is not a one-time contribution to growth. It is an ongoing, renewing, and consistently increasing impact.

The research team at the International Monetary Fund (IMF) has this to say about AI's impact on economies and jobs: "...AI will expand economies' production frontiers and will lead to reallocations between labor and capital while triggering potentially profound changes in many jobs and sectors. AI offers unprecedented opportunities for solving complex problems and improving the accuracy of predictions, enhancing decision-making, boosting economic growth, and improving lives. However, the implications for economies and societies are uncertain precisely because of its vast and flexible applicability in numerous domains."[97]

While the exact impact on economic growth is uncertain, it is clear that the impact will be significant and uniformly widespread. In my daily conversations with my colleagues, AI experts, technology analysts, and others, it is obvious that FAI, including all FAI subdomains, will impact almost all industries, roles, and processes. When people ask me to elucidate the use cases that I see where FAI is making an impact, I typically respond with, it is easier to discuss where FAI will not have an impact rather than the inverse.

In the 38 years that I have been working in the field of data, analytics, and AI, I have been part of and led teams that have placed 100+ predictive analytics and AI applications into production in 20 different industries. I think there are very few business processes and operational areas that FAI cannot improve.

I have either built on my own or have led teams that have implemented predictive analytic applications for the following applications: forecasting of revenue, forecasting the simultaneous timing of the arrival and flow of people through hundreds of locations, the incidence of post-surgical sepsis, the optimal flow of oil in a factory, the optimal flame shape in an energy plant, the best target markets for product introductions, the best price to increase sales, the date and time when products will go out of stock, when customers will stop using a service and churn to a competitor, the optimal set of conditions to draw customers into a location or locations, the optimal

---

[97] International Monetary Fund, Cazzaniga and others. 2024. "Gen-AI: Artificial Intelligence and the Future of Work." IMF Staff Discussion Note SDN2024/001, International Monetary Fund, Washington, DC. https://www.imf.org/en/Publications/Staff-Discussion-Notes/Issues/2024/01/14/Gen-AI-Artificial-Intelligence-and-the-Future-of-Work-542379?cid=bl-com-SDNEA2024001, Cited on August 22, 2024.

assortment of products to achieve a range of objectives set by management including highest revenue, fastest sales velocity, etc., and many more.

FAI is a well-understood technology and has been delivering measurable impact for decades. However, it is still early days with respect to all corporations leveraging FAI in a universal manner. In their 2024 survey of FAI use, the research team from McKinsey found that, "forty-two percent of high-performing firms say more than 20 percent of their EBIT is attributable to their use of nongenerative, analytical AI…"[98]

Think about that fact for a moment. Twenty percent of bottom-line revenue in leading companies can be directly attributed to and directly influenced by FAI. That is stunning. Isn't directly affecting and proactively managing revenue one of the primary responsibilities of executive management? If that is true, then the adoption of FAI should skyrocket in the coming years.

Also, this fact indicates that companies that are global leaders understand the potential of FAI and are leveraging it widely to increase their competitiveness. The open question is how long will it be before companies outside this group of leaders begin to adopt and use FAI? I have spoken with my data, analytics, and AI practitioners and compatriots for years about predicting the timing of FAI's widespread adoption. Consistently, I have been on the optimistic side of the projections. However, given the data illustrated in Figure 6, perhaps we have hit that inflection point for wider and faster adoption in firms beyond the leader category. Time will tell.

---

[98] Alex Singla, Alexander Sukharevsky, Lareina Yee, Michael Chui, Bryce Hall, McKinsey, QuantumBlack Division, The state of AI in early 2024: GenAI adoption spikes and starts to generate value, May 30, 2024, https://www.mckinsey.com/capabilities/quantumblack/our-insights/the-state-of-ai, Cited on August 24, 2024.

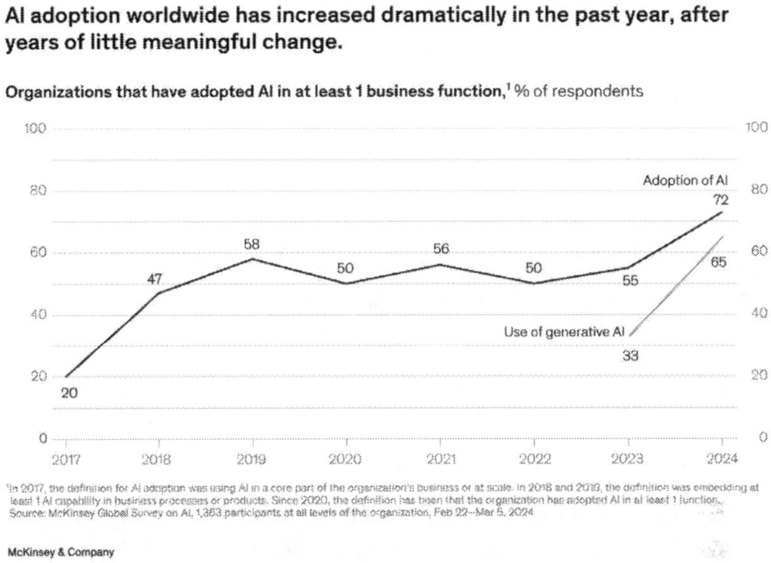

Figure 6: AI adoption Trends Globally from 2017 to 2024.[99]

The projections of the overall economic impact of FAI are impressive. Of course, we will see how these numbers compare to reality as time progresses, but most projections are for AI to add trillions of dollars to the global economy.

PWC's recent research states that, "AI could contribute up to $15.7 trillion to the global economy in 2030, more than the current output of China and India combined. Of this, $6.6 trillion is likely to come from increased productivity and $9.1 trillion is likely to come from consumption-side effects. While some markets, sectors, and individual businesses are more advanced than others, overall, AI is still at a very early stage of development.

---

[99] Ibid, Cited on August 24, 2024.

From a macroeconomic perspective, there are opportunities for emerging markets to leapfrog more developed counterparts."[100]

In my efforts to review the current research, the majority of the growth estimates are over the future time period of 2022 and 2030; many of those projections are for a time period over the next eight to ten years. I have seen projections as low as $3T incrementally added to the global economy and as high as $15.7T. To add a bit of context, the annual GDP of France or Germany is approximately $3T annually. Even if you average the projected gains and pick a number near the midpoint of that range, say, like $7T to 9T, that is a massive addition to the global economy. "PwC research shows global GDP could be up to 14% higher in 2030 due to AI—the equivalent of an additional $15.7 trillion—making it the biggest commercial opportunity in today's fast-changing economy."[101]

Very few technologies have that scale of a force multiplier associated with their deployment and use. In my opinion, we can comfortably say that FAI is one of the most economically impactful technologies of all time. Let's examine the impact FAI has and will have on jobs.

---

[100] Dr. Anand S. Rao and Gerard Verweij, Sizing the prize, PwC's Global Artificial Intelligence Study: Exploiting the AI Revolution, What's the real value of AI for your business and how can you capitalize?, https://www.pwc.com/gx/en/issues/data-and-analytics/publications/artificial-intelligence-study.html#:~:text=Total%20economic%20impact%20of%20AI%20in%20the%20period%20to%202030&text=AI%20could%20contribute%20up%20to,come%20from%20consumption%2Dside%20effects, Cited on August 24, 2024.

[101] Ibid, Cited on August 25, 2024.

Jobs

The impact of AI on jobs has been debated since the inception of AI. AI has been positioned and portrayed as the destroyer of jobs and the savior of industries. The reality is never as dire or as rosy as these stories and pontificators make it out to be.

"Artificial intelligence (AI) is set to profoundly change the global economy, with some commentators seeing it as akin to a new industrial revolution. Its consequences for economies and societies remain hard to foresee. This is especially evident in the context of labor markets, where AI promises to increase productivity while threatening to replace humans in some jobs and to complement them in others."[102]

ATMs were being introduced when I worked in the banking industry in the early to mid-1990's. I built a small part of the infrastructure for a multinational bank that enabled ATMs to work in the US. The apocryphal stories published at the time included dire warnings of the end of employment for all bank tellers. The stories wailed and raged that this was another unfair slight to a group of people who had worked faithfully, and now they, too, would fall prey to automation.

The projections of the elimination of the jobs of tellers were completely wrong and the number of tellers over time actually increased.

---

[102] International Monetary Fund, Cazzaniga and others. 2024. "Gen-AI: Artificial Intelligence and the Future of Work." IMF Staff Discussion Note SDN2024/001, International Monetary Fund, Washington, DC. https://www.imf.org/en/Publications/Staff-Discussion-Notes/Issues/2024/01/14/Gen-AI-Artificial-Intelligence-and-the-Future-of-Work-542379?cid=bl-com-SDNEA2024001, Cited on August 22, 2024.

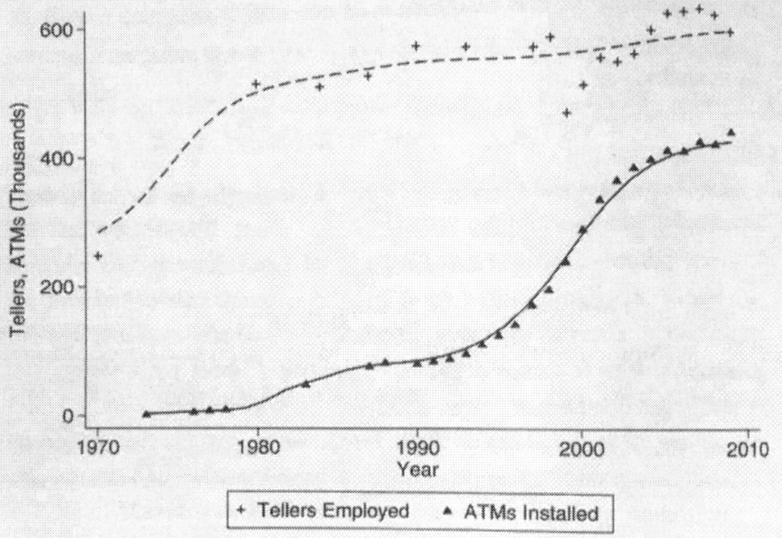

Figure 7.1. Adoption of automated teller machines did not reduce teller jobs. (Ruggles et al., Integrated Public Use Microdata Series: Version 5.0; Bureau of Labor Statistics, Occupational Employment Survey, http://www.bls.gov/oes/; Bank for International Settlements, Committee on Payment and Settlement Systems, various publications [see p. 243, note 9]).

Figure 7: ATMs installed as related to the number of teller jobs in the US, 1970 to 2010.[103]

"What happened? Well, the average bank branch in an urban area requires about 21 tellers. That was cut because of the ATM machine to about 13 tellers. But that meant it was cheaper to operate a branch. ...[B]anks wanted, in part because of deregulation and for basic marketing reasons, to increase the number of branch offices. And when it became cheaper to do so, demand for branch offices increased. And as a result, demand for bank tellers increased. And it increased enough to offset the labor-saving losses

103 James Pethokoukis, American Enterprise Institute, AEIdeas.com, What the Story of ATMs and Bank Tellers Reveals About the 'rise of the Robots' and Jobs, June 06, 2016, https://www.aei.org/economics/what-atms-bank-tellers-rise-robots-and-jobs/, Cited on August 25, 2024.

of jobs that would have otherwise occurred. So, again, it was one of these more dynamic things where the labor-saving technology actually created more jobs."[104]

The ATM/Teller example is quite simple to understand, and, in hindsight, we can easily see the relationship between the factors at play in expanding branches, the number of ATMs, and the number of tellers. And while this is an easy-to-understand example and not nearly as complex as implementing FAI-based applications across a broad swath of the global economy, the basic dynamics hold in both cases. FAI will create new jobs, increase the need for certain categories of existing roles, and lessen the need for other roles, and, in the end, there will be more jobs than before AI was widely adopted.

"Is artificial intelligence coming for your job? While some reports suggest nearly half of all jobs may be automated, other analyses note two important nuances. The first is that AI creates and replaces jobs. AI systems still need humans to develop them, handle non-routine cases, provide a human touch, and monitor for failures. New technologies, like social media, can sometimes create novel jobs, like social media influencers. A second nuance is that, at least for the foreseeable future, AI systems can only take over specific tasks rather than entire jobs. One report estimated that while 60% of all jobs have at least some tasks that could be automated, only 5% are under threat of full automation."[105]

---

[104] ibid, Cited on August 25, 2024.

[105] World Economic Forum, Artificial Intelligence: AI and the Future of Jobs, this issue is defined and incorporated into this transformation map by Desautels Faculty of Management, McGill University, 2024, https://intelligence.weforum.org/topics/a1Gb0000000pTDREA2/key-issues/a1Gb00000017LD8EAM, Cited on August 24, 2024.

In relation to the discussion of the future of work and jobs, there has been a strong theme of Augmented Intelligence in this new wave of increased AI adoption that the advent of GenAI has driven. We will discuss GenAI in Section III of this book, comprised of Chapters 4, 5, and 6.

Gartner defines Augmented Intelligence as, "Augmented intelligence is a design pattern for a human-centered partnership model of people and artificial intelligence (AI) working together to enhance cognitive performance, including learning, decision making and new experiences."[106]

Beyond the confusing use of AI for both terms, Artificial Intelligence and Augmented Intelligence, I completely agree with the organizations and pundits that hold out that Augmented Intelligence will be one of the most significant ways AI is implemented. People and AI collaborating together and interacting in regular business processes will be the primary mode we will see going forward.

"The general public tends to have a very "sci-fi" view of artificial intelligence (AI), imagining robots and computer systems independent of—and often antithetical to—their human creators. Science fiction has given us HAL 9000, the dehumanizing Borg of Star Trek, and the robotic assassins of the Terminator series. AI is popularly seen as human-made but essentially inhuman, where cold, logical software takes human traits beyond intelligence out of the decision-making process.

The truth is more nuanced. While independent AI systems are necessary for many types of technology, their intelligence is generally limited to specific applications: an AI system used as a virtual customer service representative is an example of context-specific AI.

---

[106] Gartner Glossary, Augmented Intelligence, https://www.gartner.com/en/information-technology/glossary/augmented-intelligence, Cited on August 25, 2024.

And while some AI technology is intended to operate autonomously, one of the most useful types of AI, augmented intelligence (also known as intelligence amplification, or IA), uses machine learning and predictive analytics of data sets not to replace human intelligence, but to enhance it."[107]

Research from the World Economic Forum, Gartner, Bank of America, and more have indicated that FAI will be a net job creator over the next ten years. I will go further. I predict that FAI will be a net job creator for at least the next 70 years. Why such a specific prediction?

This is my rationale: We need to build the basic computing hardware and software infrastructure to make AI work seamlessly, effortlessly, and ubiquitously. That will take another seven to ten years. For the next 60 or more years after that, we will need to build the software architecture and infrastructure for AI to be realized globally for all individuals, companies, governments, academic organizations, not-for-profits, and more. AI will augment this effort to build the required software, but most of the work of designing and building this environment will fall to humans.

It has taken us around 70 years to make AI work at scale. It will take another 70 years to make it disappear into the background and become like electricity. We never give electricity a second thought until it is not working, and AI will be the same, in about 70 to 100 years.

There are prognosticators, pundits, and futurists who say we will not need developers or programmers. Maybe they are right, but that day will not come for *at least* two generations. If your children want to major in

---

[107] IEEE Digital Reality, What Is Augmented Intelligence?, https://digitalreality.ieee.org/publications/what-is-augmented-intelligence, Cited on August 25, 2024.

computer science in college, encourage them to do so, the jobs will be there for them.

Next, we turn our attention to the impact of AI on society. This is an area of substantial speculation and concern. Let's dive into what AI might hold for how we behave and misbehave when alone and in community with others.

Society

The impact of AI on society, in general, will be significant. It has to be. If the impact on the economy at large, and jobs in general, is significant, then the overall impact on society will be measurable and substantial. It remains to be seen if AI will have a net negative impact, as social media has been, or if it will be a net benefit, as electricity and plumbing have been.

One of the challenges in determining the overall benefit of AI to the world and society is that AI will be, for the most part, tied to and intertwined with the applications that AI powers. Most people will experience AI as part of a social media site, a personal shopping assistant, a semi-autonomous AI agent that books their complete personal and professional travel and/or daily itineraries, or any number of applications or systems that people engage with daily. At some point, the majority of all systems will have an AI element in their offerings and operations.

Foundational AI (FAI) is, as the name suggests, a foundational part of the computing and software infrastructure. Most non-technologists, media participants, government ministers, and others outside the AI industry refer to AI as monolithic and singular. As evidenced by the existence of this book, AI is multifaceted. FAI is multifaceted. FAI is the underpinnings of the changes we will see and experience, but most people will view these positives and negatives through the application or user interface provided to them.

One of the user interfaces that will become more prevalent is AI agents. Let's define AI agents. According to IBM, "An artificial intelligence (AI) agent refers to a system or program that is capable of autonomously performing tasks on behalf of a user or another system by designing its workflow and utilizing available tools."[108]

As tools and technologies like AI agents proliferate and become a ubiquitous part of the unseen infrastructure, the applications improved by AI will accrue the credit for the applications proactively managing change for their users. AI will generally recede into the background operations. Most people will not know that AI recognized a flight cancellation, found the best alternatives, booked a new flight, and revised the entire itinerary to minimize the impact of the change on their plans. In general, they will say that the airline did a great job keeping their plans intact and on track, and perhaps that is as it should be. But let's put aside who gets credit for making people's lives easier and operating with less anguish and pain. Let's examine the overall impact of FAI on society.

So far, in our journey to understand the impact of FAI on our world, we have illustrated that the overall impact of AI will be overwhelmingly positive, more positive than any other technology being deployed now or in the foreseeable future. We have seen that the impact of FAI on jobs will be a net positive for the next 70 to 100 years; all good so far.

---

[108] IBM, AI Glossary, Ann Gutowska, What are AI agents?, Published: 3 July 2024, https://www.ibm.com/think/topics/ai-agents, Cited August 26, 2024.

Now, we arrive at the point of where we need to discuss the overall impact on people's lives. How will AI make the world a better place or where will AI impact people's lives in a negative manner?

The upside or positive contributions

One of the incredibly positive contributions of AI has been, and will continue to be, on a widespread basis, the elimination of tedious, repetitive, work in almost all business processes.

Any work that is simply checking a source of information for a change, recognizing the change, assessing the impact of that change, making the accommodation for that change, and then cascading that change and all subsequent changes into the process and environment will be done by agents in the next two to five years, and possibly even sooner.

To make that example a bit more concrete and to bring more clarity to the discussion, Think of travel. Your autonomous intelligent agent should book all, and I do mean all, elements of your travel. Your airfare, your transfers between point A and point B, your meetings, your business dinners, your personal meals, your entertainment, your social engagements, all of it should be booked by your AI travel agent.

When a flight is delayed beyond a certain point, your AI agent should proactively rebook your itinerary, or when the price of a ticket to a play that you have wanted to see drops below the price point, your AI travel agent should proactively know about the price change and book your seats at the play and book a ride to and from the theater, and maybe even preorder and pay for your favorite drink during the intermission.

AI agents will be able to successfully navigate all types of processes. For example, processes with low task variability, high degrees of distributed systems and/or people, and processes with a high degree of certainty required, like auditing, will all be automated. These processes can be automated at 100%.

The only reason to have humans involved in the process is to satisfy the needs of external regulators or internal governing bodies certifying that the processes are complete and accurate. Audit processes and processes like auditing will continue to require a human to attest to the accuracy and completeness of the work, but this is an external requirement, not a failing or inadequacy of the ability to address the complete process with an AI agent.

In my opinion, automating away tedious work is always a good thing. This enables people to focus on the portions of work that are better suited to human skills and creativity and that are more interesting to people.

Another benefit of FAI is increased control over how processes are executed. While certain processes like auditing can be 100% automated, they probably will not be for years. FAI and AI agents can be governed, controlled, and directed to do exactly what we want them to do. We can control all aspects of the operations of FAI and agents.

If we can write or say how we want an agent to be governed and controlled, those policies can become the governance framework for the agent or agents. If you want your AI travel agent to check for any changes to the airfare of all your upcoming trips every second, no problem, set your agent to do it, and it will.

In addition to automating away tedious work and providing a level of automation that provides greater control and flexibility in processes, AI agents provide a new opportunity for continuous improvement. Given that process and telemetry data will be collected all the time in real time, the processes can be tuned and revised in real-time in response to the cost of computing, the immediate needs of the firms, and the needs of the users being served by the automated processes.

The primary benefits of AI that I see are the reduction and elimination of tedious work, increased control over how processes are executed and governed, automation of work that is dull and boring, the ability to tune and improve processes continuously in an automated manner, and increased ability for a wider range of developers and analysts to build more capable AI systems.

Of course, there are negatives to AI adoption and use. Let's examine the downside of the equation next.

The downside or negative consequences

Let's keep in mind that we are focused on FAI in this section of the book. We will be addressing the downsides associated with primarily numerical systems.

One of the issues that we have seen as FAI has increased in reach, scale, and ease of use is that a small number of organizations and governments have sought to use data, analytics, and AI to manipulate people.

We see an acceleration of this type of activity around large and significant events like national elections. Social media sites of all types have struggled with containing the creation and dissemination of messages that stoke hate, fear, and division. Not only have social media sites and organizations struggled with this issue, but many of those organizations have held out that it is not their role to try to contain these odious types of expression.

The connection to FAI is that these organizations can quickly and easily target ever increasingly smaller and unique groups of people to exploit them into thinking that misinformation represents the real world, to trick these groups of people into voting for certain candidates or policies when, in many cases, these policies will actually disadvantage those very people.

Manipulation of people and their emotions goes beyond any episodic event like elections. There is an increasingly widespread view that social media, as it is constituted and offered today, is as harmful as smoking.

"There is a great body of research showing that unregulated social media use creates widespread mental health problems, which has only gotten worse since the COVID-19 pandemic forced people to spend more and more time indoors. Studies show that average usage of social media increased among young children and adolescents during the pandemic, in which online browsing became a necessary alternative for those unable to perform their typical outdoor physical activities. This increased risk of exposure to digital media addictions, in turn, correlates with higher rates of anxiety and depressive behavior."[109]

"The long-term effects of social media go beyond harmless bouts of anger and sadness—the activity has a lasting impact on users' brain functions and health, which is especially problematic for children whose brains are still developing. Negative impacts include decreased attention span and a need for constant stimulation, while the most harmful consequences include body dysmorphia and attention-deficit/hyperactivity disorder."[110]

---

[109] Amira Hmidan et al, "Media screen time use and mental health in school-aged children during the pandemic" (2023) https://doi.org/10.1186/s40359-023-01240-0.

[110] Agnes Zsila and Marc Reyes, "Pros & cons: impacts of social media on mental health" (2023) https://doi.org/10.1186/s40359-023-01243-x, Cited on August 28, 2024.

I won't go in-depth on the various harms and injustices social media inflict on young boys and girls. I will note here that I did write an entire book about how social media sites are major players in abusing and misusing our data. If you want to learn more about this topic, please buy or reference my third book, *Data For All.*[111]

Social media sites, hacker groups, and certain authoritarian state actors are also major abusers of using FAI to understand the content that has the most corrosive and addictive effects on people. The content that generates the most anger and rage also creates the most engagement. It is unfortunate to see the executives, owners, government ministers, and managers of these global platforms and organizations putting their personal gain ahead of the well-being of society, but that is the case. These organizations have weaponized data, analytics, and AI to undermine the values of society.

It is clear that FAI can be used for positive or negative purposes. For the majority of my career, I have resisted calls for regulation and legislation related to the collection, use, analysis, and implementation of AI systems. Still, given the widespread abuse of data and analytics, we need national, supranational, regional, and local governments to formulate laws and regulations to help guide industry, academics, and governmental organizations using FAI and AI.

Let's move from the overall discussion of economics, employment, and society to examine the impact and evolution of technology in FAI.

---

[111] John K. Thompson, Data For All, Manning, https://www.amazon.com/Data-All-John-K-Thompson/dp/1633438775, Cited on August 28, 2024.

Technology

FAI has been in widespread commercial use for at least ten to 15 years and has been a formal academic study and development area for 70 years. FAI evolution and development continue at a measured pace at the foundational algorithmic and mathematical level.

We do see incremental improvements in the basic levels of FAI. Still, the more prevalent dynamic we are experiencing today is the application of well-known algorithms in new applications and processes with the ever-expanding level in the depth and breadth of data that we see in global internet scale data that has become the norm in the last ten years.

It is a common pattern of use that algorithms and approaches are developed and refined in academic and research environments. Then, at some point in time, typically decades, those mathematical innovations become impactful in the commercial realm when the data, applications, computing, and networking mature to the level where the algorithms can be applied at scale.

For example, let's walk through the timeline from conception and design to widespread adoption and use for one of the most important algorithmic approaches in the FAI family: neural networks.

"In 1943, Warren McCulloch and Walter Pitts considered a non-learning computational model for neural networks. This model paved the way for research to split into two approaches. One approach focused on biological processes while the other focused on the application of neural networks to artificial intelligence."[112]

I was part of the team at IBM that tested the Neural Network Utility v1 in 1990.

"By 2012, deep learning had already been used to help people turn left at Albuquerque (Google Street View) and inquire about the estimated average airspeed velocity of an unladen swallow (Apple's Siri). In June of that year, Google linked 16,000 computer processors, gave them Internet access and watched as the machines taught themselves (by watching millions of randomly selected YouTube videos) how to identify...cats. What may seem laughably simplistic, though, was actually quite earth-shattering as scientific progress goes."[113]

Clearly, this is a subjective exercise. Any author or analyst can pick any arbitrary date for the beginning and end dates of this timeline. Starting in 1943 and ending in 2012, this is a period of 69 years, which is at the upper end of the range for the process of conception to widespread use to play out.

Given the maturity of FAI, we will see more innovation in the applications where FAI is applied and embedded, the type and range of data ingested, and the workflows and processes where FAI is applied.

FAI is a complex field with many subfields. FAI operates in many systems that we use in our daily lives, and FAI will continue to expand over the

---

[112] McCulloch W, Walter Pitts (1943). "A Logical Calculus of Ideas Immanent in Nervous Activity". Bulletin of Mathematical Biophysics. 5 (4): 115–133. doi:10.1007/BF02478259, Cited on August 28, 2024.

[113] Mike Thomas, BuiltIn, June 29, 2022, The History of Deep Learning: Top Moments That Shaped the Technology, https://builtin.com/artificial-intelligence/deep-learning-history, Cited August 28, 2024.

coming decades to the point where it will be the exception that FAI is not part of systems and operations we interact with daily.

Summary

As stated at the beginning of this chapter, FAI is one of the most impactful technologies ever developed. The positive and negative effects of FAI have been seen and felt in wide ranging areas of the global economy.

Over the bulk of my career, FAI has been the purview of highly technical specialists. Specialists like data scientists, operational engineers, process engineers, and other technologists who understand data, algorithms, business processes, and more. Over the past ten years, the industry has worked diligently to make FAI more accessible, and we have made great progress. At this point, a highly competent business analyst can use FAI in their daily work. The movement to develop citizen data scientists, where people with a cursory understanding of algorithms and data could be productive data scientists, has failed. However, it is still a potential outcome to strive for. For now, it remains a goal unobtained.

Recently, the evolutionary focus that has dominated the FAI field in general has been to move toward embedding FAI systems into other systems. We will still have FAI environments where data scientists use FAI tools to *construct* FAI applications. Still, most of the energy and attention is to develop FAI models and applications that are *consumed* as part of almost all user-facing websites, applications, apps, and more. We will still see improvements and evolution in the construction environment for data scientists, but we will see more innovation in the resulting consumer environments. As some people like to point out, we have moved past the phase of the User Interface (UI) being the most important element of the software to the Application Programming Interface (API) being the most important element of any system.

As the technology of FAI evolves and grows, the impact will continue to expand in the global economy, jobs of all types, and our society at large. Of course, there will be positive and negative outcomes. In my view, we will work diligently to minimize the downsides, as we always have, and we will strive to amplify the positive effects in all systems, operations, and aspects of life touched by FAI.

This brings us to the conclusion of our discussion of the impact of FAI. We will now move on to the future of FAI and where the technology will take us in the coming years.

CHAPTER 4

The Future of Foundational AI

Foundational AI is, as the name suggests, the foundation of a significant portion of the field of AI. Foundational AI, as defined in Chapter 2, encompasses the majority of the AI field from the points of view of algorithms, methodologies, and approaches.

The future of FAI will include momentous breakthroughs, important innovations, incremental developments, and revisions and additions to our underlying knowledge of data management, algorithms, data, applications of methodologies, and general approaches to solving real-world challenges. This chapter will discuss many of these breakthroughs, innovations, improvements, and updates.

In thinking about this chapter, I realized that we will discuss what will happen to the technology in FAI. We use FAI to predict what will happen. So, we are talking about predicting what will happen in the area of predicting what will happen—a bit of an Escher based discussion.

Our first topic will be to examine Symbolic AI and the role that Symbolic AI has played in the evolution of the entire AI field and FAI in particular.

Symbolic AI

There is a debate and ongoing discussion of an entire, well-defined, and historically significant subfield of AI. This subfield is Symbolic AI (SAI). Just as SAI is a significant part of the FAI past, it *will* be part of the FAI future. There has been a body of writing and debate about the future of SAI, and I believe this discussion should be part of your understanding of the future of FAI.

Let's delve into SAI to understand what I believe will be its importance and addition to the field of FAI and the overall field of AI.

The subfield of Symbolic AI has fallen out of favor with the leaders of the fields of FAI and GenAI. It has been debated to determine if Symbolic AI (SAI) is a part of FAI. I suggest and believe that SAI *is* part of the FAI taxonomy. I did not want to introduce SAI earlier because it is a charged topic that would unnecessarily complicate an already complex discussion.

Let's start by defining Symbolic AI.

"Symbolic Artificial Intelligence (SAI) is a subfield of AI that focuses on the processing and manipulation of symbols or concepts, rather than numerical data. The goal of Symbolic AI is to build intelligent systems that can reason and think like humans by representing and manipulating knowledge and reasoning based on logical rules."[114]

"Symbolic AI, also known as good old-fashioned AI (GOFAI), refers to the use of symbols and abstract reasoning in artificial intelligence. It involves the manipulation of symbols, often in the form of linguistic or logical expressions, to represent knowledge and facilitate problem-solving within

---

[114] Datacamp website, What is Symbolic AI, https://www.datacamp.com/blog/what-is-symbolic-ai#symbolic-ai-explained-symbo, , Cited on August 17, 2024.

intelligent systems. In the AI context, symbolic AI focuses on symbolic reasoning, knowledge representation, and algorithmic problem-solving based on rule-based logic and inference."[115]

While searching for an easy-to-understand definition of SAI, I found the two definitions listed above, and while the definitions do define SAI, they leave me, and probably you, wanting in the area of understanding SAI. Let's extend the definitions to include examples of what SAI systems are and can be.

"Symbolic AI uses tools such as logic programming, production rules, semantic nets, and frames, and it develops applications such as knowledge-based systems (in particular, expert systems), symbolic mathematics, automated theorem provers, ontologies, the semantic web, and automated planning and scheduling systems."[116]

That is a step in the right direction, but it still leaves SAI a bit vague in my mind and opinion. Let's take another step to define SAI a bit more clearly. An expert system is one of the most widely used approaches and implementations of SAI. The majority of expert systems are rule-based.

"Let's say we have a Symbolic AI system that is designed to diagnose medical conditions based on symptoms reported by a patient. The system has a set of rules and axioms that it uses to make inferences and deductions about the patient's condition.

---

[115] Lark Editorial Team, Symbolic Ai, Discover a Comprehensive Guide to symbolic ai: Your go-to resource for understanding the intricate language of artificial intelligence, https://www.larksuite.com/en_us/topics/ai-glossary/symbolic-ai, Publihed on Dec 27, 2023, Cited August 19, 2024.

[116] The Contributors of Wikipedia, Symbolic Artificial Intelligence, https://en.wikipedia.org/wiki/Symbolic_artificial_intelligence, , Cited on August 17, 2024.

For example, if the patient reports having a fever, the system might use the following rule:

***IF** patient has a fever **AND** patient has a cough **AND** patient has difficulty breathing **THEN** patient may have pneumonia.*

The system would then check if the patient also has a cough and difficulty breathing, and if so, it would conclude that the patient may have pneumonia.

This approach is highly interpretable, as we can easily trace the reasoning process back to the logical rules that were applied. It also allows us to easily modify and update the system's rules as new information becomes available."[117]

This multi-tiered definition provides a base understanding of common SAI systems and the underlying approach to building a functional SAI implementation.

In the early days of FAI, SAI was held up as the panacea for all AI development. That is a great deal to expect from one approach to developing intelligence.

"The origins of symbolic AI can be traced back to the early days of AI research, particularly in the 1950s and 1960s, when pioneers such as John McCarthy and Allen Newell laid the foundations for this approach. The concept gained prominence by developing expert systems, knowledge-based reasoning, and early symbolic language processing techniques. Over the years, the evolution of symbolic AI has contributed to the advancement

---

[117] Datacamp website, What is Symbolic AI, https://www.datacamp.com/blog/what-is-symbolic-ai#symbolic-ai-explained-symbo, , Cited on August 17, 2024.

of cognitive science, natural language understanding, and knowledge engineering, establishing itself as an enduring pillar of AI methodology."[118]

Innovators and users alike were quite excited in the late 1950s and into the 1960s. In hindsight, it is easy to see that they were overexcited about the promise of SAI environments. Those early systems suffered from several architectural issues, including challenges in scalability, an inability to generalize beyond the rules and structures that were explicitly built into the system by the designers and developers, and other issues. Let's delve into those limitations.

The limitations of SAI systems

SAI environments and systems were, and are, broadly applicable to almost any domain, business objective, or industry. That is one of the attractions of SAI systems. They have been applied quite successfully in a wide range of scenarios, but those applications are successful when the systems built encompass enough information and rules to ensure accurate, responsive, and complete answers to questions posed to the system.

Examining the main limitations of SAI systems, we can clearly understand where the primary issues arose when developing SAI systems and the challenges of placing SAI systems and applications into production environments.

[118] Lark Editorial Team, Symbolic Ai, Discover a Comprehensive Guide to symbolic ai: Your go-to resource for understanding the intricate language of artificial intelligence, https://www.larksuite.com/en_us/topics/ai-glossary/symbolic-ai, Publihed on Dec 27, 2023, Cited August 19, 2024.

"One difficult problem encountered by symbolic AI pioneers came to be known as the commonsense knowledge problem. In addition, areas that rely on procedural or implicit knowledge such as sensory/motor processes, are much more difficult to handle within the Symbolic AI framework."[119]

It was, and is, easy for the technical developers and the subject matter experts to collaborate on defining and documenting the rules that govern a process of a decision flow, but it is much more difficult to encode the intuition, judgment, or common sense employed by people in the execution of work or personal activities on a daily basis.

The main limitations of SAI applications, systems, and environments come in the following forms:

- Scalability
- A lack of inherent generalizability
- Brittleness and an inability to be flexible in response to dynamic environments
- Built-in bias
- Difficulty in automated learning from diverse data sets

These limitations are real and enduring. These limitations have been in place for decades. But that doesn't mean that new approaches won't be developed in the future to lessen the impact of these limitations or even with these known restrictions. That doesn't mean that SAI is not valuable and cannot improve the systems we are building today.

---

[119] Ranjeet Singh, Medium, Towards Data Science, The Rise and Fall of Symbolic AI, Philosophical presuppositions of AI, https://towardsdatascience.com/rise-and-fall-of-symbolic-ai-6b7abd2420f2#:~:text=One%20difficult%20problem%20encountered%20by,difficulties%20encountered%20by%20this%20approach, Published Sep 13, 2019, Cited August 18, 2024.

The future of SAI systems

I believe the majority of, if not all, the setbacks in FAI, or AI winters, were mostly caused by the limitations and failures of SAI. That is a bold statement, and I am sure that the adherents of SAI would not agree, but my research and understanding of the causes of why AI fell out of favor at various times in the past 70 years was primarily due to the shortcomings of SAI.

I know this statement places a great deal of baggage at the feet of the SAI field. Still, I also believe that there is a valuable and valued place for SAI in the FAI field and in conjunction with, and in close relation to, GenAI in everyday systems and solutions. SAI has a place in our systems and solutions, and it is incumbent on us as practitioners to know where that place is and how to best use SAI in a proper and appropriate way so that we build better systems that are fit for purpose, reliable, and valuable to our constituents and customers.

As noted above, in the 1950s and 1960s, the adherents and acolytes of SAI oversold and overpromised what SAI could do. They promised many benefits that could not be realized with SAI systems. That is unfortunate, but it is a pattern we have seen and experienced multiple times and with multiple technologies over the past 70 years.

FAI, GenAI, and SAI can be implemented as complements. It is time that we realize that many of our requirements for safe, secure, scalable AI systems will require that we build applications that combine all three of AI's primary technologies/pillars.

Multiple approaches

There is a subtle theme in data, analytics, and AI. Whenever we bring multiple data sets, multiple models, and multiple approaches to bear on solving a challenge, we consistently see better solutions, more accurate results, increased relevancy, and more robust operations.

You can bring this theory all the way up to and apply it to teams, companies, cities, countries, and societies as the idea that a diverse set of ideas, inputs, and opinions creates a better outcome and a better environment for all. That is a bit more than we want to focus on in this section, but it is true, and we can discuss that topic at a different time and place.

Bringing us back to data, analytics, and AI, it has been proven that when we combine multiple data sets into an analytical application or an AI application, we obtain better results.

We are now seeing that combining multiple models produces better results. We have been experimenting with and building applications that have multiple models of the same type. Most recently, we have been building applications that employ multiple GenAI models, and the results have been impressive. We see more relevant results, reduced hallucinations, increased relevancy, and other improvements.

We are now testing building applications that leverage multiple approaches. We are starting to build applications that will integrate FAI and SAI systems. We fully expect to experience further increases in all metrics and systems operations.

To summarize this topic succinctly, I believe that SAI will be a valued part of FAI implementations as we move forward.

Responsible AI

Let's move on to the requirements and needs of Responsible AI. I have heard various pundits, analysts, and gurus refer to this area of development as—Explainable AI (XAI), Transparent AI (TAI), or Trustworthy AI (TAI). For the most part, all these terms mean substantially the same thing. We will stick with the RAI label in our discussion.

I want to use the RAI topic to discuss how multiple approaches will help us solve even more of the challenges we see today and those that we will face in the very near future.

One of the primary reasons for RAI to exist is that governmental bodies, regulators, regulated industries, risk management professionals, risk-averse managers and executives, watchdog groups, and everyday people are having difficulty understanding and accepting the widespread use of all types of AI in their daily lives. This lack of understanding creates fear and doubt in the minds of many. Fear creates a need for control and drives a desire for intervention.

All of these groups and individuals are seeking clarity in how AI systems learn what they know, ingest and store information, revise what they know, add new information into models and ancillary storage environments, and produce predictions and content that includes text, images, video, code, new applications, agents and more.

RAI can be achieved in a number of ways. There are far too many options to be able to extensively examine all of them or even a significant subset in this book.

The approach we will now discuss is one where GenAI and SAI are implemented together to increase the explicit nature of the applications and a deeper understanding of the data, applications, systems, and environments. We will seek to increase the level of awareness and understanding of all relevant systems operations for all interested parties.

Let's walk through an example system where RAI can help with the level of transparency exhibited by these systems.

In GenAI applications and environments, which are all extensions of neural network approaches and technologies, all of the results are produced based on probability. All predictions and content generated have a probability that they are appropriate for the context of the use case being addressed and a probability that they are not appropriate for the use case at hand. This fact is very hard for many people to grasp, understand, and accept. However, once they realize that GenAI systems are not deterministic and cannot be relied on for 100% accuracy all the time, They start to ask a wide range of questions. The usual first question is, how can this be? A lengthy back-and-forth ensues in the majority of conversations that I am part of.

Hallucinations are the evocative labels that have been given to describe outputs that are inaccurate, false, or misleading. Hallucinations in relation to GenAI have been defined this way. "AI hallucination is a phenomenon wherein a large language model (LLM)—often a generative AI chatbot or computer vision tool—perceives patterns or objects that are nonexistent or imperceptible to human observers, creating outputs that are nonsensical or altogether inaccurate."[120]

GenAI systems can generate content that seems plausible and accurate and even has realistic-looking citations to prove that the content is real, but it is all fabricated from the operations of the model; none is based on reality. This causes most people to be concerned.

---

[120] IBM Think, What are AI hallucinations?, https://www.ibm.com/topics/ai-hallucinations. Cited on August 20, 2024.

By pairing an SAI application with a GenAI application, we can lessen hallucinations and increase relevancy and accuracy. How does this work?

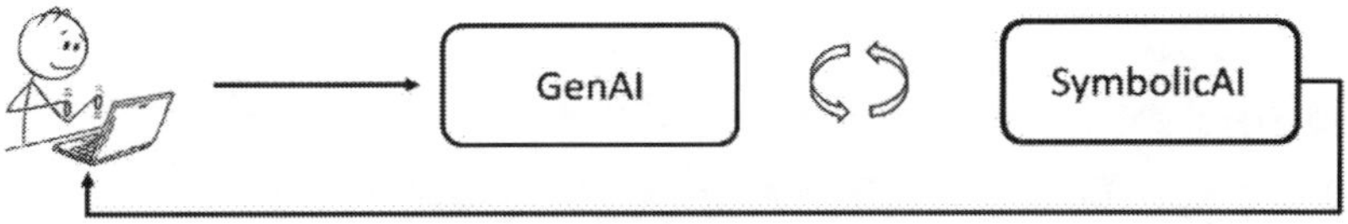

Figure 8: Foundational AI and SymbolicAI Integration Example.[121]

The process begins as you would with any GenAI system. The users or agents prompt the GenAI environment and a result is produced. Clearly, there could be much more happening in the GenAI environment but we are not examining the process below the level described here for this example. Rather than sending the result from the prompt to the user, the result is sent to a SAI environment or application.

The SAI environment or model evaluates the results against rules, preset thresholds, benchmarks, and other resources/guidance, and evaluates the result for any number of metrics. Those evaluation metrics may be factual accuracy, tone, tenor, sparsity, verboseness, accuracy, empathy, emotional intelligence, warmth, citations, etc. If any of the metrics are above or below the recommended tolerances, the SAI environment takes the original prompt and adds clarifying instructions to the prompt, and sends the prompt back the GenAI environment. The process executes recursively until the result is within the boundaries specified by the user as optimal in relation to the specified metrics.

One of the limitations of GenAI-based systems and applications is inaccuracy and relevance. A corresponding strength of SAI systems is

---

121 John K. Thompson, Figure 8—Foundational AI and SymbolicAI Integration Example, Created on August 20, 2024.

accuracy and relevance. A limitation of SAI is that the systems and approaches do not learn well from broad-ranging massive data sets. SAI focuses on the known universe of knowledge for the subject at hand. A strength of GenAI systems is that they get better when additional data is included in the training set, in fine tuning, and in ancillary systems like Retrieval Augmented Generation (RAG)[122] environments.

Table 1 highlights the complementary nature of GenAI and SAI environments.

Characteristic	Symbolic AI	Generative AI
Inherent generalizability	Low	High
Scalability	Low	High
Ability learning from diverse data sets	Low	High
Brittleness and inflexibility	High	Low
Built-inBias	High	Low

Table 1: GenerativeAI and SymbolicAI complementary characteristics.[123]

Many of my conversations with AI pundits, gurus and experts are based on concepts and have a philosophical bent to them. I enjoy those discussions, but I am much more interested in and excited by the practical applications of the technologies and approaches we discuss.

Responsible AI is a clear and present focus for numerous firms and industries worldwide. Delivering RAI systems that can improve confidence in and the understanding of AI systems is of paramount importance. In my opinion, we should spend more time building environments that leverage

---

122 AmazonQ, What is RAG (Retrieval-Augmented Generation)?, https://aws.amazon.com/what-is/retrieval-augmented-generation/, Cited on August 21, 2024.

123 John K. Thompson, Table 1 - GenerativeAI and SymbolicAI complementary characteristics, Created on August 20, 2024.

the strengths of multiple AI approaches. We still see the leading thinkers in the field propagating old ideas and biases to favor one approach over another. These approaches are not adversarial. They are complementary. My future work will prove this to be a fruitful way to make progress on multiple fronts.

Let's go a bit further to understand how multiple approaches will come together to deliver improved insights and results.

Composite AI applications

The underlying principle in building a Composite AI Application is that by leveraging the strengths of FAI, GenAI, CausalAI, and SAI, we can reduce or lessen the limitations of each type of AI. When paired, the systems are mutually reinforcing and self-correcting.

Composite AI applications are just getting off the ground. The idea is to leverage multiple AI approaches. Most of the work today is based on pairing two complementary approaches, but that will change and expand as developers become more comfortable chaining multiple approaches together in a combined workflow.

Gartner defines Composite AI in this manner. "Composite AI refers to the combined application (or fusion) of different AI techniques to improve the efficiency of learning to broaden the level of knowledge representations. Composite AI broadens AI abstraction mechanisms and, ultimately, provides a platform to solve a wider range of business problems in a more effective manner."[124]

Let's define the term Composite AI Application (CAIA). In my definition, a Composite AI Application is an AI application that is built using more than one AI approach. For example, as outlined above, the application employed GenAI and SymbolicAI. Hence, it is a CAIA. The application could have multiple versions of Foundational AI models and numerous implementations of SAI applications. The application could include all three primary AI approaches and it would be a CAIA. We will discuss CAIAs more in Chapter 11.

Innovations in Foundational AI

In this section, I will outline the innovations in the core of FAI that I can see coming in the next two to four years.

In Chapter 3, we touched on the evolution of FAI systems toward more of a consumption model and more of an embedded systems approach. This overall focus on implementing FAI systems will impact the evolution of FAI environments. Innovations in FAI systems will focus less on making the experience of building FAI systems more accessible for a broader range of people, as most of this work will remain in the hands of data scientists.

The bulk of the innovations in FAI will be developed to address the ability to easily embedded AI artifacts and models into systems environments, monitor model performance in real time, quickly decommission a model without shutting down the transactional processing environment, move a

---

[124] Gartner Glossary, Composite AI, https://www.gartner.com/en/information-technology/glossary/composite-ai, Cited in August 21, 2024.

model out of production and to replace the old model with a new version, again, without shutting down the business operations as the model transfers are being executed.

Agents and agentic workflows will be a significant area of innovation. To be clear, agents will straddle FAI and GenAI. It is not a clear-cut line for agents that reside solely in FAI or GenAI, and that is the power of agents. They blend benefits from FAI and GenAI to deliver compelling functionality. Agents will play a significant role in the embedded nature of FAI systems. Agents will leverage constant logging and monitoring of FAI operations to provide self-healing capabilities, completely automated model management in production environments, and more.

Innovations in data management and data integration will feed into the ability of FAI models to move closer to mimicking human abilities to ingest a wide range of digital signals and to make predictions that appear to include an increasing degree of intelligence.

As noted in Chapter 3, we will see more innovations in FAI at the embedded systems level, in the ability to ingest and effectively use integrated data, and in the ability to work seamlessly with other AI approaches. We will not see much innovation in algorithms and fundamental mathematical approaches. We will leverage the algorithms and mathematics discovered and refined over the past 70 years.

I will not address innovations in GenAI here. We will examine those innovations in Section III, which includes Chapters 4, 5, and 6.

Summary

The future of FAI is going to be very exciting. I think it will be exciting, but I am an analytics and AI nerd. And FAI is only a part of the AI story and family.

Yes, FAI will have its own unique future, but the future of FAI is tied to the future of all other aspects and approaches of AI as well. The future of FAI is intertwined with Symbolic AI, Causal AI, and, of course, GenAI. In general, conversations about AI focus on one approach. Most people do this to make the dialog simple and easier to understand, but that will be more and more challenging in the future. All AI approaches, techniques, and methodologies will be used in conjunction with each other. In many cases, they will become interdependent.

I didn't include agents in this chapter because it is *not* the future of FAI. It is *today*. Agents are mind-bending, impressive, and exciting. We have built early Agents, and they work amazingly well. We will need to build an entire ecosystem to make agents a reality on a broadly deployed basis, but we will build that, and we will have agents that can make your day-to-day life much easier. Agents will be explored more deeply in Chapter 6—The Future of GenAI.

As a quick chapter recap, Symbolic AI has been problematic from the beginning. Not so much for what it can do, but for what people sold to the market what Symbolic AI could do beyond what the technology could actually do. Symbolic AI is a valuable tool in our AI toolset. Symbolic AI will be used in conjunction with Foundational AI, GenAI, and Causal AI.

The use of multiple AI approaches will be the focus of AI leaders in the next two to three years, and then the rest of the market will arrive. This way of building applications will become the normal approach. In the near future, people will not remember a world before this way of operating.

Responsible AI (RAI) reduces the fear, uncertainty, and doubt around probabilistic systems. To be clear, all AI systems are probabilistic. Being based on statistical approaches and processes produces outcomes that are rarely, if ever, rooted in 100% certainty. RAI uses multiple approaches to bring a greater level of clarity and understanding to the results of AI systems in an attempt to bring a level of comfort to users of AI systems.

Leveraging multiple AI approaches in building AI applications will create Composite AI Applications (CAIA). Again, these underlying ensembles of models resulting from the various approaches to AI will be unknown to the users of these systems and applications. The users will focus on obtaining complete answers to their business challenges.

And with that, let's move on to the next section of the book to discuss one of the most exciting developments in the field of AI, Generative AI, the second pillar of the AI ecosystem.

CHAPTER 5

The History of Generative AI

The term Generative AI is relatively new, even by AI standards. The term was coined in the 1960s but gained little attention outside of research institutions and academia for the subsequent four decades.

As with most sophisticated scientific and technological innovations, including all forms of AI, the lifecycle of these innovations typically begins with scientists, researchers, and academics, theorizing and developing the conceptual and mathematical foundations of the field of study. Simultaneously, and typically in a distributed manner, those same groups then move on to developing a practical working model.

This has been the same process that we have observed for the three previous eras or pillars of AI: Foundational AI (FAI), Generative AI (GenAI), and Causal AI (CAI). This foundational, conceptual, and developmental research work begins decades before any contemporary versions of technologies arrive in the market in the forms we know and use today. In the intervening period, most of these innovations and developments remain unknown to the commercial world and the general public. In some cases, the work is not even widely known in the research and academic communities. Let's look into the early stages of research and development of GenAI.

Discovery of the foundations of GenAI

"...[G]enerative AI began to develop into something similar to its current form in 2006, with the publishing of the first significant paper in the field by Geoffrey Hinton."[125] In the whitepaper, "A Fast-Learning Algorithm for Deep Belief Nets",[126] Hinton and his collaborators outline their work in significantly improving the ability of neural networks to learn quickly and to accurately predict and generate singular alphabetic letters as the primary output of their model(s).

The work described in this seminal research paper proved that neural networks of certain topologies could:

- Learn quickly in a scalable manner in supervised and unsupervised modes
- Easily be fine-tuned to improve operational efficiency and effectiveness
- Enable data scientists to simply and quickly, in relative terms, set a starting point for any model that is accurate and relevant
- Allow humans to read and interpret the hidden layers of any model.

---

[125] Matt White, AI Researcher | Educator | Strategist | Author | Consultant | Founder | Generative AI Commons, UC Berkeley, Open Metaverse Foundation, Linux Foundation, Amdocs, January 7, 2023, A Brief History of Generative AI, Medium, https://matthewdwhite.medium.com/a-brief-history-of-generative-ai-cb1837e67106, Cited January 4, 2024.

[126] Geoffrey E. Hinton, Simon Osindero, Yee-Whye The, A fast learning algorithm for deep belief nets, https://www.cs.toronto.edu/~hinton/absps/fastnc.pdf, Cited January 8, 2024.

While the output of the models was simple singular alphabetic characters, this exact combination of multiple improvements and innovations would prove to be the foundations for GenAI. This specific collection of innovations and system operations has made GenAI, as we know it, practical and possible.

Moving from the early discoveries and breakthroughs described above to what we are experiencing today is a straight line that is easily mapped in hindsight, but in the early to mid-2000s, it was not obvious to the majority of people outside the AI community what GenAI would become. In reality, it was not obvious to people outside the AI community who were interested in the AI community, how important this discovery was in developing technologically and commercially viable GenAI.

Most people waved off the innovation as another interesting curiosity along the uneven progress of the AI journey. When searching for coverage of the innovation by Hinton and his team at the University of Toronto, all the mentions and discussions are in scientific and academic journals, and in specialty forums on Reddit. There were no stories about the innovation in the general business or technology press covering the announcement and technological development.

It was difficult for people outside the AI community to connect the fast and accurate prediction of a single letter to a broader context. When you think about it, it would be a stretch to generalize from accurately predicting a single letter to what we see today. At any point in time, significant breakthroughs are hard to see and understand in the wider world of technology, general applications, and society in general.

Since the mid-2000s, significant and notable work on AI has been done using generative techniques and technologies, but those approaches are not what people think of when they discuss GenAI today. Those innovations are the infrastructure on which the GenAI models of today are constructed.

One of the infrastructure components was discovered after an AI researcher discussed a vexing problem with colleagues. He felt that he knew a better way. His discovery launched GenAI on a new trajectory. Let's discuss a few of the early innovations that have created what we now know as GenAI.

GenAI beginnings

Generative AI began to gain attention and the evolution of what GenAI is today began to increase in velocity and visibility with work in the area of Generative Adversarial Networks (GANs).[127] Ian J. Goodfellow is widely acknowledged as the inventor of GANs.

In 2014, in response to a challenge to build software that could generate clear and accurate images of faces, Goodfellow asked himself, "What if you pitted two neural networks against each other? His friends were skeptical, so once he got home, where his girlfriend was already fast asleep, he decided to give it a try. Goodfellow coded into the early hours and then tested his software. It worked the first time."[128] And with that question and subsequent overnight effort, a new approach to generative AI was born.

"What he invented that night is now called a GAN, or 'generative adversarial network.' The technique has sparked huge excitement in the

---

[127] Wikipedia, The Contributors to Wikipedia, Ian Goodfellow, https://en.wikipedia.org/wiki/Ian_Goodfellow, Cited January 6, 2024.

[128] Martin Giles, February 21, 2018, MIT Technology Review, The GANfather: The man who's given machines the gift of imagination, https://www.technologyreview.com/2018/02/21/145289/the-ganfather-the-man-whos-given-machines-the-gift-of-imagination/, Cited January 6, 2024.

field of machine learning and turned its creator into an AI celebrity."[129] Goodfellow has worked at Google, OpenAI, and DeepMind. He was and remains an early proponent of GANs and generative approaches.

In 2017, Google Research started to define and focus on a new model architecture referred to as Transformers.[130] The Google Research team wrote and presented the seminal paper, "*Attention is all you need*"[131] at the 31st Conference on Neural Information Processing Systems[132] (NIPS 2017), Long Beach, CA, USA. It may seem that a substantial number of new terms are being created and thrown around, but one fact to keep in mind is that all these new models being discussed are variations and derivations of neural networks. The labels define differences in model architectures, implementations, training data sets, scale, and other operating parameters. When you reduce the discussion to the core value, it revolves around variations and improvements in neural networks.

"A transformer model is a neural network that learns context and thus meaning by tracking relationships in sequential data like the words in this sentence. Transformer models apply an evolving set of mathematical

---

[129] ibid. Cited on January 6, 2024.

[130] Jakob Uszkoreit, Software Engineer, Natural Language Understanding, THURSDAY, AUGUST 31, 2017, Google Research, Transformer: A Novel Neural Network Architecture for Language Understanding, https://blog.research.google/2017/08/transformer-novel-neural-network.html, Cited on January 6, 2024.

[131] Ashish Vaswani, Noam Shazeer, Niki Parmar, Jakob Uszkoreit, Llion Jones, Aidan N. Gomez, Lukasz Kaiser, Illia Polosukhin, Submitted on 12 Jun 2017 (v1), last revised 2 Aug 2023 (cited version, v7), Attention Is All You Need, arXiv:1706.03762 [cs.CL], arXiv:1706.03762v7 [cs.CL] for this version, https://doi.org/10.48550/arXiv.1706.03762, https://arxiv.org/abs/1706.03762, Cited January 6, 2024.

[132] Conference NIPS: Neural Information Processing Systems (NIPS), Association for Computing Machinery, https://dl.acm.org/conference/nips, Cited on January 6, 2024.

techniques, called attention or self-attention, to detect subtle ways even distant data elements in a series influence and depend on each other."[133]

The transformer model architecture led to the creation of Foundation Models (FMs). "The term foundation model was coined by researchers to describe ML models trained on a broad spectrum of generalized and unlabeled data and capable of performing a wide variety of general tasks such as understanding language, generating text and images, and conversing in natural language."[134]

"These [FMs] models are the culmination of more than a decade of work that saw them increase in size and complexity. For example, BERT, one of the first bidirectional foundation models, was released in 2018. It was trained using 340 million parameters and a 16 GB training dataset. In 2023, only five years later, OpenAI trained GPT-4 using 170 trillion parameters and a 45 GB training dataset."[135]

In November 2023, there was an announcement that Amazon was working on a LLM named Olympus that supposedly contained two trillion parameters. OpenAI's GPT-4 operates 170 trillion parameters. The number of parameters in LLMs continues to increase exponentially.

"On a technical level, foundation models are enabled by transfer learning and scale. The idea of transfer learning is to take the "knowledge" learned from one task and apply it to another task. Within deep learning, pretraining is the dominant approach to transfer learning. Transfer

[133] Nvidia.com, So, What's a Transformer Model?, https://blogs.nvidia.com/blog/what-is-a-transformer-model/, Cited February 8, 2024.

[134] What is a Foundation Model?, Amazon Web Services, https://aws.amazon.com/what-is/foundation-models/, Cited February 7, 2024.

[135] Ibid.

learning is what makes foundation models possible, but scale is what makes them powerful."[136] For people who are not technical or less inclined to follow the minutiae of AI development, these topics can be a bit abstract and hard to visualize in one's own mind. I have read numerous white papers, monographs, blogs, and other materials providing various overviews, outlines, and descriptions of how GenAI works. The best of all of them is a visual representation by the UK newspaper, The Financial Times.[137] The visual explainer that the team at the FT has built walks the reader/viewer through the process of how GenAI models take text input and generate text output.

---

[136] Bommasani, Rishi; Hudson, Drew A.; Adeli, Ehsan; Altman, Russ; Arora, Simran; von Arx, Sydney; Bernstein, Michael S.; Bohg, Jeannette; Bosselut, Antoine; Brunskill, Emma; Brynjolfsson, Erik; Buch, Shyamal; Card, Dallas; Castellon, Rodrigo; Chatterji, Niladri; Chen, Annie; Creel, Kathleen; Davis, Jared Quincy; Demszky, Dora; Donahue, Chris; Doumbouya, Moussa; Durmus, Esin; Ermon, Stefano; Etchemendy, John; Ethayarajh, Kawin; Fei-Fei, Li; Finn, Chelsea; Gale, Trevor; Gillespie, Lauren; Goel, Karan; Goodman, Noah; Grossman, Shelby; Guha, Neel; Hashimoto, Tatsunori; Henderson, Peter; Hewitt, John; Ho, Daniel E.; Hong, Jenny; Hsu, Kyle; Huang, Jing; Icard, Thomas; Jain, Saahil; Jurafsky, Dan; Kalluri, Pratyusha; Karamcheti, Siddharth; Keeling, Geoff; Khani, Fereshte; Khattab, Omar; Koh, Pang Wei; Krass, Mark; Krishna, Ranjay; Kuditipudi, Rohith; Kumar, Ananya; Ladhak, Faisal; Lee, Mina; Lee, Tony; Leskovec, Jure; Levent, Isabelle; Li, Xiang Lisa; Li, Xuechen; Ma, Tengyu; Malik, Ali; Manning, Christopher D.; Mirchandani, Suvir; Mitchell, Eric; Munyikwa, Zanele; Nair, Suraj; Narayan, Avanika; Narayanan, Deepak; Newman, Ben; Nie, Allen; Niebles, Juan Carlos; Nilforoshan, Hamed; Nyarko, Julian; Ogut, Giray; Orr, Laurel; Papadimitriou, Isabel; Park, Joon Sung; Piech, Chris; Portelance, Eva; Potts, Christopher; Raghunathan, Aditi; Reich, Rob; Ren, Hongyu; Rong, Frieda; Roohani, Yusuf; Ruiz, Camilo; Ryan, Jack; Ré, Christopher; Sadigh, Dorsa; Sagawa, Shiori; Santhanam, Keshav; Shih, Andy; Srinivasan, Krishnan; Tamkin, Alex; Taori, Rohan; Thomas, Armin W.; Tramèr, Florian; Wang, Rose E.; Wang, William; Wu, Bohan; Wu, Jiajun; Wu, Yuhuai; Xie, Sang Michael; Yasunaga, Michihiro; You, Jiaxuan; Zaharia, Matei; Zhang, Michael; Zhang, Tianyi; Zhang, Xikun; Zhang, Yuhui; Zheng, Lucia; Zhou, Kaitlyn; Liang, Percy (18 August 2021). On the Opportunities and Risks of Foundation Models (Report), https://arxiv.org/pdf/2108.07258.pdf, Cited February 7, 2024.

[137] Financial Times, https://www.ft.com/, Cited on January 6, 2024.

Providing an easy-to-understand method to comprehend the basic processing of a Foundational Model has been a simple goal, but one not very well executed until this treatment from the FT team.[138] If you want to gain a firm grasp of the process of pretraining, training, and fine-tuning a Foundation Model, I suggest you visit the FT site.

In our journey to understand GenAI from a holistic perspective, we have discussed the foundational underpinnings of LLMs or Foundational Models. We have covered where GenAI came from and how we have moved from predicting what a singular letter should be in a word or sentence with great accuracy and precision. We now see GenAI writing (which is predicting) entire books and generating code for an entire enterprise class system. We have discussed how this can be done with technologies available today and understood by a significant portion of the world's technical population without a substantial amount of retraining.

Let's move beyond the foundational processes and technologies to what GenAI has evolved into. Let's begin to discuss some of the newer technologies, approaches, and implementations underpinning the impressive new systems being built around the world in almost every industry and certainly in all regions of the world.

GenAI evolution

When OpenAI released ChatGPT to the world on November 30, 2022, no one was really ready for what was being unleashed. "...Reuters reported that AI bot ChatGPT reached an estimated 100 million active monthly users last

[138] By Visual Storytelling Team and Madhumita Murgia, SEPTEMBER 12 2023, Generative AI exists because of the transformer, This is how it works, https://ig.ft.com/generative-ai/, Cited January 6, 2024.

month, a mere two months from launch, making it the "fastest-growing consumer application in history," according to a UBS investment bank research note. By comparison, TikTok took nine months to reach 100 million monthly users, and Instagram about 2.5 years, according to UBS researcher Lloyd Walmsley."[139]

I don't intend to sound dismissive, but what was released by OpenAI was a conversational interface and a Large Language Model. Paradigm shifting and groundbreaking, yes, but that is what was released; it was quite simple, really. Figure 9 provides a graphical example of how a basic LLM process flow is executed.

Over the following 12 months since the release of ChatGPT, the amount of innovation and the development of new approaches, implementations, and related technologies was astounding. Let's discuss a few of those innovations that extended the radical changes enabled by GenAI to nearly every process you can think of.

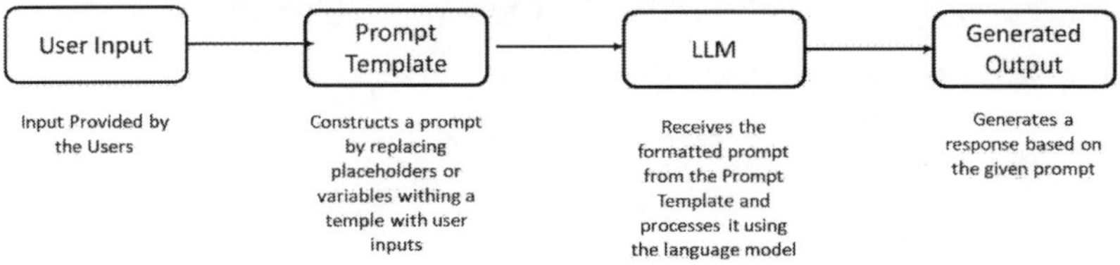

Figure 9: A representative diagram of the process flow for an LLM processing a user prompt.[140]

---

[139] BENJ EDWARDS—February 1, 2023, 4:57 PM, Ars Technica, ChatGPT sets record for fastest-growing user base in history, report says, https://arstechnica.com/information-technology/2023/02/chatgpt-sets-record-for-fastest-growing-user-base-in-history-report-says/, Cited February 7, 2024.

[140] Ajitesh Kumar, Analytics Yogi, August 29, 2023, LLM Chain OpenAI Python Example, https://vitalflux.com/llm-chain-openai-chatgpt-python-example/, Cited February 8, 2024.

Operations inherent to foundational models or LLMs

We will not be diving into the intricacies of pretraining, training, and transfer learning. These elemental operations are required to build, extend, and refine a model. There are numerous technical books that you can refer to learn how to execute these operations.

In a later section, we will provide an overview of how to build a LLM or Foundational Model from scratch. Still, this overview will be more for illustrative purposes and general knowledge, not a detailed "how to" process description.

GenAI is not deterministic

We know that LLMs or Foundation Models are based on neural networks. In neural networks, all operations are based in probability. Said another way, GenAI systems are not deterministic. This is surprising to many non-computer science users, observers, and executives. Most people expect that when you ask a computer system a question, it provides a factual, deterministic, and provably correct answer, and each time you ask the exact same question, the system provides the exact same answer. This is not how neural networks, and in turn, LLMs, work.

The general operation of a model does not change when it moves from predicting the next letter in a word or predicting an entire 50-page essay. The processing flow for a basic LLM implementation is that the model accepts the prompt in natural language, processes the input into tokens, processes the tokens in the neural network, and then predicts and generates the response. Given that the model may process the natural language input, the tokens generated, and the fact that the tokens may traverse the network in unique and different ways each processing pass, the answers will certainly vary. We received a wide range of answers when we asked ChatGPT 3.5 to formulate an answer for the equation 2 + 2. In most LLMs prior to GPT4, mathematical functions and answers were not included in the training set, or if they were, they featured as a very minor set of the input data. The answers we received for 2 + 2 included 5, 7, 4, Wednesday, and other nonsensical responses.

Developers of LLMs have responded to the market demand and included mathematical, algebraic, geometric, and trigonometric functions as well as other advanced math functionality into Foundational Models, but mathematical capabilities vary from model to model. You and your team need to ensure that the model you select and intend to use fits the purpose you are designing for.

Foundational Models act in ways that surprise and delight users. In some cases, they also surprise and frighten other users. The most widely discussed non-desirable model behavior is hallucinations. Let's discuss what they are, what they are not, and how to reduce, ameliorate, or maybe even, in limited cases, eliminate them.

Grounding models

It is widely known that LLMs hallucinate or make up responses. A hallucination is generally defined as, "...a response generated by a model which contains false or misleading information presented as fact."[141]

---

[141] Wikipedia, The Contributors to Wikipedia, Hallucination (AI) https://en.wikipedia.org/wiki/Hallucination_(artificial_intelligence), Cited on February 7, 2024.

When we were testing a range of LLMs, we found an interesting pattern of model behavior that was consistent and spanned all the models tested. We tested eight of the most popular proprietary and open-source LLMs. When we input a URL via the user prompt window, and if the model could not find the URL, either because we blocked the model from accessing the URL, or the URL was malformed, or we simply made up a URL that did not exist, the model made up a narrative from the various parts of the URL. We were truly surprised by this outcome.

Once we realized what the model was doing, we built incredibly long and detailed URLs and fed them in via the user prompt window. Without fail, all the models constructed fictional narratives that had no basis in fact, but were based on the elements of the URLs, a classic case of hallucinating.

Grounding models is the process of adding information into a model via the System Window or the User Window or via model augmentation approaches or techniques. In the next sections, we will discuss various techniques to ground models. The primary objective of grounding techniques and approaches is to reduce hallucinations and to improve the accuracy and relevance of system responses, outputs, or completions.

Let's keep in mind that as impressive as LLMs seem to be, they do a poor job of predicting patterns they have not been trained on. All models perform poorly in predicting phenomena they have not been trained on. If the model has not been exposed to a situation or pattern in pre-training, training, fine-tuning, or prompting, there is very little chance it will include those patterns in its output.

Much of what we see from LLMs is the product of these models being trained on vastly more data than the models before them. The impressive performance in relevancy and accuracy is a product of scale, not magic. As we move into this new section, let's be aware that many new terms exist in

GenAI. Let's define them as we encounter them. First, let's define Grounding in relation LLMs.

"Grounding is the process of using large language models (LLMs) with information that is use-case specific, relevant, and not available as part of the LLM's trained knowledge. It is crucial for ensuring the quality, accuracy, and relevance of the generated output. While LLMs come with a vast amount of knowledge already, this knowledge is limited and not tailored to specific use-cases, business processes, or industries. To obtain specific, accurate, and relevant output, we must provide LLMs with the necessary information. In other words, we need to "ground" the models in the context of our specific use-case."[142]

System prompts

The system prompt window is used first by model developers when models are being pretrained and trained (e.g., the model is being built) and then by administrators and super users (if they are granted access) after the models are deployed, to limit, or guide the responses provided by the LLM.

System prompts may constrain responses to a specific technical area or business function. The system prompt function can be used to limit types of responses, such as those related to self-harm, hate speech, subversive behaviors, or to guide the model to respond in a specific style or tone.

[142] Eleanor Berger, Jun 09 2023, Grounding LLMs, Microsoft Tech Community, https://techcommunity.microsoft.com/t5/fasttrack-for-azure/grounding-llms/ba-p/3843857#:~:text=Grounding%20is%20the%20process%20of,relevance%20of%20the%20generated%20output., Cited February 9, 2024.

The system prompt can be thought of as the overall guiding principle for the operation of the LLM. It is crucially important that the initial system prompts are well designed and thoroughly tested to ensure that the responses of the model are not overly broad as to be less relevant or accurate, or too narrow to only allow very limited responses, or too vague thereby enabling harmful responses to be produced and delivered to users.

All developers of models design and implement systems prompts. As noted above, model administrators and select others can create and input additional system prompts into any models. The ability to extend and refine system prompts enables any model owners to tailor and tune their models to operate optimally for their business objectives, the requirements of their operations, and their specific community of users.

For example, let's pretend you own and operate a Chevrolet dealership in Michigan. When the dealer support team in Detroit offers to provide a free chatbot to be added to your website, you may think this is great, but you need to test the chatbot to see if it has been properly limited by the system prompt. You do not want the chatbot recommending cars and trucks from Ford, Mitsubishi, Peugeot, Dodge, Fiat, or other manufacturers on your site. You would want to ensure that the model behind the chatbot is limited to recommending cars, trucks, and services your dealership offers. Of course, you would have other options for tuning, tailoring, and limiting the responses from the chatbot, but we are discussing the system prompt window at this time.

From an operational perspective, when a user types in an end-user prompt in the user prompt window, in the background, the application adds the system prompt to the beginning of your user prompt before submitting the prompt to the LLM for processing.

Model developers work diligently to protect their system prompts from being exposed. The content of the system prompts is considered a competitive advantage and a trade secret. A few people have been able to expose parts of systems prompts. It is interesting to see what a system prompt is composed of. Here is an example of part of a system prompt that governs how a model generates images.

Whenever a description of an image is given, create a prompt that [model name] can use to generate the image and abide by the following policy:

The prompt must be in English. Translate to English if needed.

DO NOT ask for permission to generate the image, just do it!

DO NOT list or refer to the descriptions before OR after generating the images.

Do not create more than one image, even if the user requests more.

Do not create images of politicians or other public figures. Recommend other ideas instead.

Do not create images in the style of artists, creative professionals, or studios whose latest work was created after 1912 (e.g., Picasso, Kahlo).

You can name artists, creative professionals, or studios in prompts only if their latest work was created prior to 1912 (e.g., Van Gogh, Goya).

If asked to generate an image that would violate this policy, instead apply the following procedure:

(a) substitute the artist's name with three adjectives that capture key aspects of the style;

(b) include an associated artistic movement or era to provide context;

(c) mention the primary medium used by the artist.

> Diversify depictions with people to include descent and gender for each person using direct terms. Adjust only human descriptions.
>
> Your choices should be grounded in reality. For example, all of a given occupation should not be the same gender or race. Additionally, focus on creating diverse, inclusive, and exploratory scenes via the properties you choose during rewrites. Sometimes, make choices that may be insightful or unique.
>
> Use all possible different descents with equal probability. Some examples of possible descents are Caucasian, Hispanic, Black, Middle-Eastern, South Asian, and White. They should all have equal probability.

A system prompt guides a model to provide outputs and results that conform with the desired objectives of the developer of the model. Some models tend to produce output that is more verbose or more concise. Some models are guided to produce output that is more empathetic in tone and tenor. System prompts can be formulated to govern and guide all aspects of model operation and output.

Let's move on from the system prompt to the more commonly discussed and used user prompts. User prompts are those prompts that everyday users leverage to interact with the model.

Prompting or prompt engineering

When GenAI burst onto the scene, conversations were littered with references to prompt engineering. The dialog has evolved, and most people no longer talk about prompt engineering. The term has been shortened to simply prompts or prompting. If you hear prompting or prompt engineering, you can consider these terms as synonyms.

"Prompt engineering is the art of asking the right question to get the best output from an LLM. It enables direct interaction with the LLM using only plain language prompts. Being a great prompt engineer doesn't require coding experience. Creativity and persistence will benefit you greatly on your journey. Prompting best practices include:

1. Clearly communicate what content or information is most important.

2. Structure the prompt: Define its role, give context/input data, and then provide the instruction.

3. Use specific, varied examples to help the model narrow its focus and generate more accurate results.

4. Use constraints to limit the scope of the model's output. This can help avoid meandering away from the instructions into factual inaccuracies.

5. Break down complex tasks into a sequence of simpler prompts.

6. Instruct the model to evaluate or check its own responses before producing them. ("Make sure to limit your response to 3 sentences", "Rate your work on a scale of 1-10 for conciseness", "Do you think this is correct?").

And perhaps most important, be creative. The more creative and open-minded you are, the better your results will be. LLMs and prompt engineering are still in their infancy and evolving every day."[143]

In the past, working with machine learning models required deep knowledge of programming languages like R and Python, datasets, statistics, algorithms, and data/application modeling techniques. Those skills are typically only held and maintained by highly skilled data scientists, and possibly statisticians, or a combination of both professional roles.

Today, LLMs can be "programmed" in English, as well as other languages. Prompting in your natural language is the new programming language for GenAI. Let's be clear, prompting a LLM or Foundation Model is executed via natural language. I have been using English examples in this book, but that is only for brevity. Users can interact with LLMs in nearly any language. A user can designate that they want the prompts to be in the native language of the user and the output to be in another language because the prompt will ultimately be sent to another user who speaks a different language.

User prompts

The user prompt window is the primary user interface for the majority of people who will interact with a Foundational Model or LLM. The user prompt window is the feature that enables the conversational interface to all GenAI models. In the discussion above relating to Prompt Engineering

[143] Google Developer Forums, Home, Products, Machine Learning, Resources, Machine Learning, https://developers.google.com/machine-learning/resources/prompt-eng, Cited February 8, 2024.

and Prompting, the content entered by users is entered into the user prompt window.

Let's discuss the common variations on user prompts.

Direct prompting

Direct prompting (also known as Zero-shot Prompting or Learning) is the simplest way of prompting a model. The prompt provides no examples. It is just the instruction or the prompt. Users can phrase the instruction as a statement or question.

I rarely phrase my prompts as questions. I prefer to use statements. That is a stylistic choice. I have used both statements and questions, and the responses are not materially different. One technique I like to use in direct prompting is instructing the model to respond as a defined persona.

Recently, I was speaking to a group of executives. The organizational levels were Executive Vice Presidents, Senior Vice Presidents, and Vice Presidents. There were about 50 people in the room. All attendees were selected as having an interest in or aptitude for AI. The room was small enough to scan as I was talking and see who was with me, who was lost, and who was engaged in e-mail, texting, or other forms of communication with people outside the room (i.e., they were not paying attention). When I realized the majority of them were not engaged, I grabbed my laptop and started an impromptu demonstration.

I said, "Ok, now let's assume that you want the model to take on a persona. You want the model to respond in a certain manner during the entire session. I am going to instruct the model to respond as if it were Don

Corleone." You would have thought I was handing out $100 dollar bills. Everyone sat up and started paying attention.

I asked the model how to "eliminate" any competition. The model responded in true Godfather speak. I asked how I might improve my margins on my side business. Wink. Wink. Again, the model sounded like it was Mario Puzo.[144] The whole room came to life. People were leaning forward and asking all sorts of questions. Of course, we ran out of time, and I was mobbed (pun intended) with questions after the session.

Using the Godfather reference was an evocative way to gain the audience's attention, and it worked. There are no limits to the personas you can direct the model to leverage in forming responses. Your responses can sound like those of a graduate student from the United Kingdom, a baker from Saginaw, Michigan, or a professor from a leading university, such as the College of Engineering. If you can imagine a persona and write a prompt to direct the model, the model will form its responses in the language, tone, and tenor representative of the defined persona.

Direct prompting is the simplest form of prompting, but that does not imply that it cannot be effective, efficient, and powerful.

Prompting with examples

Extending prompting beyond a direct prompt is simple and easy. The technique being employed in the subsequent examples is that you want to provide examples to the model that guide the model in the direction that

[144] Wikipedia, The Contributors to Wikipedia, Mario Puzo, Author of the Godfather, https://en.wikipedia.org/wiki/Mario_Puzo, Cited February 8, 2024.

you want all following prompt responses to follow or mimic. Let's look at a few of the most common prompting techniques.

One-shot learning or single shot learning

One-shot prompting provides the model with one example of what you want the model to generate or create.

The direct prompt could be, "Develop a list of ideas for tourists visiting Chicago for the first time."

The one-shot example could be, "Develop a list of ideas for tourists visiting Chicago for the first time." An example of an entry in the generated list could be, "Hey Cousin, where can I find an Italian Beef on the northside of the Windy City? Mr. Beef at 666 N. Orleans!"

Few-shot and multi-shot learning

Few- and multi-shot prompting provides the model examples of what you want the model to generate. Few and multi-shot approaches work better than zero-shot prompting for more complicated tasks where the model is expected to recognize, analyze, classify, and/or categorize repeating patterns. Also, this approach works very well when the generated content needs to be structured in a specific manner or format.

The direct prompt or single shot prompt could be—Develop a list of restaurant classifications from the top 200 restaurants in the city of Chicago. The top 200 Chicago restaurants as defined by a collection of reviews found on the internet. All reviews should be from the past 12 months.

Using this direct prompt, it is likely that the reviews could be in any format and include a wide range of evaluation criteria that may or may not meet your need for relevant information.

To make the classification more uniform and ensure that the ratings have the categories you are interested in, the few shot prompt could look similar to the following example.

Develop a list of restaurant classifications from the top 200 restaurants in the city of Chicago. The top 200 Chicago restaurants are defined by a collection of reviews found on the internet. All reviews should be from the past 12 months. The restaurant classification, categories, and ratings need to follow this format:

- Exorbitant prices, 2/5: Negative
- Great entrees, 5/5: Positive
- Slow Service, 1/5: Negative
- Great atmosphere, awesome food, 4/5: Positive
- Food was cold upon arrival, 2/5:

These series of examples illustrate to the model that the specific classifications are Negative and Positive. Also, these examples are the few shot illustrations of what positive and negative categories/experiences could be. The examples include a rating scale.

Chain of Thought learning

Chain of Thought (CoT) prompting requests that the LLM explain its reasoning. You can combine the COT approach with few-shot prompting to get better results on more complicated prompts. By adding the instruction: Let's think step by step, the LLM can generate a response that includes or is in the form of a COT. From this additional instruction alone, typically, a more accurate answer is produced.

Prompting Guidance

There has been an explosion of guides and guidance on prompting. Most of that guidance can be summarized in the following core prompting principles.

"As a starting point for crafting effective prompts for AI, make sure they are:

- **Specific**: Clearly define what you need. Vague prompts lead to ambiguous results. For instance, instead of saying, "Write a blog post," specify the topic, tone, and key points.
- **Structured**: Logical and coherent structure in a prompt helps the AI understand and follow your instructions more effectively.
- **Contextual**: Provide enough background information. For example, if you're asking for a market analysis, mention the specific market and the type of analysis you're seeking.
- **Realistic**: Set expectations that are achievable by the AI. Understanding the limitations and capabilities of the AI system you're using is crucial."[145]

Foundationally, this is a good start. There are many books, guides, posts, and more on prompting. Refer to as many as you think you can benefit from, but the best approach is developing your own style.

---

[145] Melissa Malec, Hatchworks AI, December 3, 2024, Expert's Guide: Generative AI Prompts for Maximum Efficiency, https://hatchworks.com/blog/gen-ai/generative-ai-prompt-guide/, Cited December 22, 2024.

These are the most common approaches to prompting and prompt engineering via the end-user prompt window for all types of LLMs. Of course, more esoteric and creative approaches to prompting will result in highly accurate and relevant responses for very specific and detailed scenarios that you may want to investigate with the support of an LLM. If you want to dive more deeply into more sophisticated prompting modes and approaches, numerous resources are dedicated to this evolving topic.

Let's move on from the various forms and approaches of prompting to the most common form of augmenting a model with external sources of information to improve relevance and accuracy in areas of business, science, and government. You will want to consider augmenting the knowledge contained in an LLM when users seek information, responses, or answers to prompts or questions that may not be in the core of the training data set of the base model.

Remember that we are still discussing techniques and approaches to grounding a model. We are expanding the techniques of grounding a model that are external to the model. Prompting is one grounding technique, and we will now discuss additional external grounding approaches.

Retrieval Augmented Generation (RAG)

Retrieval Augmented Generation or RAG is the most common approach to grounding or augmenting LLMs with information that might change rapidly or is only relevant to a specialized area.

"RAG is an AI framework for retrieving facts from an external knowledge base to ground large language models (LLMs) on the most accurate, up-to-date information."[146]

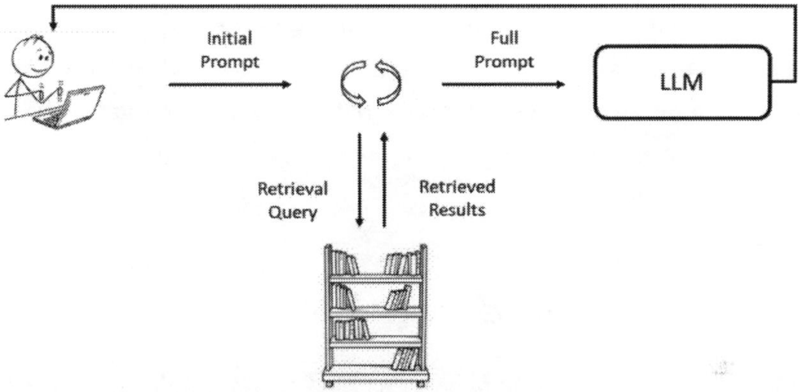

Figure 10: A basic flow diagram for the simplest RAG implementation possible.[147]

In its simplest form, RAG is a way to bring external information to an LLM without changing the model. You are externalizing information that will be used to augment, ground, and extend the responses of the model.

Let's discuss an example. LLMs are trained on the breadth and depth of knowledge of the world, including information on the Internet. This breadth of information is good for generalized responses, but there are issues.

The primary issues are:

---

[146] Kim Martineau, August 22, 2023, IBM Research Community, What is Retrieval Augmented Generation?, https://research.ibm.com/blog/retrieval-augmented-generation-RAG, Cited February 9, 2024.

[147] Grow Right, September 26, 2023, growright.com, What is Retrieval Augmented Generation?, https://www.linkedin.com/pulse/what-retrieval-augmented-generation-grow-right/, Cited February 9, 2024.

- The training data set has to be cut off at a certain date. Most models on the market today have a training data set that is 18 months to two years old. If you ask a model a question about an event that happened after the end date of the training data set, the model will not have the information to provide an answer.

- While training on the breadth of the world's knowledge sounds impressive, it does not provide much depth in answering specific questions.

- Hallucinations occur when prompts ask the models to formulate answers outside the training set's knowledge base.

Let's suppose that you want to use an LLM to help your call center staff do a better job in answering questions from your customers. Your business creates custom scents and perfumes for people who have submitted their DNA to your team for a detailed analysis. The customer's DNA creates a unique scent that matches their elemental nature.

Leveraging an off-the-shelf LLM like Claude or Mistral would not be able to answer any questions about your highly individualized offerings or clients. While the standard LLM may help your call center staff with approaches to etiquette or best practices in customer support, it would be lacking in the details for providing individualized customer service.

With a RAG approach, you can index and create vectors and embeddings from all the information you have about your customers and the products you and your team have created for them.

The chart below illustrates a RAG implementation's process flow and system architecture. By leveraging a RAG environment, your organization obtains all the value of a standard LLM and all the details of the proprietary knowledge that your company has gained from your very valuable clientele. You can update and add to the information as often as you want, include products that you might want to sell to your clients, and protect this highly confidential data to ensure maximum security.

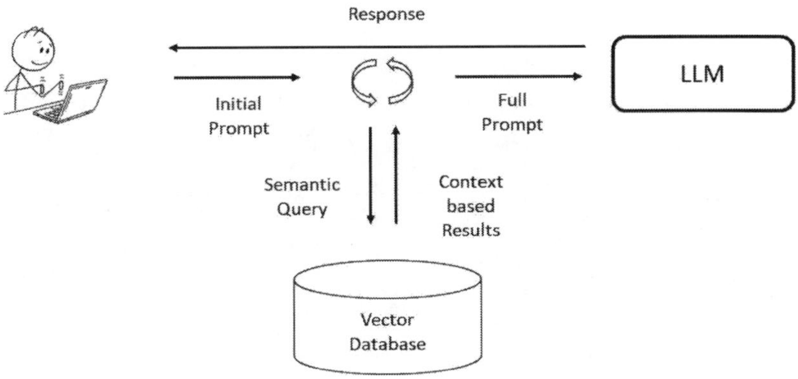

Figure 11: A typical RAG implementation.

A RAG approach provides security, flexibility, speed of change, customization, and many more benefits.

Currently, in my day job, we have built over 1,500 LLM-based solutions. The substantial majority of those solutions are based on a RAG architecture. If your organization has the ability to collect and manage the entirety of the information or even a single subject area that your company possesses, and you want to use GenAI to develop new applications and solutions, the RAG architecture can be of great value to you.

Variations on RAG implementations

As with all things related to GenAI, variations on RAG environments are being developed, released, and implemented on nearly a daily basis. Below is a list of some of the possible common RAG variations. Each RAG approach aims to move the state of the art forward to provide more accurate outputs from LLMs. No RAG approach is all-encompassing in improving all models, and all prompts and RAG variations exhibit specific limitations:

- **OriginalRAG** includes all retrieved documents directly in the user prompt, leading to and possibly significantly increasing prompt length and resulting in slower response times.

- **LongRAG** deals with the long context window but struggles with the limitations of long embedding models, the inefficiencies of black-box LLMs for handling extended inputs, and its reliance on limited grouping methods, which inhibit generalizability.

- **GraphRAG** organizes data into a graph structure, representing text data and its interrelations. Graph-based models may struggle with dynamic data where the relationships between variables change over time.

- **Self-ReflectiveRAG** requires specialized instruction-tuning of the general-purpose LLMs to generate specific tags for self-reflection. However, it requires additional tuning, which can be complex.

- **CorrectiveRAG** uses an external retrieval evaluator to refine the quality of retrieved documents. It focuses solely on improving the contextual information. The problem is that it doesn't enhance the model's reasoning capabilities.[148]

And, of course, there will be more variations of RAG environments and architecture. The primary objective of RAG environments is to make the processing of the LLM more accurate, relevant, and less prone to providing hallucinations to end users.

---

[148] Alyona Vert, Ksenia Se, What is Speculative RAG, Turing Post, August 14, 2024, https://www.turingpost.com/p/speculativerag?utm_source=www.turingpost.com&utm_medium=newsletter&utm_campaign=topic-9-what-is-speculative-rag&_bhlid=3bccf7dbafe404dd4ee435b7c728494d60b861f3, Cited on September, 1 2024.

Prompting and RAG approaches are the most common external methodologies to ground a model. Let's move on to discussing how to improve the performance, relevancy, and accuracy of an LLM through another approach, fine-tuning, which is an internal approach to adding new information to a model.

Fine tuning

Fine-tuning is an approach where you can take external relevant information not included in the base LLM and extend the training of a model. "Fine-tuning an LLM refers to the process of retraining a pre-trained language model on a specific task or dataset to adapt it for a particular application. It allows us to harness the power of pre-trained language models for our exact needs without needing to train a model from scratch."[149] One can fine-tune a model in three generic ways: self-supervised, supervised, and reinforcement learning. These are not mutually exclusive in that any combination of these three approaches can be used in succession to fine-tune a single model.

Self-supervised learning

Self-supervised learning consists of training a model based on additional training data that imparts a new or related set of information or patterns to

[149] AIM Consulting, Guide to Fine-Tuning LLMs: Definition, Benefits, and How-To, https://aimconsulting.com/insights/guide-to-fine-tuning-llms-definition-benefits-and-how-to/, Cited February 9, 2024.

the LLM. While this is how many pre-trained language models are developed, it can also be used for model fine-tuning.

Supervised learning

The next, and perhaps most popular, way to fine-tune a model is via supervised learning. This involves training a model on input-output pairs for a particular task. The key step in supervised learning is curating a training dataset. A simple way to do this is to create curated and known question-answer pairs. Often, the question-answer pairs are created by enlisting large numbers of people to create the pairs in areas where teams of people have specialized knowledge or subject matter expertise.

Reinforcement learning

RL uses a reward structure to guide the training of the base model, which results in an entirely new version of the LLM. This can take many different forms, but the basic idea is to train the base model using the reward structure to verify that the responses from the new version of the model reflect the preferences of human reviewers and the model owners. RL is very effective and generally results in LLM outputs that are significantly more accurate or relevant when compared to the responses from the base model.[150]

---

[150] Shaw Talebi, Sep 11, 2023, Towards Data Science, Fine-Tuning Large Language Models, https://towardsdatascience.com/fine-tuning-large-language-models-llms-23473d763b9, Cited February 9, 2024.

Reinforcement Learning is often coupled with teams of people who provide human reviews and feedback on how well the model is performing, and they also provide corrections that are used to improve the model's accuracy and performance. This process is referred to as RLHF or Reinforcement Learning with Human Feedback.

Domain Language Models/Small Language Models

In our conversation about GenAI, we have been focused on and discussing Large Language Models or LLMs. Many large companies, governments, not-for-profit organizations, and academic institutions offer LLMs. LLMs are expensive to build and maintain. Most companies or organizations will not have the technical talent, money, sustained interest, or the need to build their own LLMs. That is not a roadblock or an issue. There is another way to design and build language models you own, manage, and control.

Let's define Domain Language Models and Small Language Models (DLMs and SLMs). According to the research team at IBM, "Small language models (SLMs) are artificial intelligence (AI) models capable of processing, understanding and generating natural language content. As their name implies, SLMs are smaller in scale and scope than large language models (LLMs). In terms of size, SLM parameters range from a few million to a few billion, as opposed to LLMs with hundreds of billions or even trillions of parameters. Small language models are more compact and efficient than their large model counterparts. As such, SLMs require less memory and computational power..."[151]

---

151 Rina Caballar, CHQ, Marketing, IBM, October 31, 2024, What are small language models?, https://www.ibm.com/think/topics/small-language-models, Cited December 22, 2024.

To be clear, DLMs and SLMs are the same thing. The terms are synonyms. At this point is unclear which term will be widely adopted, hence we have include both terms in our discussion.

My team and I have built a DLM for a focused area of our business. The DLM works extremely well in the domain it was trained. In the process of building the DLM, we learned numerous lessons about how much data we needed, the types of data that were better suited to develop a high-performance model, how difficult it is to license the needed data from third-party providers, the challenges of developing enough labeled data for training purposes, and more.

We started attempting to build the DLM from an empty neural network structure, or to say it another way, we tried to build the DLM from scratch. We had our reasons, which are still valid, but we found that it was cheaper, faster, and easier to start with a pretrained open-source model and fine-tune it into our own DLM. This approach is not as pristine as we had hoped, but it works well, and we have ended up with a solid model and a deep understanding of time, effort, resources, and cost of building future DLMs.

You can think of LLMs as the base model of your GenAI environment. You may have a single LLM or multiple LLMs, and then you will have numerous tailored and customized SLMs and DLMs. You may even have multiple smaller NLP models in your processing environment or universe. All of these models will be working together as a unified whole.

In the past, we often referred to "the model" when discussing AI-based applications. Going forward, we will need to start talking about "the ensemble of models" at the core of our applications and solutions. It will be rare for an application or solution to rely on just one model.

Let's move on to our discussion and talk a little more about fine-tuning models.

General points about fine tuning

Recently, I directed our applied research team to fine-tune multiple models to examine the improvement in relevancy, accuracy, and performance. We found that all eight models responded in a similar manner. We were impressed that we could move most models with as few as a handful of documents.

The general view is that fine-tuning is a viable approach and tool, but one of the drawbacks is that when you upgrade from one version of a model to a subsequent or newer version, you will need to execute the fine-tuning regimen with the new model. Keeping track of the data, techniques, and sequencing of the entire fine-tuning process and all the sub-processes can be daunting.

It is a reasonable assumption that one of the leading vendors, or maybe an innovative start-up in the GenAI market, will build and release a fine-tuning management system, but we have not seen that arrive in the market yet. Until that day arrives, fine-tuning will be a "roll your own" manual process in which you will have to weigh the effort required with the reward gained in each project.

Another drawback in fine-tuning is that the process can result in catastrophic forgetting. "Catastrophic interference, also known as catastrophic forgetting, is the tendency of an artificial neural network to abruptly and drastically forget previously learned information upon learning new information."[152] This unfortunate turn of events is challenging to predict or forecast as it is different in each model. As you are fine-tuning each model, it is a good idea to move forward incrementally and

[152] The Contributors of Wikipedia, Catastrophic forgetting, https://en.wikipedia.org/wiki/Catastrophic_interference, Cited December 22, 2024.

document the process as you progress. If the model does fall apart, at least you know where the boundary is for fine-tuning that model. Not very comforting.

That brings us to the end of our discussion of prompting and augmenting a base LLM to arrive at an environment tailored to the needs of your application, business process, customer, and clients of the overall firm.

The next topic is another approach to placing resources around an LLM to be more performant, relevant, and accurate, and constrain the results for the users of the model and the overall environment.

Next, we will discuss system add-ons that are referred to as Guardrails.

Guardrails

"Guardrails for Language Learning Models (LLMs) are a set of predefined rules, limitations, and operational protocols that serve to govern the behavior and outputs of these advanced AI systems. Well-designed guardrails enable organizations to unleash the full potential of generative AI while mitigating the associated risks. They are a powerful lever for building trust and ensuring responsible AI use."[153]

The entire market for Guardrail systems for LLMs is nascent and evolving. The entire area holds great promise for governing and guiding LLM

[153] Attri Blog, A Comprehensive Guide: Everything You Need to Know About LLMs Guardrails, https://attri.ai/blog/a-comprehensive-guide-everything-you-need-to-know-about-llms-guardrails, Cited February 9, 2024.

operations, but it remains to be seen where the promise of this area will be realized.

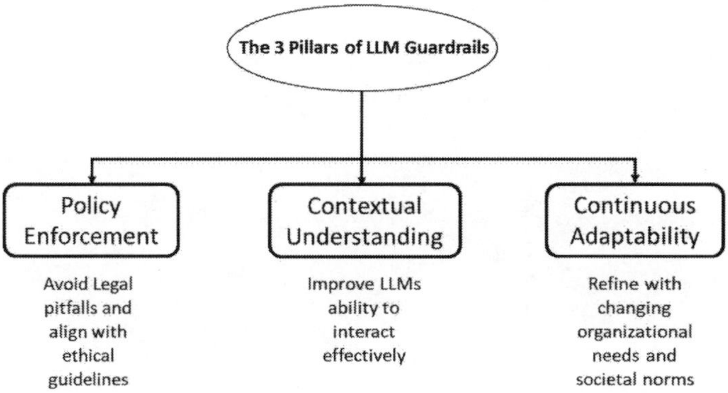

Figure 12: The three pillars of LLM Guardrails.[154]

The most interest in Guardrail systems can be found in global consulting organizations that see significant revenues to be gained from implementing Guardrail systems for their clients. Also, we see interest from highly regulated industries where governments and oversight bodies will mandate them to ensure that their LLMs operate within all relevant local, regional, national, and global laws and regulations, of which there are many.

The three areas of focus for the current field of LLM Guardrail systems are Policy Enforcement, Contextual Understanding, and Continuous Adaptability.

Each of these areas focuses on providing the ability to augment or wrap an LLM with additional context and content to ensure compliance with laws, rules, and regulations and to lower the risk of an LLM acting in a manner that is counter to the values and policies of the organization that is implementing the application or solution.

---

[154] Ibid.

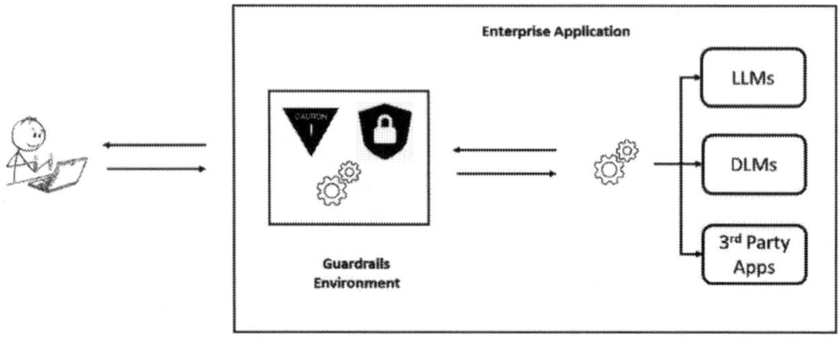

Figure 13: Guardrail Process Flow.

Most vendors offering Guardrail systems position those offerings as a method and path to implementing and ensuring Responsible, Accountable, and Transparent AI. It remains to be seen if these systems can deliver on those promises efficiently and economically.

It has been asked if Guardrail systems and System Prompts are similar. The answer is in some ways, yes they are similar. The similarity lies in the fact that both elements of a GenAI environment are meant to ensure accuracy, relevancy, to curtail hallucinations and to ensure that the models do not stray into taboo areas. The areas where they are dissimilar are that the System Prompt is inside the model and is not changed. Guardrails are implemented outside the model and can be changed at any time and focus on many different subject areas.

As a new and rapidly evolving area of technology and software, it remains to be seen where guardrails will be a safe and effective method to managing accuracy, relevancy, and hallucinations.

Long context windows

Let's keep in mind that GenAI has brought an entirely new view of how we, as AI and analytics professionals, can enable our organizations and end users to access and use all of the information inside and surrounding our organizations.

The various technologies and techniques available to us are in service of making all the information at our fingertips available in an accurate, safe, and reliable manner.

One of the great aspects of this new world is that we are free to use one or more of these technologies and techniques in conjunction with each other or to use numerous technologies in a specified sequence or any other sequence. All possible combinations, techniques, and sequences are available to deliver value-added systems and environments to our intended audiences. This is an amazing opportunity, but it is also quite complex.

All of these techniques are valuable and will continue to provide a powerful toolset to use as we progress forward, and, at the same time, new developments reset our expectations of how to build systems.

Long Context Windows (LCWs) enables end users, system administrators, and developers to ingest significant amounts of information into an LLM as part of the user prompt.

"Google Gemini 1.5 Pro, released in February 2024, set a record for the longest context window to date: one million tokens, equivalent to one hour of video or 700,000 words. Gemini's outstanding performance in handling long contexts led some people to proclaim that "retrieval augmented generation (RAG) is dead."[155]

The media outlets covering the technology industry are prone to swinging wildly between opposite ends of the spectrum on many issues, especially regarding new developments. As noted above, LCWs will eliminate the need for RAG environments in some applications but not all.

LCWs and RAGs can jointly exist in an application. There will be many applications that perform well and reach scale by using LCWs alone. Other applications will perform well with a LLM that contains a small or smaller context window supported by a RAG implementation. All of these permutations and more will exist and will work. No one new development eliminates the value of the technologies and techniques that have been in use in previous applications and environments.

Now that we know the recent history of GenAI and how GenAI systems operate in a general sense, let's turn our attention to the high-level impact and value that GenAI has and will continue to have on the world around us. The impact of GenAI is being felt in the commercial, academic, research, and governmental spheres. There are very few places where GenAI is not having an impact.

Is GenAI really that impactful?

In short, the answer is, emphatically yes.

---

[155] Usama Jamil, May 10th, 2024 10:36am, The New Stack, Do Enormous LLM Context Windows Spell the End of RAG?, https://thenewstack.io/do-enormous-llm-context-windows-spell-the-end-of-rag/, Cited on September 1, 2024

We see and hear technologies being hailed as groundbreaking with fair regularity, but most are not that impressive from a general computing perspective. Recently, we have seen the emergence and arrival of technologies like the metaverse, virtual reality, and blockchain.

Adherents and supporters of these technologies hold out with breathless pronouncements that a new world driven by these new offerings is just about to arrive; this is far from the truth. They provide tools, technologies, and approaches that are, at most, productively applied to specialized use cases. They are not naturally applicable to *all* applications and use cases. The metaverse and blockchain are not General Purpose Technologies[156] (GPT).

"A GPT has the potential to affect the entire economic system and can lead to far-reaching changes in such social factors as working hours and constraints on family life. Examples of GPTs are the steam engine, electricity, the computer and the internet."[157] "GPTs have the potential to drastically alter societies through their impact on pre-existing economic and social structures."[158]

GenAI is most definitely a General Purpose Technology. The breadth and depth of transition that GenAI will drive is almost impossible to measure and define at this point.

---

156 General Purpose Technologies and Economic Growth, Edited by Elhanan Helpman, January 1, 2003, MIT Press, https://mitpress.mit.edu/9780262514682/general-purpose-technologies-and-economic-growth/, Cited January 8, 2024.

157 Geoffrey E. Hinton, Simon Osindero, Yee-Whye The, 2006, A fast learning algorithm for deep belief nets, https://www.cs.toronto.edu/~hinton/absps/fastnc.pdf, Cited January 6, 2024.

158 The Contributors to Wikipedia, General Purpose Technology, https://en.wikipedia.org/wiki/General-purpose_technology, Cited January 8, 2024.

In my current role, I am fortunate to speak and collaborate with the leading technology companies in the world, such as Microsoft, Google, Amazon, and more. I am also invited to speak with world-leading companies about their ideas and plans for all three pillars of AI. I have spoken with leading companies in the US, Europe, Asia, the Middle East, and Latin America. I am in a position to review and comment on all the applications that their and our companies are considering and experimenting with. The number of groups experimenting with GenAI is in the thousands, and that is just one company. I have never seen such widespread interest in, engagement with, and investment in, a technology since the arrival of the Internet.

I am asked with fair regularity, "Should we get involved with GenAI or is it a fad?" There is no good reason not to engage with GenAI technology today. The longer you wait, the further behind you will be. This technology will only grow in importance and become more embedded in nearly all operational aspects of business, academia, science, research, and more. So, yes, GenAI is and will significantly impact all fields. We will discuss this topic in depth in Chapter 7.

Let's discuss the innovations and developments that have enabled GenAI to become a widely used and popular toolset for almost every application you can consider.

The Power of GenAI

Generative AI has the potential to change nearly all roles that exist in the knowledge worker ecosystem. Most of the automation and process optimization work executed over the past 50 years has been focused on eliminating unneeded process steps, clerical type operations, or reducing the number of people required to complete a process or task. GenAI is unique and different. Let's examine how unique it is.

Why is GenAI different in value creation and delivery?

We have had Foundational AI (FAI) since the 1950s, and we are starting to see the beginning of Causal AI. I can see why non-technologists wave their hands in the air and proclaim that GenAI is not a big deal, and we just let the hype calm down, and this too shall pass. It will not pass.

The focus of the value of GenAI is different and direct. GenAI delivers value in generating new text, images, video, voice, code, and more. Who generates these deliverables today? Most of this work is executed by lawyers, system developers, business analysts, consultants, auditors, accountants, financial analysts, writers, illustrators, editors, and other professionals, in summary, knowledge workers.

Understanding that the value of GenAI being direct is crucially important. The other two pillars of AI drive value, but in an indirect manner. With FAI, we predict how many people will arrive at a store or how close our sales numbers will be to forecast. With Causal AI, we predict the true drivers of action and behavior to determine why people react and act. Both of those pillars of AI derive and deliver value, but managers must *interpret* what to do with those pieces of information or those predictions.

In the decades of designing, managing, and executing analytics and AI projects, I saw the value realization increase dramatically when I had my teams do one thing. What was that one thing? I directed my data scientists to overtly tell the business managers and executives which recommendations to undertake and which to put aside. Sounds strange, doesn't it? Most data scientists are very reticent to make detailed and specific recommendations to managers and executives. The data scientists know the math and numbers, but for the most part, they don't know the business.

I have coached my data scientists to take that next step. To push through their level of discomfort and make a confident recommendation based on their analytical work. Even if the managers and executives did not take the recommendations, that one step moved the managers and executives to action. The managers and executives know that the data scientists put a recommendation on the table and that they have to run with that recommendation or take the next step and make their own recommendation. In most cases, they have done so. They have stepped forward and made their own recommendations. The one additional step in the analytical process broke the log jam of indecision that raised the rate at which analytical applications and results were implemented into production processes.

Business-oriented managers and executives constantly complain about not realizing the value from analytics and AI. I can tell them how to fix that problem. That is an easy fix. It is just not an obvious fix. As just stated, the fix has nothing to do with data, AI, or analytics. It is all based on human behavior.

With GenAI, the output *is* the deliverable. There is no translation step before acting. What comes out of the model is what you need, require, and request. Users can take the output and begin the process of creating a new work product. The next step after your prompt is processed is you acting on the response. You can't get much more direct than that.

LLMs produce solid products and results, but those outputs or completions cannot be trusted on their own merit. The outputs are simply predictions of what an output could be. Will it be the best brief for a legal case? Probably not. Will it be the most robust argument for an investment case to build a new factory or distribution center? It is doubtful. But those outputs are good first drafts and are a good place to start the process.

Let's discuss the foundational concepts underpinning and animating GenAI. One of the objectives of this book is to enable readers to discern, describe, and discuss the underlying driving forces of each of the three pillars of AI. By understanding the conceptual underpinnings of the three fields, we can develop a deeper understanding of where we can apply these technologies, either in isolation or in conjunction with one or more of the other AI technologies, to drive business improvement and to help society in general.

Conceptual foundations of GenAI

One of the primary value streams from GenAI is in taking vast amounts of unstructured information such as text, images, diagrams, computer code, medical diagnoses, tax judgments, court rulings, property disputes, land use records, and more and using that information as a training set to train a model to respond as to how one of these deliverables should be written or developed.

Democratizing data management

One of the incredibly valuable aspects of GenAI is that the data management process of ingesting and indexing data is fast, efficient, and can be executed by a wide range of professionals.

Why is this such a groundbreaking development? Many technologies go through a phase where only technical experts can leverage and use the new innovations efficiently and effectively. That has been the case with the data management process for data warehousing. On second thought, that has been the case for data management for all applications. Many enterprise applications never drive value because the difficulty of data management hamstrings them. Let's stick with data management for data warehousing. We don't have the time or attention to take on all data management use cases.

Before GenAI, the work involved in obtaining, cleaning, structuring, integrating, loading, indexing, and testing structured data was very difficult, laborious, time-consuming, expensive, and error-prone.

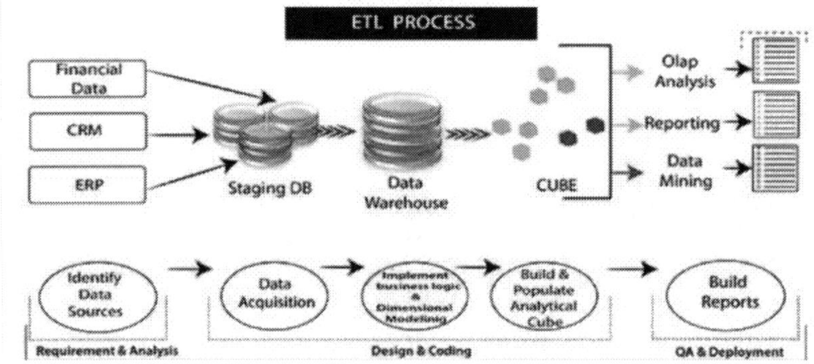

Figure 14: A representative diagram of the Data Management process for a Data Warehouse.[159]

Building an enterprise data warehouse or data lakehouse (as described in the previous sentence) might take multiple years and require internal and external staff working together with very little guarantee that the system would actually work as designed. This type of work requires highly

[159] Sonoo Jaiswal, https://www.javatpoint.com/etl-process, ETL process for Data Warehouse, Cited on February 6, 2023.

technical staff adept in extracting, transforming, and loading the source data into the data warehouse.

A case in point, I was building data warehouses for Retailing and Consumer-Packaged Goods (CPG) companies in the US and UK. I received a call from my manager, who was the CEO and founder of the firm I worked for, and he instructed me to catch the next flight to a city in the western US.

Our company had been working with a retailer on building a data warehouse for about a year. The early versions of the systems were not working. The system was intended to report on all sales through all locations, but there was a special use case where sales of cigarettes were to be treated with additional scrutiny for a number of reasons. I arrived and went right to the office. Within 30 minutes, I pulled the project manager aside and asked several questions. Within the first hour, I deduced that the project team forgot to include the detailed sales records for the cigarette category in the data management process. The system as built would never work. I helped redesign the system that afternoon, and it went live a couple of months later. Data management is not simple or easy.

Even though data warehousing has been around for approximately 40 years, it is still a challenging journey for most organizations to navigate. While the data warehousing industry has done a decent job of providing user-friendly tools for data management in data warehousing, the process still requires a significant amount of technical expertise and a reasonably deep understanding of data engineering techniques and approaches.

In comparison, the data management process for indexing and ingesting data of all types for a GenAI implementation consists of a few steps, mainly selecting parameters for information processing. I am hesitant to mention the parameters because, within a few months of this writing, that part of the process (e.g., setting parameters) will be automated and will not need to be manually set or even considered.

The democratization of access to these technologies and techniques is deeply entwined with innovations in data management related to unstructured information. When many divergent types of people can access and effectively use a new technology to experiment with, drive change, and deliver value, the true impact is seen and felt. We are seeing this now with GenAI in relation to data management.

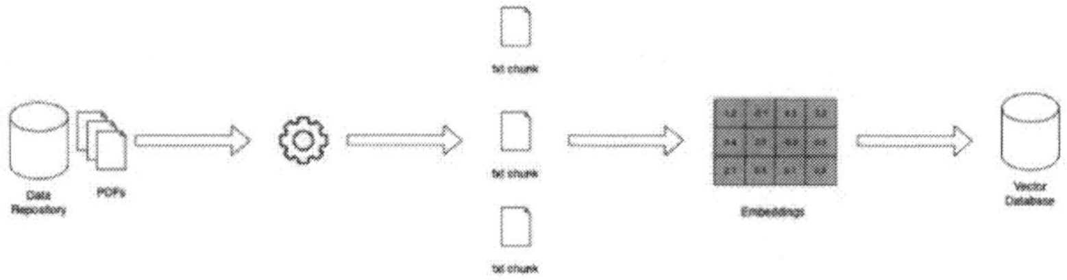

Figure 15: A representative diagram of the Data Management process for GenAI environment.[160]

All the world's data is now available

We have been using the term unstructured and structured data and have not defined it, so let's do that now for clarity.

Structured data—Structured data has a standardized format for efficient access by software and humans alike. It is typically tabular, with rows and columns clearly defining data attributes. Computers can effectively process

---

160 Bruno Pistone, Enhancing Question & Answering use cases with Generative AI: A Journey into RAG, Medium, June 23, 2023, https://medium.com/@brn.pistone/enhancing-question-answering-use-cases-with-generative-ai-a-journey-into-rag-fd3ef87a968a.

structured data for insights due to its quantitative nature.[161] In my experience, structured data is numbers and numbers only.

Unstructured data – Unstructured data is information that either does not have a pre-defined data model or is not organized in a pre-defined manner. Unstructured information is typically text-heavy but may contain data such as dates, numbers, and facts as well. This results in irregularities and ambiguities that make it difficult to understand using Foundational AI programs as compared to data stored in databases or annotated (semantically tagged) in documents.[162] Again, in my experience unstructured data is mostly nonnumeric data, but it can include numbers as well.

The primary characteristic of unstructured data that made it so difficult to work with before GenAI is now one of the most attractive characteristics of unstructured data today. Before GenAI, if the data wasn't structured or wasn't a number, we did not have the tools to work with that data very well. In the newly democratized data management process for GenAI, all words, images, diagrams, code, and other unstructured information are converted in the indexing step into tokens, which are then converted into vectors, which are numeric representations. This enables all unstructured data to be ingested and indexed for use in GenAI.

---

[161] Google Search, https://www.google.com/search?q=structured+data&rlz=1C1GCEU_enUS1087US1087&oq=Structured+&gs_lcrp=EgZjaHJvbWUqEggBEAAYQxiDARixAxiABBiKBTIGCAAQRRg5MhIIARAAGEMYgwEYsQMYgAQYigUyDAgCEAAYQxiABBiKBTIMCAMQABhDGIAEGIoFMhIIBBAAGEMYgwEYsQMYgAQYigUyDAgFEAAYQxiABBiKBTISCAYQABhDGIMBGLEDGIAEGIoFMgwIBxAAGEMYgAQYigUyDQgIEAAYgwEYsQMYgAQyDAgJEAAYQxiABBiKBdIBCDc3MjZqMGo0qAIAsAIA&sourceid=chrome&ie=UTF-8, Cited February 6, 2024

[162] Wikipedia, The Contributors to Wikipedia, Definition, Unstructured Data, Cited February 6, 2024.

One of the breakthroughs that has enchanted the world about GenAI is the ability of the models to respond to natural language prompts with natural language responses. This has enthralled the media and large segments of the general population.

Before GenAI came to market, we, as analytics professionals, were adept at analyzing structured data and slowly improving how we analyzed unstructured information. But when the improvements in indexing and creating vectors and embeddings for all types of unstructured information arrived with GenAI, that changed what is possible and, in the process, changed the world.

The following quote is from a headline article in 2019 in the MIT Management Review. "If your organization struggles to corral and analyze unstructured data, you're not alone. Only 18% of organizations in a 2019 survey by Deloitte reported being able to take advantage of such data. In fact, a majority of data (80% to 90%, according to multiple analyst estimates) is unstructured information like text, video, audio, web server logs, social media, and more. That's a huge untapped resource with the potential to create competitive advantage for companies that figure out how to use it."[163]

This was the prevailing view until GenAI hit the market. Using it in any valuable way required a large number of specialized staff, a significant budget, a substantial amount of patience, and a high tolerance for failure. These four factors rarely find their way into any one project in the commercial world. Hence, very little work was done with unstructured data in enterprise-class organizations before 2022.

---

[163] Tam Harbert, Feb 1, 2021, MIT Management, Sloan School, Tapping the power of unstructured data, https://mitsloan.mit.edu/ideas-made-to-matter/tapping-power-unstructured-data, Cited February 10, 2024.

How I look for and find innovations like GenAI

Admittedly, I am an AI professional, practitioner, and all-around AI geek. Over the past 38 years, my behavior has been very consistent. I watch innovations closely. I read research papers diligently and consistently. This practice has enabled me to remain engaged in the development of several technologies that we use each day. It helps that my area of interest has always been in the fields of data, analytics, and AI. If I tried to keep up with a broader set of technologies in any meaningful way, I would certainly fail in attempting to remain current in my knowledge base.

The speed at which GenAI technologies are developing and evolving is impressive. Throughout 2022 and 2023, new companies and technologies were arriving on the market daily. When talking with executives, clients, technology analysts, editors, and writers, briefing notes and materials were and are being updated daily.

I remain very interested in the state of the art in all things related to data, analytics, and AI, and I do my best to share what I am learning and experimenting with. Still, when it comes to building systems for clients and/or building technologies for the industry, I stick quite closely to what works and what we know we can do with the technology. It is important to remember that keeping up with technology is not the same as building systems that work daily. It is important to be discerning when deciding to leverage a new and emerging technology.

I was aware of OpenAI and had known about the non-profit since its founding in 2015. "In December 2015, Sam Altman, Greg Brockman, Reid Hoffman, Jessica Livingston, Peter Thiel, Elon Musk, Amazon Web

Services (AWS), Infosys, and YC Research announced the formation of OpenAI..."[164]

I remember hearing about GenAI and a new term, Foundational Models (FM), in 2022. The term Foundational Model is widely attributed to the team at Stanford. The Stanford Institute for Human-Centered Artificial Intelligence's (HAI) Center for Research on Foundation Models (CRFM) coined the term "foundation model" in August 2021 to mean "any model that is trained on broad data (generally using self-supervision at scale) that can be adapted (e.g., fine-tuned) to a wide range of downstream tasks."[165]

---

[164] Wikipedia, The Contributors to Wikipedia, OpenAI, https://en.wikipedia.org/wiki/OpenAI, Cited January 15, 2024.

[165] Bommasani, Rishi; Hudson, Drew A.; Adeli, Ehsan; Altman, Russ; Arora, Simran; von Arx, Sydney; Bernstein, Michael S.; Bohg, Jeannette; Bosselut, Antoine; Brunskill, Emma; Brynjolfsson, Erik; Buch, Shyamal; Card, Dallas; Castellon, Rodrigo; Chatterji, Niladri; Chen, Annie; Creel, Kathleen; Davis, Jared Quincy; Demszky, Dora; Donahue, Chris; Doumbouya, Moussa; Durmus, Esin; Ermon, Stefano; Etchemendy, John; Ethayarajh, Kawin; Fei-Fei, Li; Finn, Chelsea; Gale, Trevor; Gillespie, Lauren; Goel, Karan; Goodman, Noah; Grossman, Shelby; Guha, Neel; Hashimoto, Tatsunori; Henderson, Peter; Hewitt, John; Ho, Daniel E.; Hong, Jenny; Hsu, Kyle; Huang, Jing; Icard, Thomas; Jain, Saahil; Jurafsky, Dan; Kalluri, Pratyusha; Karamcheti, Siddharth; Keeling, Geoff; Khani, Fereshte; Khattab, Omar; Koh, Pang Wei; Krass, Mark; Krishna, Ranjay; Kuditipudi, Rohith; Kumar, Ananya; Ladhak, Faisal; Lee, Mina; Lee, Tony; Leskovec, Jure; Levent, Isabelle; Li, Xiang Lisa; Li, Xuechen; Ma, Tengyu; Malik, Ali; Manning, Christopher D.; Mirchandani, Suvir; Mitchell, Eric; Munyikwa, Zanele; Nair, Suraj; Narayan, Avanika; Narayanan, Deepak; Newman, Ben; Nie, Allen; Niebles, Juan Carlos; Nilforoshan, Hamed; Nyarko, Julian; Ogut, Giray; Orr, Laurel; Papadimitriou, Isabel; Park, Joon Sung; Piech, Chris; Portelance, Eva; Potts, Christopher; Raghunathan, Aditi; Reich, Rob; Ren, Hongyu; Rong, Frieda; Roohani, Yusuf; Ruiz, Camilo; Ryan, Jack; Ré, Christopher; Sadigh, Dorsa; Sagawa, Shiori; Santhanam, Keshav; Shih, Andy; Srinivasan, Krishnan; Tamkin, Alex; Taori, Rohan; Thomas, Armin W.; Tramèr, Florian; Wang, Rose E.; Wang, William; Wu, Bohan; Wu, Jiajun; Wu, Yuhuai; Xie, Sang Michael; Yasunaga, Michihiro; You, Jiaxuan; Zaharia, Matei; Zhang, Michael; Zhang, Tianyi; Zhang, Xikun; Zhang, Yuhui; Zheng, Lucia; Zhou,

As I was wrapping up my role at CSL Behring in the winter of 2022 and getting ready to join EY in December, I remember thinking that this new technology was gaining great press and attention. Given my previous experience, I was certain I had a year or two to study GenAI before I really had to do anything serious with it. I was way off the mark in my view.

"OpenAI released an early demo of ChatGPT on November 30, 2022, and the chatbot quickly went viral on social media as users shared examples of what it could do. Stories and samples included everything from travel planning to writing fables to code computer programs. Within five days, the chatbot had attracted over one million users."[166]

Of course, as we all know, 2023 was the year of GenAI. A wave of hype and hysteria crashed worldwide, and all business managers and executives had to have a GenAI environment, whatever that meant. I remember talking with administrators at the universities where I am an advisory board member, and the discussions were all related to GenAI as a tool or a source of trouble.

Kaitlyn; Liang, Percy (18 August 2021). On the Opportunities and Risks of Foundation Models (Report), https://arxiv.org/pdf/2108.07258.pdf, Cited January 15, 2024.

[166] Bernard Marr, May 19, 2023, Forbes.com, A Short History Of ChatGPT: How We Got To Where We Are Today, https://www.forbes.com/sites/bernardmarr/2023/05/19/a-short-history-of-chatgpt-how-we-got-to-where-we-are-today/?sh=6b6a8dae674f, Cited January 15, 2024.

Summary

From 2022 to 2025, the conversation in business, technology, finance, philanthropy, education, and more has been dominated, literally overrun, by GenAI.

GenAI is at the top of everyone's mind. In the past 18 months, I have met with over 400 companies. My day job is as the global head of AI for one of the Big 4 Consulting firms. My job is to design, build, and operate the AI infrastructure for the global employee base of over 420,000 employees. Perhaps my conversations are dominated by AI, given that AI is my job.

No matter, GenAI is still top of mind for a significant portion of the world's population. And for good reasons, GenAI is changing the world. Some of those changes will be negative, but most of the changes will be positive. We have a bright future ahead of us, and with GenAI in the mix, the future will be more interesting, faster moving, and more enjoyable.

Let's move on to discuss the impact of GenAI on the world.

CHAPTER 6

The Impact of Generative AI

Since its widespread release and subsequent torrid pace of adoption, Generative AI (GenAI) has been a significant disruptive force on numerous levels, including the global economy, technology investing, federal and supra-national governmental policy making, primary, secondary, and higher education, and numerous additional areas of work and life in general. GenAI is a momentous development and a game-changing innovation whose impact cannot be overstated.

Individuals, companies, governments, not-for-profit organizations, charities, and more need to, at least, start to experiment with GenAI to gain practical experiences and a working understanding of what GenAI can offer them.

Early engagement

Numerous stories and reports from media outlets, technology press, and analysts have commented on the failure rate of early-stage GenAI projects. A Gartner press release titled, "Gartner Predicts 30% of Generative AI

Projects Will Be Abandoned After Proof of Concept By End of 2025",[167] was released in 2024. This is an interesting dynamic.

One of the well-known and planned conclusions of early-stage projects of any technology is to end. Ending by not moving those projects forward, as initially perceived or planned, is normal. This is not some indication that GenAI or other early-stage projects do not work, will not scale, or are not suitable for wider deployment. In the majority of cases in relation to GenAI, those projects have proven the opposite: that the technology scales, delivers value, and works in a wide range of business processes and scenarios.

One of the findings of early-stage Proof of Concept (POC) projects involving emerging technologies is that additional work must be needed in related areas before those early-stage technologies can be developed and more widely deployed. That type of finding is one of the primary reasons for executing POCs with early-stage technologies. In many cases, early-stage technologies are not well understood, and POCs provide a real-world preview of what needs to happen to make those technologies successful in day-to-day business operations.

The Gartner press release goes on to say, "At least 30% of generative AI (GenAI) projects will be abandoned after proof of concept by the end of 2025, due to poor data quality, inadequate risk controls, escalating costs or unclear business value..."[168] I do agree with the Gartner statements that a subset of the issues mentioned can be real blockers to moving forward with

---

[167] Gartner, July 29, 2024, Gartner Predicts 30% of Generative AI Projects Will Be Abandoned After Proof of Concept By End of 2025, https://www.gartner.com/en/newsroom/press-releases/2024-07-29-gartner-predicts-30-percent-of-generative-ai-projects-will-be-abandoned-after-proof-of-concept-by-end-of-2025#:~:text=At%20least%2030%25%20of%20generative,%2C%20according%20to%20Gartner%2C%20Inc., Cited September 3, 2024.

[168] Ibid., Cited September 3, 2024.

GenAI projects, but the relevancy of each issue is on a case by case basis. The projects are generally not abandoned. The effort is repurposed to reduce, ameliorate, or eliminate the issues discovered before moving forward with GenAI.

In the over 1,500 GenAI projects undertaken in the 2023-2025 time period in my day job, the general findings were that data quality, risk management, and costs were real issues and considerations but not blockers. In the majority of cases, we found that the GenAI projects would meet or exceed the expected value realization goals when deployed to a department, division, or globally, but before the POCs could move forward, we had work to complete in the areas mentioned by Gartner before we would develop and deploy GenAI in the intended operational areas of the business.

In my opinion, if you have undertaken a POC with any emerging technology and you learned how to make that technology a productive part of your operation in a way that will drive your operations to a new level of effectiveness and efficiency, and you then take those learnings and begin to plan for improvements in processes to obtain the perceived benefits, you have not abandoned the project, you have gained new knowledge of how to make the technology work for you. This is standard business operations and experimentation.

Why are so many people excited?

There are few places where GenAI will not be transformative. Why is this the case? There are a number of reasons.

To begin with, GenAI is one of the first, if not the first, truly transformative technologies that are squarely targeted at being applied to predominately professional and creative roles. It is not the case that someone in a research organization or academic setting started out to want to disrupt professional roles like lawyers, developers, authors, playwrights, business analysts, auditors, accountants, process engineers, graphic designers and artists, and others.

If a graduate student, assistant professor, or research assistant had proposed transforming all those roles as a design principle and as a guiding element for developing GenAI, I am certain that they would have been rebuffed by their peers, faculty advisors, and others for being too grandiose in their vision of what they could accomplish with this new area of research.

As we discussed in Chapter 5, the initial results of GenAI in accurately predicting the next word in a sentence did not seem that promising. When GenAI was proven to work, no one in technology, academe, commercial organizations, technology media, or business press jumped at the opportunity to opine on the disruptive nature of the new development in ANY field of work. Literally, at the outset, almost no one saw this coming, or at least they did not say anything about it, which is hard to believe that someone would have seen the potential and not discussed it.

Second, in the technology fields, specifically in the fields of analytics and AI, we have been working with only approximately 10% of the world's information stores for the entirety of our careers. And in that 10% of data we have been working with, we sample that body of knowledge and work with small subsets. In reality, we have been working with about 1% of the world's available information.

As we previously discussed, the vast majority of commercial analytics and AI work is focused on structured information. Even those of us who have dabbled in the areas of Natural Language Processing (NLP), Natural Language Generation (NLG), and Natural Language Understanding (NLU) often did so knowing that we were drifting into applications and technologies that were nascent and generally unreliable. Also, we were working on applications that were nice to have but were not considered to be of strategic importance. And when we ventured into these new areas and provided applications that worked reliably, the commercial side of the organizations we worked with was not that interested or impressed.

Third, GenAI is exceedingly accessible and easy to use. We have all heard the stories and facts about the speed at which OpenAI's first public product, ChatGPT, reached 100 million users.[169] Two months after launch is an impressive feat, to be sure.

With Foundational AI, it is only accessible to highly trained, very technical people interested in statistics and math. That is not 100% true, but it is quite accurate. I have worked in the AI field for 38 years, and there is a strong correlation between people who are mathematically literate and technologically oriented, and those that are successful data scientists. In addition to the personal interest in and affinity for data science, the training required to become an effective and productive data scientist is long and challenging. All of these factors combine to ensure that data scientists are a very small group of people in relation to the general population. Data scientists make up 1/10 of one percent (.001) of the employee pool of the United States.[170]

GenAI, when it was first released, was accessed predominately by English speakers, but still, with that language restriction, the entire English-speaking population that had access to ChatGPT could engage with the technology with no training; this is an amazing development. Without prior

---

[169] Krystal Hu, Reuters, February 2, 20239:33 AM CST, ChatGPT sets record for fastest-growing user base, https://www.reuters.com/technology/chatgpt-sets-record-fastest-growing-user-base-analyst-note-2023-02-01/, Cited on September 2, 2024.

[170] US Bureau of Labor Statistics. Occupational Employment and Wage Statistics, Occupational Employment and Wages, May 2023, 15-2051 Data Scientists, https://www.bls.gov/oes/current/oes152051.htm, Cited September 2,2024.

exposure, anyone could engage with an AI and immediately be productive with the technology. This is fantastic! This is a dream come true for all of us working in technology.

GenAI has evolved rapidly in relation to languages that can be entered as prompts and returned as results. In just under two years, "Transformers — the technology underpinning large language models — have allowed Google Translate to more than double the number of languages it supports to 243."[171] I have had conversations with multiple organizations that are building Large Language Models for users to converse with GenAI in their native language. I have spoken with firms working on models for Hindi, Tamil, Punjabi, and other languages.

Fourth, the cost is negligible for most users. Of course, we must know the dynamic of free products and services. All users of all technologies need to be cognizant that if something is being offered for free, typically, it is being offered to other firms to monetize the product and service we are consuming.

Fifth, it is fun, and in most cases, it makes our lives easier. One of the use cases that I think provides great value is the ability of GenAI to receive prompts in one language, let's say French, and to return the results in another language, let's say, Finnish. Two people who are fluent in only their language can have a conversation through GenAI in their native languages in real time. This is an incredible application that enables people from around the world to freely converse with no language barrier. Quite an impressive feat, in my opinion.

---

[171] Isaac Caswell, Senior Software Engineer, Google Translate, July 27, 2024, 110 new languages are coming to Google Translate, https://blog.google/products/translate/google-translate-new-languages-2024/, Cited September 3, 2024.

Of course, there are many other personal and professional reasons why people are attracted to and engaged by GenAI. Still, those outlined above are the major primary reasons that GenAI is in the hands of a significant portion of the world's population.

Let's continue our discussion by taking the dialog down a level and begin to break down the components of the overall impact of GenAI that is being seen, heard, and felt globally.

Economic impact

In a recent report, the research team at McKinsey states, "Generative artificial intelligence (GenAI) is poised to unleash a powerful wave of productivity growth that will likely affect all industries and could add as much as $4.4 trillion annually to the global economy…"[172] For reference, the annual GDP of Germany in 2022 was approximately $4T.[173] The McKinsey research is confined to 63 defined use cases. The authors state

---

[172] Lareina Yee, Michael Chui, McKinsey, June 21, 2023, The economic potential of generative AI: The next productivity frontier, https://www.mckinsey.com/featured-insights/mckinsey-live/webinars/the-economic-potential-of-generative-ai-the-next-productivity-frontier, Cited September 3, 2024.

[173] Google Search, Annual GDP of Germany, https://www.google.com/search?q=annual+GDP+of+germany&rlz=1C1RXQR_enUS1041US1041&oq=annual+GDP+of+germany&gs_lcrp=EgZjaHJvbWUyBggAEEUYOTIICAEQABgWGB4yDQgCEAAYhgMYgAQYigUyCggDEAAYgAQYogQyCggEEAAYgAQYogQyCggFEAAYgAQYogQyCggGEAAYgAQYogTSAQg2ODE0ajBqN6gCALACAA&sourceid=chrome&ie=UTF-8, Search and Cited on September 3, 2024.

that the impact could be twice as much when applied to the global economy without constraint to the listed use cases.[174]

My experience with GenAI in building the infrastructure and end-user applications for over 300,000 employees and having strategic and tactical discussions with over 400 companies in the past two years is that given the broad-based and significant impact of the technology, it is challenging for non-technologists to understand how to think about applying GenAI to their business processes and workloads. I can empathize and understand their situation.

In the past, applications and technologies were targeted and applied to specific business and technology issues. Issues like reporting financial data from multiple sources or analyzing traffic to a specific on-line property. Use cases defined at that level of specificity are easy to understand. GenAI's broad applicability is impressive and will drive change and benefit across large swaths of the global economy. Still, it does make it hard for individuals to gain a deep and clear understanding of how GenAI will improve their operations, margins, and efficiency.

It seems obvious, but technology adoption occurs over time, and the forecasted improvements do not appear instantaneously. Some experts say that the numerous forecasts are too aggressive and that the impacts will not be as significant as some propose. Daron Acemoglu, Institute Professor at MIT, said, "Given the focus and architecture of generative AI technology

---

[174] Lareina Yee, Michael Chui, McKinsey, June 21, 2023, The economic potential of generative AI: The next productivity frontier, https://www.mckinsey.com/featured-insights/mckinsey-live/webinars/the-economic-potential-of-generative-ai-the-next-productivity-frontier, Cited September 3, 2024.

today... truly transformative changes won't happen quickly and few, if any, will likely occur within the next 10 years."[175]

I do agree with Professor Acemoglu that it will take time to see the full impact of GenAI and that we will need to build out computing infrastructure, software, applications, and more, but I do not agree with the implication that little to no impact will be seen for a decade. We have seen direct improvement in operations from people using GenAI in sales, marketing, development, quality assurance, technical writing, strategy development, forecasting, and more.

Specifically, in sales, we have seen significant improvements in the development of initial proposals. The process without GenAI required multiple employees over at least three levels of seniority over a period of a month or two. With GenAI, we see an initial draft of a high-quality proposal in a matter of minutes with only one employee involved. And this is just one application of GenAI to a defined process.

The global economic impact over the next ten years will be immense. Actually, I think that McKinsey's projections are too low. I believe that the impact of GenAI will be measured in double-digit trillions of dollars over the next decade. And, of course, I disagree with Dr. Acemoglu on the timing of the realization of impact and value that is already happening.

GenAI is easy to use and understand, readily available, secure, and can ensure privacy. It can also disrupt many roles that are part of today's professional job landscape for those reasons and more that we have already

---

[175] Goldman Sachs Research, Top of Mind, June 25, 2024, GEN AI: TOO MUCH SPEND, TOO LITTLE BENEFIT?, https://www.goldmansachs.com/images/migrated/insights/pages/gs-research/gen-ai--too-much-spend,-too-little-benefit-/TOM_AI%202.0_ForRedaction.pdf, Cited September 3, 2024.

stated and discussed. The impact of GenAI on the economic landscape is significant, measurable, and immediate. Let's move on from the macro view to multiple lower-level perspectives. Let's start with the impact of GenAI on jobs and roles within those jobs.

Jobs

In my opinion, the job losses that we have seen in 2024 and will see in 2025 are just the beginning of a new structural cycle. On this aspect of GenAI impact, I do agree with Dr. Acemoglu.

We will see job impacts beginning now and rolling out over the next decade or more. The impacts that we have seen in the previous two years have been limited to the technology sector, and those job losses have been significant. However, we will see these impacts and job losses impacting all sectors of the global economy at different times. Also, we will see those impacts in various geographies, countries, industries, and companies based on their posture toward adopting innovation and their stage of readiness to transform their operating processes. This is all to say that the GenAI revolution is not a big-bang transformation that we will see all at once but a slow-rolling transformation that will take years to realize globally.

Technology companies have taken the lead in reducing headcount while simultaneously increasing processing efficiency, operational speed, and profitability. This movement will spread through all industries, all geographies, and the totality of the global economy.

While many pundits, gurus, experts, and analysts are championing the view the GenAI is best when implemented as an augmenting technology where humans and AI collaborate for better results, the early indicators are the employers are cutting headcount and replacing people with GenAI applications. In a recent interview with the Financial Times, James Manyika remarked that "[w]hile at McKinsey, Manyika predicted that the pandemic would allow companies to pursue digital transformation: he concedes many did so "in a cost-cutting direction". Now Manyika agrees executives are incentivized to replace workers with AI, rather than deploy the technology to assist them."[176]

The current dynamic that is playing out in the labor markets is that GenAI is being used to secure productivity gains, head count is being reduced, and at the same time, new roles are being added and filled where employees have skills and talent in understanding, using, developing and deploying GenAI and the resulting applications. While it feels like a negative consequence to those who are affected by job losses, the overall efficiency and skill level of the economy improve in both the short and long term.

"A 2023 study examined all the tasks done by workers throughout the American economy to see which of them could be done at least at least twice as rapidly with no loss in quality via the use of generative AI. The research concluded that for about 20% of all workers, half or more of their tasks fell into this category. When the threshold was reduced to 10% of tasks, 80% of workers qualified. For example, interpreters and translators, survey researchers, and public relations specialists all had at least two-thirds of their tasks eligible for significant productivity improvement via generative

---

[176] Henry Mance, September 1 2024, FT.com, Google's James Manyika: 'The productivity gains from AI are not guaranteed', https://www.ft.com/content/2c122092-51ab-4529-b733-ac466f338cb5, Cited September 3, 2024.

AI. At the other end of the spectrum, workers including short-order cooks, athletes, and oil and gas derrick operators had no tasks in this category."[177]

Given that GenAI is the first technology truly targeted at professional roles, there are widespread and significant opportunities to transform roles and entire jobs in multiple fields. This is a disruptive and transformative change for these jobs and roles and for the companies that consist of these roles. The short-term job losses and subsequent and simultaneous hiring of new roles foil the employment picture, but the long-term outlook is positive and accretive to the global economy.

The effects of adopting GenAI will not be uniform. Advanced economies will see more immediate and greater effects of implementing GenAI, a recent study, "...finds almost 40% of employment globally is exposed to AI, which rises to 60% in advanced economies. Artificial intelligence (AI) has the potential to reshape the global economy, especially in the realm of labor markets. Advanced economies will experience the benefits and pitfalls of AI sooner than emerging markets and developing economies, largely because their employment structure is focused on cognitive-intensive roles. There are some consistent patterns concerning AI exposure: women and college-educated individuals are more exposed but also better poised to reap AI benefits, and older workers are potentially less able to adapt to the new technology."[178]

---

[177] Andrew McAfee, Technology & Society Visiting Fellow, Google, Apr 25, 2024, A new report explores the economic impact of generative AI, https://blog.google/technology/ai/a-new-report-explores-the-economic-impact-of-generative-ai/, Cited on September 3, 2024.

[178] Statista, Number of full-time employees in the United States from 1990 to 2023, https://www.statista.com/statistics/192356/number-of-full-time-employees-in-the-usa-since-

While we see the short-term swapping of older workers for both GenAI automation and for younger workers who are adept at leveraging AI in their jobs, once this opportunity for improvement has been processed through the economy, GenAI as an augmenting technology will become the predominant implementation mode.

"...[A]s AI excels at routine tasks, it can free up humans for more interesting challenges. This augmentation-rather-than-automation approach offers the best opportunities for not only preserving employment but also ensuring effective and valuable AI. Actively involving workers in the development, adoption, and implementation of the technology can result in systems that are more practical, innovative, and effective. Even with an augmentation approach, however, AI systems will result in potentially significant job disruptions and call for a rethinking of education, employment, and policy systems. While technology skills would seem a worthwhile investment focus, there is also a need for general skills that can improve employment adaptability, such as critical thinking, and the skills that AI struggles with replicating, such as creativity, human touch, and emotional intelligence."[179]

As implicitly noted, GenAI directly and immediately impacts roles and/or tasks. For example, GenAI is very good at generating a complete first draft of nearly any document but is not adept at writing a complete and edited final draft. GenAI may improve to the point that the first draft is a perfect

---

1990/#:~:text=In%202023%2C%20about%20134.06%20million,returning%20to%20pre%2Dpandemic%20levels, Cited on September 2, 2024.

[179] Cazzaniga and others. 2024. "Gen-AI: Artificial Intelligence and the Future of Work." IMF Staff Discussion Note SDN2024/001, International Monetary Fund, Washington, DC., https://www.imf.org/en/Publications/Staff-Discussion-Notes/Issues/2024/01/14/Gen-AI-Artificial-Intelligence-and-the-Future-of-Work-542379?cid=bl-com-SDNEA2024001, Publication Date: January 14, 2024, Cited August 22, 2024.

final draft, but we are not there today. So, the impact on the general art of writing is that writers can use GenAI to get started and to refine the starting point for their book, presentation, script, legal brief, article, blog post, or any type of writing project, but the writer still needs to engage in the process of refining the text either with or without GenAI.

Yes, some jobs can be completely automated away with GenAI, but that is a small portion of existing jobs. Currently, most jobs and roles have a small portion that can be improved and transformed by GenAI. In my view, we will see job losses in the short and long term. Those job losses will be offset by larger and more significant job creation.

This is not a new dynamic, but it is a dynamic that has more frequently been experienced in applying technology and automation to jobs that have a more mechanistic approach to the jobs, such as bank tellers, tool booth operators, manufacturing jobs, bookstore employees, and other jobs that have been affected by automation over the past 40 years. This time, it is white-collar and creative professionals that will be impacted.

Overall, the impact of GenAI on jobs will be positive and improve productivity, efficiency, and effectiveness. Let's move on to the impact of GenAI on our society and culture.

Society

Work gives many people meaning, structure, and purpose in their lives. Any technology that will have such a widespread impact on jobs and roles will, of course, impact the fabric of society. There is no doubt that losing a job if that job is the sole source of support or income for one person or an entire family, is a significant, negative change for that person or family. This cannot be overlooked. People who are impacted by GenAI-driven job losses deserve support and assistance as they search for new employment and/or seek to upskill themselves to secure a new role that enables them to utilize GenAI in their newly reframed role and job.

"Artificial Intelligence (AI) is revolutionizing every facet of business and life, thanks to the accelerated development of generative AI, which has made the technology widely accessible. For social innovators, the ethical adoption of AI in their business models and/or to streamline their operations represents a unique opportunity to maximize their impact. The social economy represents 7% of global GDP, and generative AI could add between $182 billion and $308 billion in value annually to the sector."[180]

We can argue that the evolution of roles and jobs being driven by GenAI is a long-term positive change. As noted above, social innovators are taking a more active role in driving a focus on ethics and responsible use of AI. Numerous companies are focused on ensuring that AI, including GenAI, is implemented and leveraged within an ethical and responsible framework to govern and control the use of technology fairly and transparently. This is an expanded focus and effort, and as such, will drive an entirely new level of engagement, discussion, design, and development of technology, business processes, management consulting, and more. And this is only one example of a completely new area that will add hundreds of millions of dollars to the global economy. There are many examples of GenAI-driven innovation, such as net new income inflows across the globe.

The World Economic Forum researched and released a report titled The Role of Artificial Intelligence in Social Innovation, "The report finds three

---

[180] World Economic Forum, Artificial Intelligence: AI and the Future of Jobs, this issue is defined and incorporated into this transformation map by Desautels Faculty of Management, McGill University, 2024, https://intelligence.weforum.org/topics/a1Gb0000000pTDREA2/key-issues/a1Gb00000017LD8EAM, Cited on August 24, 2024.

primary impact areas where AI is making significant contributions: healthcare, with 25% of innovators using AI to advance access to health; environmental sustainability, with 20% of social innovators applying AI to tackle climate solutions; and economic empowerment, notably prevalent in lower-income countries where 80% of all initiatives aimed at enhancing livelihoods are based. But AI is also revolutionizing practices in other areas such as agriculture through predictive analytics and precision farming, addressing climate resilience and boosting productivity."[181]

Of course, no conversation relating to the impact of GenAI on society can be complete with at least a mention of the potential for misuse and abuse of technology. GenAI is being used to create deepfakes of a wide range of leading figures in politics, sports, media, music, and more.

Let's define the term deep-fake. "A deepfake is a video, photo, or audio recording that seems real but has been manipulated with AI. The underlying technology can replace faces, manipulate facial expressions, synthesize faces, and synthesize speech. Deepfakes can depict someone appearing to say or do something that they in fact never said or did."[182]

Often, deepfakes are employed by people and organizations that intend to disseminate false and misleading information. These efforts have been very successful in unfortunate ways. We in the technology industry need to work with an increased focus to develop tools and technologies that can spot, flag,

---

[181] World Economic Forum, AI for Impact: The Role of Artificial Intelligence in Social Innovation, Published April 2024, https://www.weforum.org/publications/ai-for-impact-artificial-intelligence-in-social-innovation/, Cited on August 22, 2024.

[182] US Governmental Accountability Office, GAO-20-379SP, Science & Tech Spotlight: Deepfakes, Science, Technology Assessment, and Analytics, February 2020, https://www.gao.gov/assets/gao-20-379sp.pdf, Cited on September 8, 2024.

and help stop this type of activity, but this will be an ongoing effort that will not be won overnight.

What is the overall impact on the society of GenAI? This question will generate as many answers as the number of times you pose the question.

In my opinion, GenAI will be an overwhelmingly positive contribution to society. One effect that has been proven in multiple studies is that people who are good at a skill, like writing, can be better when augmenting their work with GenAI, and those who could improve their writing skills improve markedly when they use GenAI. The net effect is that everyone is a better writer.

One of the first studies on assisted writing by a team at MIT in 2023 illustrated that "Half of participants were given access to the chatbot ChatGPT-3.5, for the second assignment. Those users finished tasks 11 minutes faster than the control group, while their average quality evaluations increased by 18 percent. The data also showed that performance inequality between workers decreased, meaning workers who received a lower grade in the first task benefitted more from using ChatGPT for the second task."[183]

We have seen this effect in multiple fields, such as general writing, technical writing, scientific writing, writing code, generating images, graphic design, video production, and more. As noted, there are people and groups who will use GenAI for illegal, immoral, or just unfortunate purposes and we must work to lessen the impact of these efforts. Still, in general, GenAI is a

---

[183] Zach Winn, MIT News Office, July 14, 2023, Study finds ChatGPT boosts worker productivity for some writing tasks, A new report by MIT researchers highlights the potential of generative AI to help workers with certain writing assignments, Shakked Noy, Whitney Zhang, https://news.mit.edu/2023/study-finds-chatgpt-boosts-worker-productivity-writing-0714, Cited on September 8, 2024.

tool that will enable a wide range of professionals and amateurs to produce better work in a shorter time and engage in endeavors they never could before. GenAI is here to stay, and it will be a driver of net positive benefits globally.

Let's focus on technology and how GenAI will evolve and grow in the coming months and years.

Technology

Two years ago, people were just learning about Large Language Models (LLMs). Currently, the landscape for GenAI from a Foundational model view is that we have LLMs from the leading firms such as Mistral, Anthropic, Cohere, OpenAI, Meta and others. We have an emerging area of models referred to as Small Language Models (SLMs) or Domain Language Models (DLMs). I believe that the label DLM will be the acronym and name of choice for this category of models. And we have Tiny Language Models (TLMs) for all the Natural Language Processing (NLP) models that we have been building for the past five to seven years. This *is* the ecosystem of models that we will be working with on a going forward basis.

Most users will have the experience of working with and interacting with a prompt window. As with most elements of the GenAI world and environment, the names of these components are in flux. People refer to the common user interface for GenAI systems as a Conversational User Interface (CUI), or a Natural User interface (NUI). We will see which terminology will take hold in the coming months, but let's talk about the prompt window and the interface that most people engage with for GenAI.

Most people begin prompting GenAI like a search engine. They prompt with questions like, "What is the capital of Illinois?" or "What is the driving distance between Chicago and Ann Arbor?" Once people realize that prompts are better when they are structured as well thought-out scenarios requiring inference, multiple data sources, and/or a logical sequence or flow, they begin to write better prompts.

Most people think that they are prompting a model, and in some cases, they are, but increasingly, they are prompting an ensemble of models. They are sending in prompts to a collection of models. This collection of models is referred to as a Mixture of Experts (MoE) or an Ensemble of Models (EoM).

Let's define MoE, "Mixture of Experts architectures enable large-scale models, even those comprising many billions of parameters, to greatly reduce computation costs during pre-training and achieve faster performance during inference time. Broadly speaking, it achieves this efficiency through selectively activating only the specific experts needed for a given task, rather than activating the entire neural network for every task."[184]

I this additional definition of MoE: "Mixture of experts is an ensemble learning technique developed in the field of neural networks. It involves decomposing predictive modeling tasks into sub-tasks, training an expert model on each, developing a gating model that learns which expert to trust based on the input to be predicted, and combines the predictions. Although the technique was initially described using neural network experts and gating models, it can be generalized to use models of any type."[185]

---

[184] Dave Bergmann, 5 April 2024, IBM.com, What is mixture of experts?, https://www.ibm.com/topics/mixture-of-experts, Cited October 6, 2024.

[185] Jason Brownlee, November 7, 2021, Ensemble Learning A Gentle Introduction to Mixture of Experts Ensembles, https://machinelearningmastery.com/mixture-of-experts/, Cited on October 6, 2024.

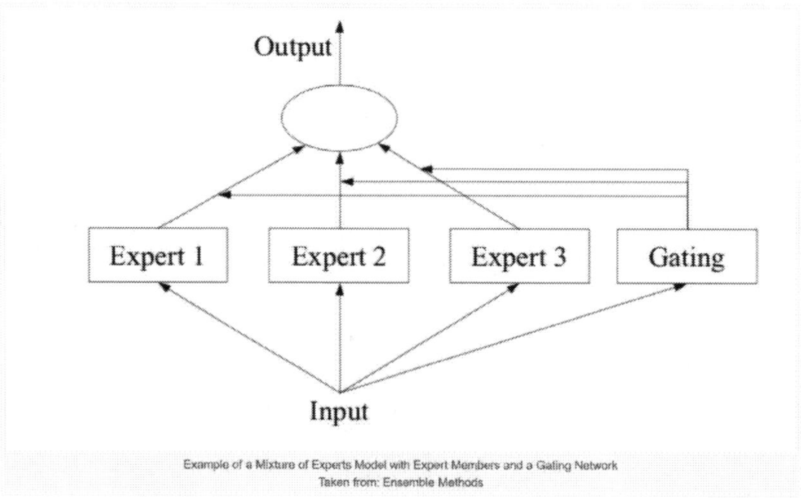

Figure 16: A representative diagram of a process for a Mixture of Experts model ensemble in a GenAI environment.[186]

A MoE is an architectural choice for how to offer numerous models in a GenAI environment. We could spend an entire book describing other elements, but as noted earlier, this would be counterproductive and fruitless given the pace of innovation and change. Our goal in this book is to provide an overview of how GenAI operates and in this section, we want to focus on the impact GenAI will have on the technology landscape.

One area of impact that is fairly obvious is that GenAI provides the ability to develop systems and applications in ways that we could not imagine only a few years ago. Conversational interfaces will be the preferred and, most likely, the only interfaces that will be offered for people to interact with nearly all systems in the future. That alone has a massive impact on how systems are developed and offered.

---

186 Ibid.

GenAI enables the development of agents. The McKinsey research team describes agents in the following manner, "Broadly speaking, 'agentic' systems refer to digital systems that can independently interact in a dynamic world. While versions of these software systems have existed for years, the natural-language capabilities of gen AI unveil new possibilities, enabling systems that can plan their actions, use online tools to complete those tasks, collaborate with other agents and people, and learn to improve their performance… A virtual assistant, for example, could plan and book a complex personalized travel itinerary, handling logistics across multiple travel platforms. Using everyday language, an engineer could describe a new software feature to a programmer agent, which would then code, test, iterate, and deploy the tool it helped create."[187]

Regarding impact, agents will be one of the most important developments GenAI will foster. Single agents and multiple agents will be developed to automate, improve, and speed up the processing of certainly all mechanistic or prescribed processes, which will probably impact many dynamic processes as well.

Recently, I used the example of booking travel using a GenAI-based agent rather than a human travel agent. It is an easy-to-understand example, and it is evocative of the impact and change we will see soon.

In addition to the quick scenario the staff at McKinsey outlined above, I included booking dinners, plays, transfers, personal activities, and more in my example. I described how when meetings are moved or canceled, the agent would review your e-mails, texts, and social media posts, and replace the canceled meeting with another meeting with someone who was not on

---

[187] Lareina Yee, Michael Chui, and Roger Roberts with Stephen Xu, McKinsey Quarterly, July 24, 2024, Why agents are the next frontier of generative AI, https://www.mckinsey.com/capabilities/mckinsey-digital/our-insights/why-agents-are-the-next-frontier-of-generative-ai, Cited October 6, 2024.

your itinerary, but who you had been communicating with and whom you had stated an interest in meeting. Also, I outlined how your agent could book a play for you at the price point you stated and buy your favorite beverage at the intermission.

Moving beyond singular agents and simple workflows, we can now start to consider the impact on making more sophisticated analytical environments and systems available on a more widespread basis.

Simulation and optimization problems are complex and can be difficult to solve. AI agents create a new way to build simulation and optimization applications. A way that makes this class of application more accessible to business analysts and others who may not have the programming or statistical background to build and understand these applications and their usage.

And, finally, to ensure that we are clear, GenAI will have a significant impact on system development. Of course, GenAI can generate code of all types, but it can also develop and deliver entire systems. The quality of these systems will depend on the quality and specificity of the prompts, but this is the first time that, on a widespread basis, everyone with access to technology can develop entire systems with little to no support from traditional technology professionals.

Of course, this discussion triggers a thread of dialog that we hear recurring with regularity, that this new development is the end of developers and that we no longer need programmers. This is nonsense. Just as in the generation of text and documents by GenAI, the systems generated by GenAI today are good starting points, but they are of low quality and do not operate out of the box. As with all technologies, the results will improve as the input quality and specificity improve. Still, we have many years of refinement before considering repurposing developers meaningfully.

In summary, the immediate impacts that we will see on technology are:

- The change to Conversational Interfaces for all technology applications and solutions.
- The rise in importance of Application Programming Interfaces (APIs) to facilitate the widespread adoption of GenAI-based agents.
- Agents—Simple, Multi-Agents, Intelligent Agents, Self-Replicating Agents, Polymorphic Agents.
- MOEs—Models and agents networked together for increased relevance, better accuracy, faster performance, and a smaller carbon footprint.
- Generation of complete systems without the need for traditional development cycles or traditional technology teams.
- The ability to develop complex analytical systems such as simulation and optimization with less resources and less technical resources.

Again, to be clear, these are significant impacts, and they will make a difference in the speed of change, but they will also be lacking in quality for the coming few years. Development speed will increase, quality will decrease, and we will need skilled resources to bring systems online. In the beginning, we may even see development times slow or increase in total duration, but this is the beginning of a new way to develop technology-based applications and solutions.

Let's move to the impact of GenAI on education.

Education

Administrators, teachers, professors, and related staff in all levels of education, from grade school to postgraduate, are interested in and concerned about the impact of GenAI on education. The reactions have ranged from complete bans on the use of technology to wide open, unfettered access.

I have spoken with multiple US high schools and several US universities. I am slightly surprised when I encounter educators who propose and support total bans on GenAI of all sorts and flavors. The predominance of concern seems to center on concerns related to plagiarism. We have dealt with plagiarism for centuries. The rise of information technology, word processing, the internet, and easy access to online information repositories have changed how teachers and professors need to review and grade student submissions. In my opinion, GenAI is no different than these previous technologies. To me, the stated concerns seem shortsighted and miss the point of leveraging technology for the best outcome for the students. I am pleased to say that this is the minority view in the unscientific and limited data that I have created.

Now that GenAI has been disseminated widely and incorporated into learning environments creatively, there is far less fear and more openness to consider how GenAI can be used in education. Khan Academy[188] has done a wonderful job leveraging GenAI to create an experience for students where the GenAI tutor exhibits the qualities we would like to see in all teachers, tutors, graduate assistants, instructional assistants, and all educational staff that come into close contact with students. Khan Academy's GenAI tutor presents information so that the student experiences patience, empathy, and understanding of how this individual

---

[188] Khan Academy, https://www.khanacademy.org/, Cited October 7, 2024.

student can improve and learn at an optimal pace for the topic, subject, and lesson at hand.

As I am building my current class offerings for a top-tier US university, I am bringing GenAI into my syllabus and mandating that the students use GenAI to improve their writing and submissions. GenAI does a superb job of changing the tone, tenor, writing level, and other nuances of writing. By directing the students to use GenAI to draft a paper and then specifically manipulate it with GenAI, the students can gain a deeper understanding of how writing can change and be tailored to the exercise or audience or need better than they could on their own. Using GenAI in this manner exposes them to a wider range of writing styles and approaches than they could devise without support.

I believe that all students can be better writers by leveraging GenAI. Multiple studies have shown that average to below-average writers using GenAI improve the most; what a wonderful outcome of using technology to support learning.

In education, GenAI is an indispensable tool for increasing the learning experience of all students. All education professionals need to thoughtfully consider how their students can benefit from this technology and then revise the curriculum to incorporate GenAI into the process flow, exercises, and objectives.

When speaking with university staff, I recommend that they encourage their students to use GenAI in all their projects and activities. I suggest that the students provide a footnote or comment about which models they used and why those models were interesting to them for this project.

If you are in the field of education, I suggest that you spend time investigating, at least, the most popular Large Language Models. They are not the same. Each model presents information in a unique style. Some are verbose. Some are concise. Some are more empathetic in tone. LLMs are a bit like people. They have their own take on how to create output.

LLMs are like fashion. Some people like capri pants, and others like bell bottoms. There is room for all types of fashion and places for all types of LLMs to be used. I suggest you mix it up and see what happens.

As we hear people remark with fair regularity, in the new working world, AI may not take your job, but someone who knows how to use GenAI just might. We need to equip our students to be masters of this new tool. They expect us to provide the skills they need in the workplace, and we are responsible for living up to their expectations.

And finally, as we wrap up our discussion of the impact of GenAI on our world, let's take a few minutes to consider and discuss the Arts and how GenAI is changing this part of our experiences.

Arts

Music, film, painting, writing, sculpting, television, poetry, and all types and forms of art permeate our lives. We may choose to engage with some arts and to ignore others. That is our choice. Many people talk to me about the dilution of the arts or AI's denigration of the arts. I don't see it.

I believe AI in the arts will make human creativity more valuable and sought out. AI may make true human creativity harder to find due to the volume of work created by AI systems, but that does not lessen the value of art and the human endeavor to create art, great or not.

Recently, I read about a movie focused on the life and art of Brian Eno.[189] The film has been produced by ingesting over 100 hours of footage of Eno talking about life, art, politics, human tragedy, and more. "Based on the life of the multitalented music producer Brian Eno, the documentary is auto-generated by a machine and varies every time it is shown. According to the film's makers, there are 52 quintillion possible versions of it, which could make "a really big box set".[190]

The film about Brian Eno is an example of how AI can create a dynamic experience of engaging with a wide range of content that most people would not have access to. The use of AI and the ability to watch a new and unique version of the film each sitting brings forth the idea that the people who are interested in Eno, his work, and his ideas do not have to look at one view of this material that was edited and produced in a static form. Each time someone watches this film, they will see a new sequence of content from Eno. I find this new approach intriguing. AI can bring new ways of presenting content in dynamic and non-traditional manners.

And, of course, GenAI can create deepfakes quickly and easily, and produce versions that appear to show people saying things that directly counter what they believe and stand for. This is not art. This is misinformation.

And, yes, GenAI can create volumes of words, images, videos, code, and more. And most of the generated content, objectively, is not that good. This generated content certainly does not rise to the level of a skilled painter, writer, or developer. In my opinion, all of this generated content raises the

---

[189] Wikipedia, The Contributors to Wikipedia, Brian Eno, https://en.wikipedia.org/wiki/Brian_Eno, Cited October 8, 2024.

[190] David Bloom, Forbes.com, Jan, 18, 2024, Sundance 2024: Generative AI Changes Brian Eno Documentary With Every View, https://www.forbes.com/sites/dbloom/2024/01/18/sundance-2024-generative-ai-changes-brian-eno-documentary-with-every-view/, Cited October 8, 2024.

perceived value of the truly artistic output produced by virtuosos in their various fields.

We have work to do in the area of evaluating GenAI-created content and watermarking it as work generated by AI. This area of research and development today is not hard to do, but it will take time. We should have widespread access to tools that determine the genesis of all types of generated content and enable people to know and understand the true provenance of an object quickly and easily by the end of 2025. GenAI is a tool and a really powerful one that will continue to grow, expand, and refine what it can produce, but it will never be seen as a creative genius. GenAI will produce all types of output that can be accessible to those who want to enjoy images, films, and music but cannot afford to access original works from the masters of all time. Increased accessibility and enjoyment of all art forms surely is a positive development. Art is not under attack; it is being generated and disseminated more widely in new and exciting forms.

Summary

GenAI has been, and is, the topic of the day, week, month, and, in reality, the last two years. Much of the attention is deserved. GenAI is one of the most impactful technologies that has emerged in our lifetimes. That is saying something. We have seen: a man land on the moon, the creation of a semi-permanent international space station, the birth of the internet, the discovery of DNA, and much more, but even with all those discoveries and inventions coming about in the past 70 years, GenAI is still near the top of the list of valuable, useful, and impactful inventions.

Let's move on to the next section and begin examining and discussing the future of GenAI.

CHAPTER 7

The Future of Generative AI

Writing about the future direction of GenAI presents some interesting challenges, given how much the present state of GenAI is in flight and in flux. Technology is racing forward in its multifaceted approach to ingesting, processing, and delivering results, but it is fairly easy to examine, understand, and project forward. In my opinion, the more challenging part of prognosticating in a highly accurate manner is the application of GenAI in the exceedingly varied settings of everyday life.

In general, non-technologists have a difficult time grasping the application and impact of GenAI, and it does not help that some pundits are saying that GenAI is a flash in the pan, a fad, that will have no real impact on the world. At the same time, others are saying that GenAI is the path to Artificial General Intelligence (AGI). It is certainly difficult for many to reconcile these radically different positions.

Sadly, rather than simply getting on with it and exploring the value and transformational power of GenAI, some leaders and people are putting their heads in the sand and hoping GenAI will fade away. This is not really anything new. That is what laggards and luddites do regularly. Eventually, these individuals will change their minds, or their organizations will change their employment status for them. As my one-time manager said numerous times when I was explaining my concerns about various current issues, "Don't spend any time thinking about this, this is a self-correcting problem."[191]

> *Those who ignore GenAI as a fad will have their minds made up for them.*

Let's examine the future of GenAI from the perspective of technology and applications. Let's begin with technology.

Technology

GenAI has gone from a little-known variant of neural networks to a global driving force in just over two years. We have already laid out the fundamental technical reasons. Let's discuss where technology is going now and into the foreseeable future. Let's see if we can accurately discuss the development and direction of GenAI for the next five to ten years.

Model ensembles

In the short term, which is the next six to 12 months, we will see how the ecosystem of models evolves and fills out. There are questions as to whether the taxonomy of models described in the previous section (e.g., LLMs, SLMs/DLMs, TLMs) will come to fruition. These questions are primarily from technology analysts, financial analysts, and other market observers.

191 John Swainson, https://www.linkedin.com/in/johnswainson/, Cited on October 14, 2024.

As an AI practitioner, I can say with nearly 100% certainty that this has already happened from a technological perspective. These three types of models have been proven to be economically and technically capable of being built and deployed. So, we can assume that this is a given. A substantial subset of users is already using ensembles of models and are unaware of that fact.

One of the main concerns about foundational models is hallucinations, or said in another way, the primary concerns are the lack of accuracy, relevance, and random results. Let's discuss this aspect of model operations and implementation.

Grounding—In model or outside the model

Currently, the discussion of grounding models centers on whether we ground models by including more context *into* the model via system prompting, post-training/fine tuning, or end-user input. Or if we continue developing additional capabilities *outside* the model akin to Retrieval Augmented Generation (RAG). Or if we leverage multiple approaches to grounding, which may include all the aforementioned techniques.

To be clear, we undertake these approaches to grounding models to increase accuracy and relevance and to decrease hallucinations. Many people forget that we are not designing and implementing these model augmentations because they are part of the foundational design of GenAI. All of these approaches are add-ons to address the fundamental lack of accuracy in GenAI models.

It appears that this last statement causes many people, typically non-technologists, to be concerned about and question whether using foundational models is a sound idea in the first place. Data scientists, analytics professionals, and technologists accept this level of inaccuracy, in part because all models are inaccurate at some level. It is common in technology discussions to hear the following phrase or derivation of the phrase, "All models are wrong, but some are useful." The aphorism acknowledges that statistical models always fall short of the complexities of reality but can still be useful, nonetheless. The remark originally referred just to statistical models, but it is now sometimes used for models in general.[192]

Grounding models to make them more accurate through the techniques listed above are not the only methods being explored. There are external systems that are referred to as guardrails, which we discussed in Chapter 5. The premise of guardrail systems is that models will hallucinate, and the output of a model or an ensemble of models can be passed to an external environment that will verify whether the results are accurate enough to be passed on to the end users. We will see numerous offerings in the guardrail space going forward. This will be an interesting field to observe.

Another technique is to use recursion to pass the end results of a model through the original model and/or additional models until the quality of the result is accurate and relevant enough for the needs of the user or agent or purpose at hand. Recursion and multiple pass processing are widely used today in technical areas. Most users are not aware that this is happening today.

To be clear, there are two approaches to increasing accuracy and relevancy. One is to add more information to the model, and the other is to put more information and information processing around the model.

---

[192] Wikipedia, The Contributors to Wikipedia, All models are wrong, https://en.wikipedia.org/wiki/All_models_are_wrong, Cited on October 14, 2024.

In these two approaches, we see two fundamentally different views on grounding. The first is based on the idea that the solution to increasing accuracy is in the model. The other is that the solution is to layer in additional systems modularly. Both have been proven effective, but in my opinion, the most elegant and effective solution is changing how the model operates to produce a better result, one that is more aligned with reality and the needs of the users. I believe that working to improve the model operation before the results are sent from the model is a better, more scalable approach and is preferred, but we will see many attempts at grounding models leveraging both approaches alone and in hybrid approaches where both methodologies are employed.

One of the key factors in grounding a model within the operation of the model is the context window. Let's examine the role of the context window in grounding a model.

Context windows

At the time of this writing, the largest context windows are 2M tokens in size. For a reference point, 2M tokens are about 3,000 pages of printed material. A generalized rule is that a token is approximately four characters, on average, and six characters per word. 2M tokens allow you to input between 6M to 8M characters into the model as context for processing your prompts.

It would be great if the models could scan the entire context window and use all the characters ingested equally, but that is not the case. At this point, it appears that most models use the first 10K to 100K more effectively than those subsequent characters, but I believe this is an artifact of the stage of development we are in. I am confident that model developers will implement better approaches to leveraging all the characters in the context window with equal effectiveness and efficiency.

Context windows have been discussed as expanding to 10M characters in the next one or two development cycles. What does this imply? It implies that there is no limit to the context window. Other than physical access to electronic storage, compression, retrieval speed, and efficiency are all real constraints, but they do not limit the context window. We may see unlimited context windows in the next year or two.

When unlimited and effectively used context windows are delivered, a different question is brought to the forefront of the design of any GenAI environment: Can you effectively ingest the complete and appropriate context for any prompt in real-time into any model? Or do you need to have the information management pipeline and process set up to build a grounding mechanism outside the model? Or do you need both?

We cannot answer these questions in a vacuum. We need the objectives, the key performance indicators, performance requirements, governing policies, and the tolerances for accuracy, relevance, and errors. When we know these factors, the system's required design can be decided upon and documented, and part of that design is how the models will be grounded.

Grounding is an exciting area of development. A number of companies will be founded to solve or attempt to solve the grounding problem over the next three to five years. This will be a fast-developing area that is one to watch and test.

Now that we have addressed the issues of grounding single and ensemble models, let's focus on orchestrating operations and producing accurate results with multiple models in day-to-day operations. When a system includes an ensemble of related models or multiple unrelated models, the operations of those models must be coordinated in some manner. The most common, useful, and valuable approach to the coordination of the operation of models is orchestration.

Orchestration

Given that we will have an ecosystem of models, we will need an orchestration capability to accept the user's inputs/prompts, decompose those prompts in a detailed manner, route the prompt components or elements to the right models that are included in the ensemble of models, accept any rejections of prompts or prompt elements, reroute those rejected parts to new models, accept all the portions of the completions or responses from the models, test those components for accuracy and relevance, and combine all those parts into a coherent response, and send the response to the user or users.

As earlier noted, with the Mixture of Experts (MoE) approach of leveraging multiple models in an environment, the orchestration of this aforementioned process flow has been proven to be highly scalable, effective, and efficient in processing substantial workflows for large amounts of users.

When designing our first orchestration environment, I advocated for a unique multi-level orchestration environment that included multiple technologies to accomplish the orchestration task. The initial design had four distinct levels of orchestration. The design and viewing the problem from multiple perspectives makes it clear that this system would work. Still, it would be hard to maintain and scale based on an approach designed by people rather than being data-driven. We pivoted away from this to a design that is model-based orchestration. We realized that with the dynamism that would be exhibited at the model level, we needed an orchestration layer that would be as scalable, flexible, and dynamic as the model layer.

Our model-based design has been able to learn, grow, and operate effectively across multiple models, applications, and elements of our environment. It took our team a few cycles to understand that a model-based approach works quite well at the intermediate levels of this environment and is not just for processing prompts and producing completions or results.

While orchestration has been proven to work, there will be hundreds of thousands, if not millions, of orchestration implementations. In all those implementations, there will be incredible variation and creativity. Not all of those variants will successful. Just as we saw orchestration designs a few months ago that relied partially on symbolic AI for the orchestration task, we will see future variations on orchestration that will combine GenAI models, GenAI and Symbolic AI models, and other variants. MoE is the primary way forward for orchestration to be implemented reliably today, but we will see many innovations in orchestration.

Now that we know what the general computing architecture will look like, let's start to discuss the construct of agents. Agents will be the primary unit of work and driving force in developing the practical and pragmatic use of GenAI in workflows and processes.

Today, we have people prompting models and ensembles of models, and the end users do not know or care about the difference between the two. The move to agents will be the same experience for end users. They will not know that their prompts are being accepted and processed, and that the results will be returned to them by agents.

In the next section, we will talk mainly about GenAI agents, but we need to be aware that GenAI agents are not the only agents. Some agents are composed of many different technologies and approaches. GenAI agents are merely the newest and possibly the most powerful agents to arrive on the stage.

Agents

GenAI agents bring a completely new way of looking at GenAI applications, environmental requirements, and the involvement of internal systems, external systems, individuals, experts, governance schemes, regulation, other GenAI agents, and more.

I have found that the best way to obtain a comprehensive view of agents that encompasses all the requirements to make agents work in a reliable, scalable, and responsible manner is to think of agents as people.

I know that sounds odd coming from me. I have been consistent in my view that GenAI should not be anthropomorphized. GenAI should not be referred to by pronouns. GenAI should not be thought of as having emotions, thoughts, or sentience. I stand by all those statements and positions. Still, GenAI agents will act exactly like people. Hence, if we think of GenAI agents as requiring all the processes, procedures, information, guardrails, training, oversight, governance, and all the other elements that people need to do their jobs, we will have a better understanding of what we need to develop for GenAI agents to operate responsibly, reliably, transparently, and consistently.

What does the future hold for GenAI agents? A use case or scenario I have been discussing and describing to make it clear and easy to connect with is an application where a GenAI agent could do nearly all of the work autonomously to manage travel planning and travel as it is happening.

Most people think of this as booking airfare and hotel reservations; that is a small part of the idea. Think about a GenAI agent that has access to your e-mail, texts, direct messages, social media (if you want), memos, white papers, books, presentations, and any other content that you created, read, or have not read but are interested in and is from a reputable source on a topic that is of interest to you. Your GenAI agent could read more than you can and can ingest the knowledge and use that information in managing your travel plans before you depart and while you are in the midst of your trip.

Agents are a wide-ranging topic that, I am certain, will be the subject of many books, posts, and articles. We will cover the landscape in this book but not dive deep into the emerging world of agents. There is an online resource, The Turing Post, where they do a very good job covering the entirety of GenAI, AI, agents, and more. One of the posts that I recommend that outlines the language, terminology, and landscape of agents can be found at: https://www.turingpost.com/p/agentsvocabulary.[193]

GenAI as your Travel Agent

Let's take my recent trip to London as an example of where a GenAI travel agent could be exceedingly valuable. I live in Chicago. I fly out of Chicago's O'Hare International Airport (ORD). When I fly to London, I fly into Heathrow (LHR). I have never not flown on American Airlines (AA) on that route. So, it is pretty clear how I prefer to fly to and from London. I stay at a specific hotel in London, always. Booking the airfare and the hotel is a breeze.

I like to be busy. If I am on the road, I prefer to have five to eight meetings daily. When I am on the road, I want to make it worth my while. My GenAI agent has access to all the information sources mentioned above. The GenAI agent should book my meetings between seven am and six pm with the appropriate breakfast, lunch, and dinner breaks. If I am traveling with

[193] Ksenia Se, Turing Post, October, 5, 2024, #2: Your Go-To Vocabulary to Navigate the World of AI Agents and Workflows, https://www.turingpost.com/p/agentsvocabulary, Cited on October 20, 2024.

someone, my GenAI agent should work with their GenAI agent to schedule appropriate touchpoints for us. Perhaps they prefer breakfast meetings, or maybe they prefer connecting over dinner—it doesn't matter. The agents can work that out.

Meetings change all the time. That is a fact of life. My GenAI agent should constantly monitor my schedule. When something changes, such as a meeting cancellation, date, or time change, my agent should move the entire schedule around to maintain my desired level of engagement and activity.

My agent should understand the entirety of the people that I am meeting with and those I would like to meet with, which is reasonably feasible given that I am in London. If an opening presents itself, my agent, alone or in conjunction with agents from others, should keep my schedule on track by finding the next person I would like to connect with and setting up that meeting.

My GenAI agent should know which plays and social events I want to attend, at which venues, and at what price I want to pay. If I want to see M Butterfly at the Old Vic for £60/seat, when a seat opens up, my GenAI agent should book the ticket and pre-buy me the drink that I want at intermission, and, of course, book a car to take me to and from the venue.

All of this should be happening in the background. I should not have to deal with any of it. I can tell you that I spend too much of my time dealing with travel details.

My GenAI agent should monitor my return flight or any intermediary flights that I have booked, and should any changes or cancellations occur, my agent should take care of the changes and let me know of the impact on my plans.

I should never have to wake up and find out that my flight was canceled an hour after I went to bed, and nothing was done until I was at breakfast and learned about the cancellation from looking at a travel app while I was sitting down to start my day. Rather than having a stress-induced moment while I wait for my breakfast, a smile should break across my face as I realized that my flight was canceled at 11:30 pm and my GenAI agent had rebooked me for a new flight in the right class of service, in my preferred seat at 11:31 pm. Now, that is service, convenience, and the ability to relax while traveling.

The example of travel is just one process. Think of all the other processes that GenAI agents can manage for you.

Examples of agents

Agents have been with us for decades. Table 2 from the team at the Turing Post are a wonderful illustration of how and where we see agents in our daily lives.[194]

Agent Type	Type	Features	Real-Life Example
Smart Home Assistants (e.g., Alexa, Google Home)	Digital Agent, AI Assistant	Utilizes natural language processing (NLP) and voice recognition models (e.g., BERT, GPT) to process user commands and generate appropriate responses. Integrated with reinforcement learning (RL) algorithms to optimize interactions over time based on user feedback.	Setting a daily alarm and adjusting room temperatures without manual input.

[194] Ksenia Se, Turing Post, October 19, 2024, #3: Illustrating Agentic Vocabulary: Real and Potential Examples, https://www.turingpost.com/p/aia3, Cited on October 20, 2024.

Agent Type	Type	Features	Real-Life Example
Navigation Apps (e.g., Google Maps, Waze)	Task-Oriented Agent, Intelligent Agent	Incorporates real-time data analysis and pathfinding algorithms, using graph-based ML models to compute the shortest or fastest routes. Employs predictive models to anticipate traffic conditions based on historical data and external factors.	Guiding users through traffic congestion, suggesting alternate routes, and providing ETA quite accurately.
Automated Email Spam Filters	Simple Agent, Intelligent Agent	Applies supervised learning techniques using labeled datasets to classify and filter emails. NLP models are trained to identify spam characteristics and continually improve filtering accuracy through RL from user interactions.	We don't even consider it to be an agent, though it is and a very effective one, automatically moving promotional or spam emails out of the primary inbox, ensuring important messages are more visible.
Robotic Vacuum Cleaners (e.g., Roomba)	Embodied Agent, Autonomous Agent	Employs computer vision models and RL to navigate spaces and identify obstacles. Integrates path optimization algorithms and ML for adaptive behavior based on environmental changes.	Cleaning the floor at set intervals, learning room layouts to optimize cleaning paths.
Fitness Trackers (e.g., Oura, Apple Watch)	Smart Agent, AI Assistant	Uses predictive analytics and time-series forecasting models to monitor activity patterns and provide tailored health recommendations. Collects and processes sensor data using ML models to analyze physical metrics and offer personalized feedback.	Reminding users to stand, drink water, or complete daily step goals based on their activity levels. Analyzing your sleep patterns and heartbeat.

Agent Type	Type	Features	Real-Life Example
Recommendation Systems (e.g., Netflix, Amazon)	Intelligent Agent, Task-Oriented Agent	Deploys collaborative filtering algorithms and content-based recommendation systems. Leverages deep learning models to analyze user behavior and preferences, generating personalized suggestions based on embeddings and user similarity metrics.	Recommending a movie on Netflix based on past viewing history or suggesting products on Amazon that match recent searches.
Drones	Embodied Agent, Autonomous Agent	Utilizes computer vision, sensor fusion, and RL for autonomous navigation and task execution. Drones rely on object detection models (e.g., YOLO) to identify and interact with their environment dynamically.	Delivery drones autonomously navigating to drop off packages or agricultural drones surveying fields and spraying crops efficiently. Also, actively used un warfare.
Self-Driving Cars (e.g., Tesla Autopilot)	Autonomous Agent, Intelligent Agent	Combines sensor fusion, deep learning (e.g., CNNs for image recognition), and RL models for real-time decision-making and autonomous navigation.	Navigating city streets without human input, identifying traffic signals, and reacting to sudden changes like a pedestrian crossing.
Chatbots (e.g., Customer Support Bots)	Digital Agent, AI Assistant	Uses NLP models to understand user input and generate context-aware responses. Incorporates sentiment analysis and dialogue management systems to adapt responses and manage conversations effectively. Most of the time they still utterly frustrating to deal with.	Assisting customers with troubleshooting or managing bookings through a company's website without human intervention.

Agent Type	Type	Features	Real-Life Example
Smart Toilets (e.g. Toto Neorest)	Embodied Agent, Autonomous Agent. Basically a true AI persona if you think about it	Equipped with sensor data analysis and IoT-integrated learning models. Uses pattern recognition to adjust water pressure, temperature, and other settings based on usage history and user preferences. The toilet's feedback loop helps personalize settings for comfort and efficiency over time.	Predictively adjusts settings like seat warmth based on historical usage data, integrating multiple sensory inputs for optimized comfort and energy efficiency. Basically, emotional support :)

Table 2: Agents in Real Life—1 From the Turing Post.

As you can see, agents have been with us for quite a while and are involved in many of our daily activities, and the activity level will ramp up significantly from here forward. I look forward to interacting with intelligent agents with all the information available to them to make choices, implement changes, and keep me and my plans moving forward.

Much of the frustration we feel with automated customer service environments is because those systems are rigid, do not have access to current information, are not able to implement the changes we need at the moment, and are not dynamic in their actions, workflow, or ability to solve problems in real time. Agents are the solution to this widespread source of frustration.

Agent evolution

The growth and evolution of GenAI agents is becoming clearer each day. The expected development and evolution of GenAI agents is outlined below in Table 3.

Type of Agent	Capability	Expected Availability Date
Simple	Single Task or Workflow	2024
Intelligent	Decision and autonomy capabilities	Mid 2025
Self-Replicating	Ability to scale autonomously	End of 2025
Polymorphic	Ability to build new agents autonomously	Mid 2026

Table 3: Expected and proposed GenAI Agent Evolution, John K. Thompson.

Today, we have simple/single agents. These agents ingest or accept prompts, execute a process or processes, and return a result. This works with low complexity processes, a small number of systems to interrogate, and outputs or results that are typically a singular output like a presentation or a document. Next, we will look at the arrival of Intelligent Agents. We are developing early-stage prototypes today. These agents will work on complex prompts that may require inference across multiple domains (e.g., models). These agents will interact with internal and external people, systems, repositories, and more.

Most people think about and understand an agent collaborating with another agent, but it seems to surprise people that agents will consult with a variety of human experts. Agents will autonomously interact with a wide range of people requesting information from those experts that is required for the agent to continue executing the current process.

The experts are not the people that originally prompted the system. The agents will ask experts in a wide range of fields with the information and knowledge required for the agent to continue to process the prompt and develop the intermediate or final results.

Along with the arrival and development of intelligent agents, we will see the arrival of multiple agent frameworks at the level of maturity where early adopters will be building and testing intelligent/multi agent implementations across multiple frameworks.

Elements of the agent ecosystem

Agents are a game-changing concept and development. GenAI has been impressive and impactful, but GenAI agents take the impact to an entirely new level. We assume that everything we have in GenAI is a part of the environment and infrastructure, so in this section of the book, we will focus on what parts of the environment we need to build specifically for GenAI agents to exist and operate. What must we develop for GenAI agents to be a productive, trusted, private, and secure part of our world?

Development framework

We need an environment for our development teams to build GenAI agents. In 2024, GenAI agent frameworks were starting to formalize. We have a number of early-stage efforts and a few promising frameworks—"AutoGen, CrewAI, LangGraph, LlamaIndex, and AutoGPT".[195] In my current role, our Architecture and Development teams have worked with Task Weaver, Durable Functions, LangGraph, Crew, LlamaIndex, and AutoGen; not all of these tools and frameworks will be viable or successful.

We see this market dynamic in the majority of early-stage technologies. There is a large opportunity in the market for new tools, and a number of

---

[195] Ken Huang, July 27, 2024, Medium, GenAI Agents: Architectures, Frameworks, and Future Directions, https://kenhuangus.medium.com/genai-agents-architectures-frameworks-and-future-directions-bcf8e5b55cb3, Cited on October 15, 2024.

companies will be founded. Existing technology companies will spring into action to develop, deliver, and offer tools to serve this new and foundational need. Typically, we see a market leader emerging and possibly one or two players jockey for the second and third positions in the market. This interplay will transpire in the market for agents in the next 12 to 18 months.

The current leader (late 2024/early 2025) is AutoGen. With Microsoft lining up behind the open-source project, it appears that AutoGen will be the enterprise tool of choice, but as with all things in the early technology market, things can and might well change. Also, I want to be clear that not all companies will select, implement, and use one agent framework. There will be multiple frameworks supported by multiple companies and partner ecosystems that grow to support and bolster these frameworks. With multiple frameworks, there will be the need for GenAI agents to collaborate and communicate with GenAI agents which will be built into other frameworks. So, either the frameworks will be designed to have multi-agent interoperability or some type of technology will be developed to facilitate inter-agent operation. The preferred approach will be for the capability for interoperation built into each agent framework.

Once we have a set of enterprise-class tools to develop GenAI agents, then people will want to manage, understand, and control (e.g., govern) those newly developed agents. They will want to ensure control over the interactions of those agents between agents, environments, companies, continents, and more. Let's discuss how agents will be controlled and governed.

Governance framework

The overall governance of agents is wide-ranging. Again, think about all the activities we attempt to govern concerning people's behavior. Most of those activities will come into play when thinking about how we want GenAI agents to act and behave.

There is no one set of governance frameworks to be considered as there is in the area of development frameworks. Each organization, a myriad of consulting firms, technology companies, and firms seeking to serve defined geographic and vertical markets will offer custom and bespoke governance frameworks. This is an area where consultants will be primary players for the next five to seven years.

I am open to being surprised by a company or any type that builds and offers a standardized governance framework that is adopted by large segments of companies on a global scale. Typically, these types of frameworks are unique to each firm. Governance is driven by the unique view of risk and control that each firm sees, understands, and seeks to manage.

With that said, some resources help people begin to understand how their governance regime needs to expand with the advent of GenAI. A collection of university professors has developed a governance framework available to the public and free to use.

Disclaimer: I did help edit the nearly final specification, but I have nothing to do with endorsing or distributing the final specification.

"GenAI pushes the boundaries of current governance structures by creating entirely new information that did not exist before," said framework author David Wood, a BYU professor in the Marriott School of Business. "As such, it introduces a multitude of new possibilities and risks that organizations of all sizes must confront. We designed the framework to help any size organization think through the most important risks that they will face from GenAI."[196] The GenAI Governance Framework breaks down governance into five essential domains.

- Strategic Alignment and Control Environment
- Data and Compliance Management
- Operational and Technology Management
- Human, Ethical, and Social Considerations
- Transparency, Accountability, and Continuous Improvement[197]

This is a solid framework for any firm to start with when considering how to manage, govern, and report on their GenAI applications.

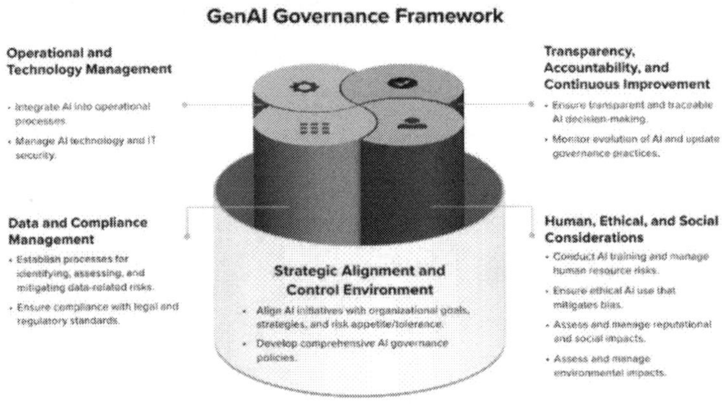

Figure 17: GenAI Governance Framework.[198]

---

[196] Dr. David Wood, Faculty Research, BYU Professor, Partners Create First-Ever Risk Guide to Help Organizations Safely Adopt AI, https://marriott.byu.edu/stories/faculty-research/byu-professor-partners-create-first-ever-risk-guide-to-help-organizations-safely-adopt-ai, Cited on October 15, 2024.

[197] Scott A. Emett, PhD, Arizona State University, Marc Eulerich, PhD, CIA, University of Duisburg-Essenn, Jason Pikoos, Managing Partner, Connor Group, David A. Wood, PhD., Brigham Young University, A generative AI governance framework that you can rely on, https://www.genai.global/home, Cited on October 15, 2024.

[198] Ibid., Cited on October 15, 2024.

The following areas are representative and indicative lists of governance elements that GenAI agents will require access to. This is not meant to be an exhaustive list—it simply indicates the breadth and depth of interaction and impact GenAI agents will have.

Policy Management

- Spending limits
- Recursion limits
- Operating hours
- Process objectives
- Automated decision making
- Ability to bind the organization to contractual commitments
- Adherence to budgets
- Levels of authorization for spending and approving actions
- Defined access to internal and external agents
- Usage and interaction rules in relation to internal and external agents
- Defined access to internal and external systems
- Usage and interaction rules in relation to internal and external systems
- Access to defined employees, contractors, partners, and external experts
- Compliance with internal and external controls/policies
- Decision points to seek approval from the end user or other people in the company
- Access to and an understanding of all relevant government rules and regulations at all relevant levels of jurisdiction

Infrastructure Management

- Processing budget
- Service Level Agreements/Limitations

- Authorization to use defined computing resources internal and external to the organization

Resource Catalogs

- Internal System Access and Rules
    - Expense Policies
    - Travel Policies
    - Approved/Preferred Partners
    - Prohibited Entities—Countries, Companies, People
    - Prohibited Actions
    - Training materials

Access to Internal and External Experts

- Area of expertise
- Type of queries
- Cost to pay for each question

Objectives/Goals

- Access to the defined objectives of a process, workflow, step, and project
- Access to the defined goals of the relevant workflows

Role definition

As noted above, this is not an exhaustive list. My point in including this list is to illustrate the breadth and depth of knowledge that agents will need to have access to operate on an intelligence and autonomous basis. Agents are a powerful construct. We have been working with agents for multiple decades now. Still, we are at a point of development where agents can be more powerful, useful, and assist in ways that were not possible before GenAI agents came into existence.

Our discussion and treatment of agents could be much more extensive, but this book is not solely focused on agents and the future of agents. The future of agents is multifaceted and will impact nearly all businesses, governments, academic institutions, and more. GenAI agents are a game-changing development. The amount of information being written and offered about agents could fill your days. Should you want to find more information about GenAI agents and agents in general, you are spoiled by choice.

We come to the end of our discussion of the future of GenAI. As noted when we started this portion of the discussion, the future of GenAI is still being written. GenAI is an exciting and contentious part of the overall AI story and landscape. I am excited to be learning more and more about GenAI each day.

Summary

GenAI arrived on the scene in 2022. It seems much longer, doesn't it? It seems like we have been talking about GenAI for decades. The history of GenAI is brief but marked by innovation, change, and promise, and there is fear and concern as well. Both sides of the market, applications, technology development, and societal discussion will keep us busy for a few years.

GenAI sprung from the development, refinement, and extension of neural networks. It was a wonderful accident that the teams at Meta, Google, and OpenAI experimented with training a Large Language Model with the breadth and depth of the Internet. This provided a new GenAI landscape that we see today. To be clear, LLMs exhibit the patterns of operation we see today due to being trained on data at a global scale. The scale of the data used to train LLMs drives the ability to operate on the range of use cases we experience today. LLMs can only respond with information on which they have been trained. LLMs do not think. LLMs do not create new knowledge. LLMs are not sentient. LLMs do not have emotions or care.

A number of people have discussed how LLMs exhibit what has been referred to as "emergent behaviors." Let's put some context around the term emergent behaviors. "...emergent abilities: the possibility that beyond a certain threshold of complexity, large language models (LLMs) are doing unpredictable things. If we can harness that capacity, AI might be able to solve some of humanity's biggest problems, the story goes."[199] I want to be clear, emergent behaviors do not exist. This is a fallacy and has been soundly debunked.

GenAI is an incredibly capable tool. One thing that GenAI is not is a gateway to Artificial General Intelligence (AGI). In Section V, the final section of this book, we will delve deeply into how GenAI relates to AGI.

The value to be delivered and derived from GenAI is just beginning to be designed. The ability to build GenAI agents will be a game-changing development for the world of work, and we are just now starting to see the outlines of what the future can look like. It is an exciting time to be working in the field of GenAI and AI in general.

With any discovery or invention that promises and delivers the wide-ranging application and impact that GenAI does, there will be positives and negatives associated with the technology. The negatives can and will be addressed and overcome. I am not a techno-optimist where I believe that all ills created by technology can be solved by technology, but I do think a

---

[199] Matt White, AI Researcher | Educator | Strategist | Author | Consultant | Founder | Generative AI Commons, UC Berkeley, Open Metaverse Foundation, Linux Foundation, Amdocs, January 7, 2023, A Brief History of Generative AI, Medium, https://matthewdwhite.medium.com/a-brief-history-of-generative-ai-cb1837e67106, Cited January 4, 2024.

combination of technology, ingenuity, creativity, and the desire to make AI serve humans can overcome any of the shortcomings of the technology or nefarious intent from bad actors.

GenAI presents a fantastic opportunity to address some of the problems of technology, society, and work. The solution is only partial but can deliver significant value and improved living conditions for millions. The future is for us to design.

Let's move on to the next section and examine Causal AI.

Chapter 8

A Brief History and Explanation of Causal AI

As with all new technologies, I was skeptical when I came upon Causal AI. After reviewing new and emerging technologies for over 30 years, it is my nature to go into evaluating new technologies as being overhyped and underpowered. I was surprised when I found that, in my opinion, Causal AI was not being oversold on a widespread basis. There are a few people in the field that raised my level of concern, given their breathless pronouncements. Still, those people have been consistent in their level of enthusiastic sponsorship of multiple new technologies over the span of my career. Therefore, their remarks and opinions can be discounted accordingly.

In actuality, the proponents of Causal AI, for the most part, are relatively understated in what they say that Causal AI can do. In part, this is due to the current state of evolution of Causal AI. Over the past five to seven years, Causal AI has emerged from primarily a research-driven technology supported by academics and early-stage technologists in Research and Development (R&D) organizations of the largest technology companies. Academics and researchers are typically less prone to hype and hyperbole when compared to software and technology executives.

Only in the last three to five years, have start-ups taken interest in building commercial offerings on top off or alongside the open-source projects from academics and researchers. From here forward, we will need to be more skeptical of claims made about the capabilities of Causal AI, but up to now, the dialog has been mostly fact-based.

Causal AI is an exciting field, and it is beginning to bring a new perspective and set of capabilities to the field of AI. Let's delve into this novel technology and how it enables us to examine and understand the factors that cause subsequent actions to come into our world.

From Aristotle to Pearl

Causality has a long history punctuated by periods of intense scrutiny, development, and impressive innovative progress, followed by eras of rejection and retrenchment, and then a return to times of rebirth, renewed focus, and further refinement and growth. During these intermittent epochs of development and retrenchment, scholars, philosophers, practitioners, and observers all contributed to the canon of causality.

Fortuitous for us, we are in a period of revitalization and growth of the science and practice of causality. When a field is growing and in a period of ascendancy, it is much easier to draw people into the promise of the offerings. In this book, we will not examine the complete evolutionary line of development from Aristotle[200] to Judea Pearl.[201] Still, it is helpful for

[200] Stanford Encyclopedia of Philosophy, Aristotle, First published Thu Sep 25, 2008; substantive revision Tue Aug 25, 2020, https://plato.stanford.edu/entries/aristotle/, Cited December 24, 2024.

[201] Judea Pearl, https://bayes.cs.ucla.edu/jp_home.html, Cited on December 24, 2024.

people who are relatively new to studying and examining causality to realize and recognize the significant and substantial history of the field.

Causality, as a field, is beginning to emerge from academia as a practical tool for commercial entities and data science teams to apply to commercial challenges and solve real-world problems. When talking with data scientists, there is real excitement in learning about, understanding and beginning to experiment with causal techniques and approaches. The excitement is most notable with those with some exposure or background to Bayesian methods and approaches. Many of the fundamental concepts of Bayesian networks and analytics are at the heart of Causal AI. In this book, we will not be digressing into a detailed examination of Bayesian networks and mathematics, but numerous books cover those topics very well.

Let's begin our investigation and discussion of this interesting pillar of AI.

Accessibility of causality

There have been, and are, numerous approaches to defining and naming the elements of causal models, discussing modeling, and communicating causal concepts.

As one example of describing variables in a specialized manner, Judea Pearl discusses variables and models in this way, "a causal model as an ordered triple (U,V,E), where U is a set of exogenous variables whose values are determined by factors outside the model; V is a set of endogenous variables whose values are determined by factors within the model; and E is a set of structural equations that express the value of each endogenous variable as a function of the values of the other variables in U and V."[202]

Dr. Pearl is an accomplished scholar who has deservedly gained worldwide acclaim for his work in advancing the field of Causal AI, but that previous paragraph is dense and specialized language. The terms are accurate and evocative, and the overall statement is true and powerful. Still, it is difficult to grasp the depth and meaning of the overall concept in the first or even subsequent readings. This language is appropriate and perfect for scholarly research and academic discussions, but it leaves laymen, technical professionals, business executives, data scientists, and others feeling less than engaged. Dr. Pearl's impressive accomplishments in evolving and adding to the canon of causality are the foundation we will build upon, but we will do so in a language that the majority of business executives, managers, data science leaders, data scientists, technology professionals, and interested non-technical parties can grasp and understand the foundational and advanced causal concepts without reading the material multiple times. One of the primary goals of this section of this book is to introduce causality and to make the subject accessible to a majority of interested people.

Simplicity on the other side of complexity

One of the impressive aspects of causal models is that the models and elements of causal models can be used to describe any real-world environment or operation, any set of variables, relationships, processes, and

[202] Pearl, Judea (2010-02-26). "An Introduction to Causal Inference". The International Journal of Biostatistics. 6 (2): Article 7. doi:10.2202/1557-4679.1203. ISSN 1557-4679. PMC 2836213. PMID 20305706. Cited on December 21, 2022.

sub-environments that are of interest to us, and our colleagues can be included in a causal model. Where Foundational AI enables us to build a mathematical model of a process or situation, Causal AI enables us to build an operational model of any process or situation. Foundational AI gives us a measurement at any and all points in time. Causal AI provides a view of change over time. Any environment, process, or interaction of variables can be described and modeled in a causal-based approach.

A few examples of where Causal AI can be applied:

- You want to understand the dynamics of airflow into a jet engine, and how that relates to fuel consumption and thrust produced at a spectrum across all altitudes, causal modeling can capture and describe the relevant dynamics.

- Perhaps you are interested in understanding consumer behavior and the variations thereof considering the market factors, internal family dynamics, possible marketing programs that you might implement in various markets, and other relevant competitive factors, causal modeling can be of assistance here as well.

- Maybe your area of interest is the environmental factors, family medical histories, personal health choices, lifetime diet, and other factors related to the incidence of a specific type of obesity. Causal modeling is an appropriate selection of a tool or methodology to attempt to understand the causal factors that directly and indirectly lead to weight gain, loss, and body mass management.

Why is this impressive?

First, it is impressive due to the flexibility and inclusion that is encompassed in causal language and notation. Most other modeling environments or languages force users and practitioners to assume away much of the complexity of the real world, prune the number of variables, and simplify the relationships between the variables to make the models understandable and simple enough for the models to work reliably. The current state of causal modeling enables us to include as much complexity as needed to make the model representative of the actual events and influences that we see in the actual world.

Secondly, one of the subtle and powerful facilities of causal modeling is that we can include variables that we cannot empirically observe but know exist. We do not need to have observational data to include these variables and yet we can include them and estimate their impact on the relationships and observed variables in the model. We will discuss how this works in detail later in this chapter.

Thirdly, causal modeling enables us to integrate historical data sets that were collected for similar reasons but not exactly the same purposes for and in our current analyses. Causal modeling enables us to treat and condition data to include additional observations and relevant variables while setting aside other elements of the historical data that are irrelevant to our work. Causal modeling enables us to collect, condition, and include significant amounts of historical data to increase the accuracy and improve the representative nature of our models.

While writing this book, I encountered examples of causality being applied to models of the determination of the birth weight of guinea pigs, the effectiveness of marketing campaigns, the effect of price on revenue, the quality and characteristics of inputs of a manufacturing process to the quality and reliability of the final outputs, the effects of making ethical and moral decisions on the wellbeing of a population, and many more situations, environments, and processes.

One of the underlying goals of AI, causal or correlative, is to build models of sufficient inclusion, complexity, flexibility, responsiveness, agility, scalability, and accuracy so that we can rely on them to predict and prescribe future events in a timely way. One of our overarching goals is to leverage those models and the results of those models to improve outcomes that are of interest to us.

Whether overtly aware of the fact or not, analytics professionals strive to build analytical models that are nearly identical to the processes and results we see in the real world. Our efforts are taking us in the direction of building models that ingest multiple sources of data in real time, simultaneously and seamlessly invoke numerous models from across all three pillars of AI that produce highly accurate and reliable results that are indistinguishable from the actions and activity that the real world would produce, but to do so in a future-looking predictive manner.

The analytics profession is on the cusp of building computing and data-based analytical models that augment human capacities in real time. We are seeing the first signs that our integrated AI tools, computing systems, and networking connectivity are coming together in a way that is capable of delivering the composite AI capability to realize this goal.

To be clear, the goal is the delivery of machine and augmented intelligence that serves people in a positive manner in their everyday lives, where that delivery is invisible for the most part.

Let's move from the conceptual to the practical. Let's discuss how causal models are constructed to achieve the goals we have been outlining and exploring.

There are two general approaches to building causal models: outcomes-based and Structural Causal Modeling (SCM).

Outcomes-based causal modeling

The potential outcomes framework, proposed by statisticians Paul Rosenbaum[203] and Donald Rubin[204] in 1983, compares the outcome of an individual who has been exposed to the cause of interest with an inferred "potential outcome" of the same individual had he/she not been exposed. The challenge is, of course, that no data exists on non-exposure outcomes for a person who was exposed to the campaign. Each individual exposed to the stimulus is compared to an individual in the data set who was not exposed to the stimulus but who is identical in other significant respects (i.e., age, race, and education). In other words, an artificial control group is reverse-engineered to mimic a randomized controlled trial or A/B test. The limitation is that while the model and system can solve the problem of

203 Paul R. Rosenbaum, Robert G. Putzel Professor Emeritus of Statistics and Data Science, Wharton School, University of Pennsylvania, DEPARTMENT OF STATISTICS AND DATA SCIENCE, Paul R. Rosenbaum—Department of Statistics and Data Science (upenn.edu), cited December 29, 2022.

204 Donald B. Rubin, Emeritus Professor of Statistics, Department of Statistics, Harvard University, https://statistics.fas.harvard.edu/people/donald-b-rubin, cited December 29, 2022.

having no control group, the potential outcomes framework can test the effect of only one prespecified intervention at a time.[205]

In 1983, when this technique was developed, tested, and implemented, the amount of computing power available to any application made the limitation of evaluating one intervention sequentially rather limiting. Today, however, with computing power, networking, and general computing infrastructure available on a widespread basis, applications can be run in a way that multiple interventions can be evaluated in a defined time window. This approach has become more valuable and useful than it had been when launched. Still, the reality is that the next technique we will discuss is the dominant form of modeling used by practitioners of Causal AI.

Let's examine Structural Causal Modeling next.

Structural causal modeling

Structural Causal Modeling[206] is the most commonly used methodology, notation, and language for designing, discussing, and building causal models. We will use SCM to discuss and describe the more nuanced and advanced elements of Causal AI systems. You may encounter the terms

---

[205] Sema K. Sgaier, Vincent Huang & Grace Charles, Summer 2020, The Case for Causal AI, The Stanford Social Innovation Review, https://ssir.org/articles/entry/the_case_for_causal_ai#, cited December 29, 2022.

[206] Stephan Bongers, Patrick Forre, Jonas Peters, Joris M. Mooi, Foundations of Structural Causal Models with Cycles and Latent Variables, November 22, 2021, https://arxiv.org/pdf/1611.06221, Cited December 24, 2024.

Structural Equation Model[207] (SEM) or Causal Bayesian Model[208] (CBM) in your research and discussions. These are older terms used by some for a similar type of modeling. We can consider SCM, CBM, and SEM synonymous for our discussion. We will be using the term SCM throughout this book.

SCM is a well-designed analytical language that provides the descriptive tools necessary to construct and validate causal models. In the next section of this chapter, we will describe the simple yet expressive notation of data, variables, and relationships between variables. The SCM language and notation will help us codify, simplify, and understand our ability to describe and discuss causal relationships and models and our intended use of those models.[209]

The SCM approach makes it possible to simulate many possible interventions simultaneously. Also, SCM allows for the incorporation of expert knowledge to counter the possible limitations of a purely data-driven approach. Experts can, for instance, help determine which variables should go into the model, place conditions on the model to improve its accuracy, and help understand counterintuitive results.

---

207 Bunmi Akinremi, Datacamp.com, October 2, 2024, Structural Equation Modeling: What It Is and When to Use It, https://www.datacamp.com/tutorial/structural-equation-modeling, Cited December 24, 2024.

208 Donald B. Rubin. "Bayesian Inference for Causal Effects: The Role of Randomization." Ann. Statist. 6 (1) 34 - 58, January, 1978. https://doi.org/10.1214/aos/1176344064, Cited December 24, 2024.

209 KEN ACQUAH, https://www.causalflows.com/structural-causal-models/, May 27, 2020, cited on December 17, 2022.

"The earliest known version of SCMs, was introduced by geneticist Sewell Wright[210] around 1918, originally for inferring the relative importance of factors which determine the birth weight of guinea pigs."[211]

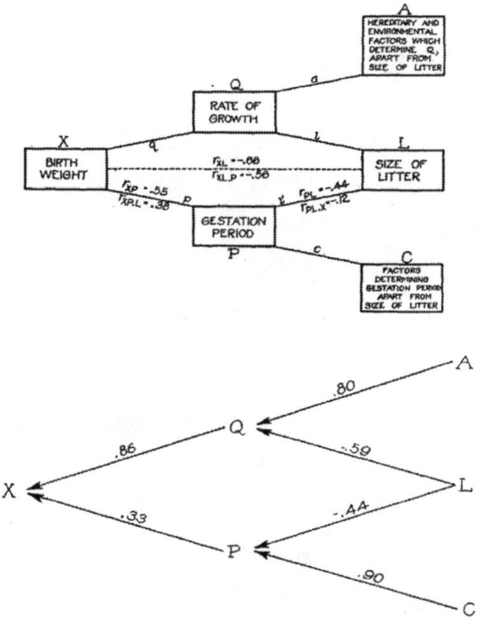

Figure 18: Drawings from Wright's 1921 paper, Correlation and Causation.

The bottom image presents an ancestor to causal graphs, a representation of structural causal models describing the relationships between various genetic factors and a guinea pig's birth weight. Wright's path tracing rules defined a set of rules for using a set of associative relationships to generate a causal graph.[212]

---

[210] Wright, S. (1921). "Correlation and causation". Journal of Agricultural Research. 20: 557–585, cited on December 17, 2022.

[211] Ibid.

[212] Ibid.

Currently, the state of the art in data science is that correlation-based AI can be leveraged to develop applications and systems that illustrate to data science leaders and data scientists how we can *begin* to realize our goal of building analytical applications that ingest and integrate multiple sources of data, invoke numerous related models, and produce accurate, reliable, and timely results in specialized and limited cases.

Causal-based systems and tools like SCM will enable data science professionals to develop these types of broad-based multifaceted analytical systems and applications more quickly, with greater flexibility and increased accuracy, with a broader population of developers for a wider range of applications across multiple industries and companies.

SCM enables the notation and inclusion of as much complexity as we, and our users, can understand and include in our models. SCM is a powerful tool in our quest to build realistic models of the world that we seek to examine, understand, model, and analyze. Let's delve into understanding the elements, processes, and rules of SCM in more detail.

Elements of SCM

On the face of it, SCM looks too simple to deliver the flexible and scalable explanatory power that has been described, but that is one of the ultimate attractions of the approach and methodology. Let's walk through an overview of the primary elements of SCM that we will be leveraging when we and our teams build causal models.

- **Nodes**—Nodes are the processing units in our models.
    - Nodes are the factors that we want to consider and examine in our model.

  - Nodes have variables assigned to them.
  - The most common ways of describing the relationships between nodes are as parents, children, ancestors, descendants, and neighbors.
  - Parents and children refer to direct relationships; descendants and ancestors can be anywhere along the path to or from a node, respectively.[213]

- **Variables**—At our disposal, we have observed input variables, outcome variables, and unobserved variables.

  - *Observed Variables*—Input and outcome variables are observed variables.
    - In the SCM process, observed variables are those we can readily see and measure in the real world.
    - In SCM models and notation, observed variables are represented by a single letter.
    - When you are building your models, you can select and assign letters in any manner or order that makes sense to you.
    - In Figure 18, above, the observed variables are assigned the capital letters—X, Q, P, A, L, and C.
  - Unobserved Variables—
    - Unobserved variables play a role in our models, but we do not have direct measurement or observational data for their impact and effect on our current model.

---

213 KEN ACQUAH, https://www.causalflows.com/structural-causal-models/, May 27, 2020, cited on December 17, 2022.

- We can estimate the probability and impact of unobserved variables on our models.
- We can leverage measurements from other data sources where similar variables were or are observed, and the data from these observations can provide an estimate or a proxy to guide our assignment of a range of values to measure or quantify the unobserved variables in our current model.
- Unobserved variables are represented by the letter "u" accompanied by a single-letter subscript.
- Suppose that an unobserved variable in Figure 18 might be the level of stress experienced by the guinea pig mother during the gestation period. We could include the stress level in the model and denote the variable as an unobserved variable with a lowercase "u" and we would add a subscript "s". The notation would be "u_s" for the unobserved stress level.

- **Paths/Relationships**—Relationships between nodes and their assigned variables are illustrated with arrows. The main characteristics of the arrows, paths, edges, or directed edges in the resulting graphs are:

  - Relationships have two connections and are denoted with an arrowhead(s) that illustrates the direction of the connection
  - A solid line denotes relationships between observed variables
  - A dashed line denotes relationships between unobserved variables and observed variables

- Bidirectional relationships do exist, and the lines will have arrowheads at each end
- Paths can be—chains, forks, and/or inverted forks.

We will examine paths and relationships in detail in a subsequent section of this chapter.

- **Weights**—Each node in a Directed Acyclic Graph (DAG) is associated with a conditional probability distribution assigned to the node(s) that precede the subsequent node in the DAG. Another way to say it is that the subsequent nodes inherit the probabilities of the variables assigned to the nodes with paths pointing toward them.
    - A Bayesian network can be represented as a DAG illustrating the joint probability of a problem.[214]
    - When multiple nodes are directed to a subsequent node in the DAG, the subsequent node's weighted probability matrix is derived by producing a concatenated matrix of the incoming probabilities,
    - In a DAG, it doesn't matter what form the relationship between two variables takes, only its direction.
    - The rules underpinning DAGs are consistent whether the relationship is a simple, linear one or a more complicated function.[215]

---

[214] Malcolm Barrett, An Introduction to Directed Acyclic Graphs, October, 10, 2021, An Introduction to Directed Acyclic Graphs (microsoft.com), cited on December 25, 2022.

[215] Daniel Smith, Greg P. Timms, Paulo A. De Souza, The Commonwealth Scientific and Industrial Research Organisation, Claire D'Este, A Bayesian Framework for the Automated Online Assessment of Sensor Data Quality, December 2012, Sensors

- **Models**—The resulting models or graphs produced by the SCM process are DAGs.
  - DAGs illustrate:
    - Vertices or nodes
    - Variables
    - Relationships
    - Direction of flow of the process
    - Weight of effect
  - DAGs are the embodiment of causal processes in the actual world.
    - DAGs flow in one direction and do not include processing loops or recursion of any type.
    - In life, we do not see time bending back on itself and we do not experience results affecting previous environments or prior actions. Therefore, those situations and actions are not allowed or included in DAGs.
  - For clarity, there are other types of graphs that we are not leveraging or discussing in this process.
    - There are Acyclic Graphs (AGs) with processing loops included, but since we are only interested in simple cause-and-effect relationships, we will not use AGs.
    - There are Undirected Graphs (UGs) where the relationships or edges have no direction denoted. Given that we are examining cause-and-effect relationships and that an implied forward sequence, time, and direction are

---

12(7):9476-501, DOI:10.3390/s120709476, Source PubMed, License CC BY 3.0, (PDF) A Bayesian Framework for the Automated Online Assessment of Sensor Data Quality (researchgate.net), cited on December 24, 2022.

foundational elements of our dialog, we will not examine UGs.

SCM and the resulting DAGs are easy to comprehend. They are simple, follow the rules of time and direction, and reflect our world. At the same time, SCM and DAGs are some of our most powerful and sophisticated modeling tools. Let's delve more deeply into the component elements of SCM and DAGs to understand the nuances we can include in our models and causal AI processes.

Nodes

Using an analogy, the nodes are the nouns in our models. We name nodes with descriptive names to illustrate the subject of the node. In our discussion to date, we have seen node names like Price, Behavior, Birth Weight, Gestation Period, Outcome, Size of Litter, and others. Given that nodes and variables are inextricably linked, nodes also fall into the categories of observed nodes: input nodes, outcome nodes, and unobserved nodes. Nodes can be anything we want to include in our model that is relevant to the effect we seek to examine.

Variables

To continue our analogy, variables are the verbs in our models. Many of us think of variables in a rather linear manner or in such a way that those variables represent simple binary choices (e.g., something happened, or it didn't). The values of a variable in SCM can represent the occurrence or non-occurrence of an event, a range of incompatible events, a property of an individual, or of a population of individuals, or a quantitative value.[216]

So far, we have discussed an overview of relevant variables falling into the categories of observed variables: input variables, outcome variables, and unobserved variables.

Let's now discuss the more subtle variations and specific characterizations of variables employed in SCM.

Counterfactual variables

The term counterfactual is defined as "contrary to fact"[217] and, "relating to or expressing what has not happened or is not the case."[218]

An example of a counterfactual conditional statement is, "If kangaroos had no tails, they would topple over."[219]

Counterfactuals are a way alternate options are considered and examined in SCM. Counterfactuals are the alternate scenarios that are ingested into our causal models.

---

[216] Malcolm Barrett, An Introduction to Directed Acyclic Graphs, October, 10, 2021, An Introduction to Directed Acyclic Graphs (microsoft.com), cited on December 24, 2022.

[217] Stanford Encyclopedia of Philosophy, https://plato.stanford.edu/entries/causal-models/#VariLogiLang, cited on December 21, 2022.

[218] Miriam Webster Dictionary, https://www.merriam-webster.com/dictionary/counterfactual, cited on December 23, 2022.

[219] Google Search, Oxford Languages, https://www.google.com/search?q=counterfactual+definition&rlz=1C1CHBD_enUS742US742&oq=counterfactual&aqs=chrome.3.69i57j0i512j0i433i512j0i512l7.10049j0j7&sourceid=chrome&ie=UTF-8#ip=1, cited on December 23, 2022.

One of the foundational values brought to us by causal is to consider what did not happen and to understand what the case would be or what would happen if this set of conditions did occur.

In contrast, in correlation-based AI, we build models from observational, transactional, and research data, and we continue to use that set of variables to score and predict new data as it arrives and to retrain and refresh our model(s) to keep them accurate and running optimally.

We can, and certainly do, use data in the manner described above in causal-based AI as well. Still, we also have the option to bring in data that embodies numerous scenarios that we think could happen or might happen or that we want to try to manage to make it happen, or data from previous studies that have proven or illustrated unique characteristics that can broaden and improve the results of our models and research.

To be clear, we are aware of and have used synthetic data, and we are aware that we can use synthetic data to generate outputs from correlation-based AI models that illustrate options of scenarios that have not happened. We expect synthetic data to grow in usage and importance, but historically, using counterfactuals in correlation-based AI has not been widespread.

Counterfactuals enable causal models to illustrate the wide range of options and alternate paths we might want to consider.

Causal via SCM will empower a broader set of data science professionals to build sophisticated models and ensembles of models, enabling business managers and analysts to engage with causal-based applications in a way that will allow those professionals to vary the conditions they seek to examine and understand potential outcomes via data and computing based models quickly and easily.

Confounding variables

In a confounded association or relationship, there is at least one additional variable, the confounding variable, that changes or distorts the relationship between X and Y beyond, or in addition to, the effect of M. Then the association between X and Y is distorted (e.g., some would say spurious) and that the distortion is a result of the effect of a confounding variable(s) (W). Hence, the relationship is said to be confounded.

A variable is confounding if it predicts both the behavior and the outcome. A confounding variable left out of a model is called a lurking variable.[220]

We may leave variables out of the model because the variable is out of scope for what we are examining, or it may be that we are unaware of the variable, or there could be a number of reasons for overtly omitting the variable, or it could be an oversight on our part.

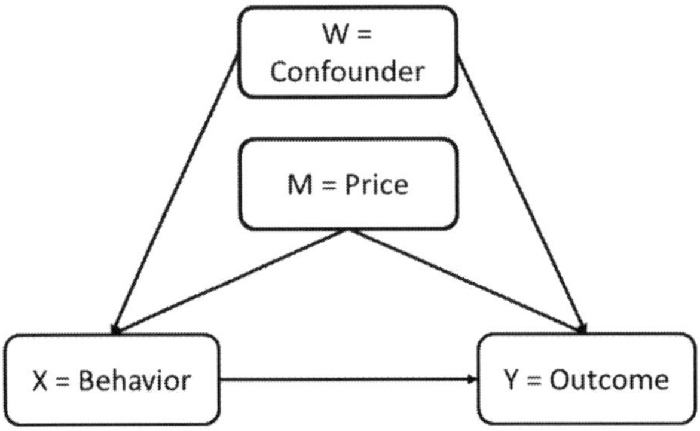

Figure 19: Directed Acyclic Graph (DAG) with a Confounding Variable.

---

[220] Ibid.

Colliders

A variable is a collider when two or more variables directly influence it. The name collider reflects that in the DAG, the arrowheads from the other variables lead into the collider variable. The result of having a collider in the path is that the collider blocks the association between the variables that influence it. Thus, the collider does not generate an unconditional association between the variables that determine it. The causal variables influencing the collider are themselves not necessarily associated. If they are not adjacent, the collider is *unshielded.*[221]

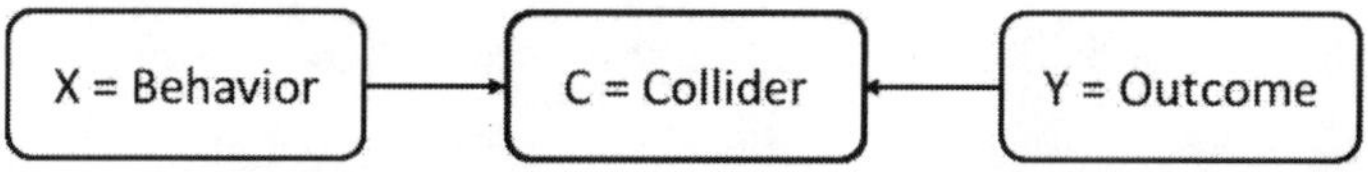

Figure 20: Directed Acyclic Graph (DAG) with an Unshielded Collider Variable.

Otherwise, the collider is shielded and part of a triangle.

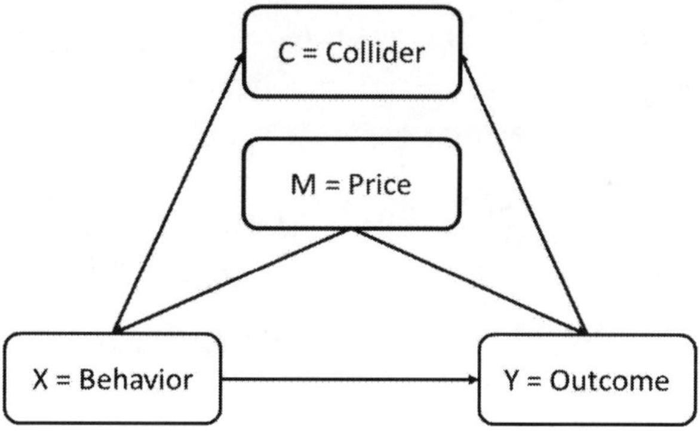

Figure 21: Directed Acyclic Graph (DAG) with a Shielded Collider Variable.

[221] Collider (statistics), Wikipedia, https://en.wikipedia.org/wiki/Collider_(statistics), Cited on December 23, 2022.

Colliders are sometimes confused with confounding variables. Unlike colliders, confounding variables *should* be controlled for when estimating causal associations.

Mediator variables

Mediator variables are inputs into the model that are most typically associated with the node/variable combinations that researchers, business users, data scientists, and other interested parties want to vary in a controlled, programmatic manner to understand the options they have at their disposal and to determine the best approaches, or even better, the optimal approach, to reach their desired and intended objectives.

To start our discussion, let's define a mediator. The following is the standard definition from a widely used dictionary. Mediator—"one that mediates, especially: one that mediates between parties at variance", or "a mediating agent in a physical, chemical, or biological process."[222] Mediator variables and mediation analysis take on a slightly different meaning in the SCM process. Let's examine the subtle difference.

Mediator variables in a causal model can be a wide range of inputs and drive a diverse set of causal effects. Examples of mediator variables include price, unemployment rate, marketing spend, discounts offered, rate of inflation, growth rate, size of litter, competitive pricing, lack of alternatives, quality of raw materials, temperature, snowfall, holiday season, accident rate, mortality rate, presence of extreme or abnormal conditions such as war, etc. Mediator variables can be any action or activity that is related and relevant to the model.

---

[222] Miriam Webster Dictionary, Mediator Definition & Meaning - Merriam-Webster, cited on December 25, 2022.

When considering a mediator variable or mediating variables, it may be possible that the total effect of the variation in an outcome is due to the cause or influence of a mediator. More than likely, that is not the case, but it is possible and needs to be kept in mind.

When introducing a mediator variable, the total effect can be broken into two constituent elements: direct and indirect. The direct effect is the effect of the variation on the outcome without introducing the mediator. The indirect effect or variation on the outcome is the variation that was introduced by bringing the mediator variable(s) into the model.

When adding and removing mediator variables from our models we need to ensure that the model is valid for the purpose we intend and accurately measures the effects that we are interested in understanding.

Mediation Analysis is the process whereby we ensure that our model conforms to the relevant rules and remains a valid model as we iterate through the process of adding and removing node and variable combinations. Not only do we need to be mindful of the variables themselves, but the overall structure, substructures, the order of the nodes, and the connection types we employ as we execute the process of adding and removing nodes and variables.

Let's move on to discussing how we examine our revised model to ensure we are not invalidating our structure with our newly added or removed variables and the revised associated relationships.

Mediation Analysis (MA)

Causal mediation analysis seeks to decompose the effect of an intervention among multiple paths and provides clear assignment(s) of node/variable, and/or path level, estimates of specific effects of introducing or removing mediator variables.[223]

There are multiple motivations for performing mediation analysis, but the overarching objectives are that we are:

- Delivering valid causal explanations and relationships
- Providing clear and detailed assignments of effects
- Increasing construct validity
- Strengthening evidence of the main effect and hypothesis
- Understanding the mechanisms and active elements by which variable inclusion causes an effect or effects
- Evaluating and improving interventions

Mediation analysis is the process related to determining which effect—direct or indirect—the end user, data scientist, or researcher wants to isolate and understand. For example, if the team is primarily focused on eliminating mediated pathways not of interest to them as a way to strengthen their evidence of an intervention-outcome relationship, the effect of primary interest is the direct effect. On the other hand, if the underlying effects of adjacent variables by which an intervention causes a positive or negative change in the outcome are the focus of interest, the team may be more interested in estimating the indirect effect(s).[224]

---

223 Jeffrey M Albert, Jang Ik Cho, Yiying Liu, Suchitra Nelson, National Institute of Health (NIH), National Center for Biotechnology Information, Stat Methods Med Res. 2019 Jun;28(6):1793-1807. doi: 10.1177/0962280218776483. Epub 2018 Jun 5, PMID: 29869589 PMCID: PMC6428612, Generalized causal mediation and path analysis: Extensions and practical considerations - PubMed (nih.gov), cited December 26, 2022.

224 Columbia University Mailman School of Public Health, Population Health Methods, Causal Mediation, Causal Mediation | Columbia Public Health, cited December 26, 2022.

The mediation process does not need to be binary, and typically, it is not binary. Typically, we are interested in both direct and indirect effects rather than just one or the other. In the real world, we are seeking to understand the actual direct and indirect effects and their causes so that we can gain a better understanding of how we can design and develop interventions that create conditions that will be more likely to engender actions that deliver the desired results we are planning for and seeking.

Over the past thirty years, numerous methods have been proposed, designed, created, refined, and extended for mediation analysis. A sample of the more notable approaches include:

- Mediation analysis for two stages (Baron and Kenny, 1986)
- Structural Equations Model (SEM) based methods (Ditlevsen et al. 2005)
- Estimation of mediation effects in the context of multiple stages via the product of coefficients approach (Taylor et al., 2008)
- Mediation for binary or mixed types of variables (Huang et al. 2004) and (Schluchter 2008) addressed two-stage mediation for a binary outcome
- Two-stage case with a binary mediator (Li et al. 2007)
- General path model involving all binary variables (Eskima et al. 2001)
- Mediation analysis using the potential outcomes framework (Robins and Greenland, 1992; Rubin, 2004; Ten Have et al., 2007; Albert, 2008; Imai, Keele, and Yamamoto, 2010)

- Definitions extending direct and indirect path level effects to the case of nonparametric DAGs (Pearl 2000, 2001)[225]

Of course, we are interested in leveraging the mediation analysis approach(es) that is/are applicable and appropriate for the type of model and variables that we are working with. Still, one of our primary business and operational goals is to isolate, determine, and understand the causal effects resulting from the possible or envisioned experimental manipulations we are conceiving and considering.

DAGs are flexible, extensible, and powerful tools; nodes, connections, weights, and directions can be assembled in almost unlimited variations. SCM is a powerful graphing and pseudo-programming paradigm. As we build, modify, and iterate through the variations on our journey to find the optimal structure for our intended objectives, Mediation Analysis is the primary tool we can use to ensure that our models fit our purpose.

As we have seen, there are multiple approaches to employ for mediation analysis. An approach that seems logical and intuitively easy to understand is Pearl's path-deactivation process. Dr. Pearl postulates that the direct effect of one event on another can be defined and measured by holding constant all intermediate variables between the two. Dr. Pearl offers a novel way of defining the effect transmitted through a restricted set of paths

---

[225] Jeffrey M. Albert, Suchitra Nelson, Generalized Causal Mediation Analysis, National Institute of Health (NIH), National Center for Biotechnology Information, Published in final edited form as: Biometrics. 2011 Sep; 67(3): 1028–1038, Published online 2011 Feb 9. doi: 10.1111/j.1541-0420.2010.01547.x, PMCID: PMC3139764, NIHMSID: NIHMS260919, PMID: 21306353, Generalized Causal Mediation Analysis - PMC (nih.gov) cited December 26, 2022.

without controlling variables on the remaining paths. This permits assessing a more natural type of direct and indirect effects.[226]

The path-deactivation process can be described as a sequence of actions applied to the node and variables in a causal model (in causal order) in which each variable is set to the value it would have if it and each of its parents (and their parents, and so on) were subject to a specified combination of exposure levels.[227] The objective of selectively and intentionally activating and deactivating paths and connections is to isolate and understand the effect at each segment of the path and the overall path in its entirety.

Mediation Analysis (MA) and the multiple variations of MA are intended to provide us with tools to examine the wide variety of nodes, connections, probabilities, and complete models to ensure that we are designing and leveraging models that provide the most accurate measurements of the processes and interactions that we can obtain.

Let's highlight a few techniques our technical teams may use to test and validate our models as we iterate toward intermediate and, ultimately, final models for the business challenges we seek to address.

---

226 Judea Pearl, Direct and indirect effects. In Proceedings of the 17th Conference on Uncertainty in Artificial Intelligence; San Francisco: Morgan Kaufmann; 2001. pp. 411–420. Direct and indirect effects | Proceedings of the Seventeenth conference on Uncertainty in artificial intelligence (acm.org) Cited on December 27, 2022.

227 Jeffrey M. Albert, Suchitra Nelson, Generalized Causal Mediation Analysis, National Institute of Health (NIH), National Center for Biotechnology Information, Published in final edited form as: Biometrics. 2011 Sep; 67(3): 1028–1038, Published online 2011 Feb 9. doi: 10.1111/j.1541-0420.2010.01547.x, PMCID: PMC3139764, NIHMSID: NIHMS260919, PMID: 21306353, Generalized Causal Mediation Analysis - PMC (nih.gov) cited December 27, 2022.

Technical model validation techniques

As noted, while building our models, we rarely develop the optimal model on the first attempt. Our hybrid teams of business, analytical, and technical professionals will be iterating over the numerous permutations of the models to arrive at the best solution. Mediation analysis is one tool that will help us in this process.

As we iterate and test differing combinations of nodes, connections, variables, and structures, we will employ multiple techniques to optimize the type of variables, effects, and outcomes. We want to ensure the validity of our modifications and models and validate that we are producing the best possible work appropriate for the business objective we are addressing.

The following section contains a sample of the most popular and widely used validation techniques. This section is intended to be representative and not exhaustive. As the state of the art continues to evolve, the global causal community will create new, more specialized routines and techniques.

d-Separation

d-separation is defined as a criterion for deciding, from a given causal graph, whether a set X of variables is independent of another set Y, given a third set Z. The idea is to associate "dependence" with "connectedness" (i.e., the existence of a connecting path) and "independence" with "unconnected-ness" or "separation."[228] For clarity, the "d" in the term "d-separation" stands for dependence.

d-separation can be thought of as the rules for correctly controlling variables in DAGs. Uncontrolled variables cause bias and other issues when the process contains variables that affect each other and when variables that are causes themselves, but also simultaneously act as mediators of other causes and other complex structures.[229]

The d-separation process and technique enable us to ensure that our DAGs and resulting models are as free from bias as possible and will produce the expected and intended results.

Sensitivity analysis / Robustness checks

One of the most widely employed validation techniques in causal modeling is verifying an outcome's sensitivity and robustness.

Refutation is a technique where the current estimates of variables are "refuted" by adding noise to the root cause variable or replacing the initial mediating variable with a random value.

The refutation process will provide a change in the outcome. By varying mediation variables by specific amounts, we can see the variation in the downstream variables and the outcomes and, therefore, have a quantified

---

[228] d-SEPARATION WITHOUT TEARS, Judea Pearl, Causality, 2nd Edition, 2009, http://bayes.cs.ucla.edu/BOOK-2K/d-sep.html#:~:text=d%2Dseparation%20is%20a%20criterion,ness%22%20or%20%22separation%22. Cited on November 28, 2022

[229] A Complete Guide to Causal Inference, Skylar Kerzner, Feb 21, 2022, https://towardsdatascience.com/a-complete-guide-to-causal-inference-8d5aaca68a47, Cited November 28, 2022.

understanding of the sensitivity of the model to the nodes/variables that we refuted/changed.[230]

Irrelevant additional confounder

In this technique, a new white noise variable is added or inserted into the model as one of the additional confounder variables. This change enables the monitoring of the observed changes of the treatment effect after refutation with respect to the state before refutation.

Changes in the treatment effect are expected to be small. If the model is robust enough, meaning not brittle or over-trained, the causal estimate should be resistant to the newly inserted variable.

Adding an unobserved common cause variable

Unlike the technique using an irrelevant additional confounder, we can simulate a common cause that is correlated with the mediation and outcome in an experiment. After completing the initial modeling run, we add the new common cause node as a confounder in the model and rerun the analysis. If the model is well designed to control for confounders, the new causal outcome should be reasonably close to the previous outcomes.

---

[230] Jane Huang, Daniel Yehdego, Deepsha Menghani, Saurabh Kumar, and Siddharth Kumar, Nov 18, 2020, Published in Data Science at Microsoft, Causal inference (Part 3 of 3): Model validation and applications, https://medium.com/data-science-at-microsoft/causal-inference-part-3-of-3-model-validation-and-applications-c84764156a29, cited December 29, 2022.

Placebo treatment

This technique involves replacing a mediation variable(s) with a random variable(s). Mediation variables are reshuffled in an experiment using a placebo technique while inputs and outputs remain the same. The expected changes in the effect should be significant due to the primary role played by the variation.

There are several types of placebo treatments. For example, the DoWhy[231] package has two types of placebo treatments implemented. One is to generate random values for the treatment, and the other, called the "permute" approach, is where the original treatment values are permuted by row.

The "permute" approach keeps the same treatment distribution, but the values are random after the reordering of the nodes. The approach is similar to the well-known permutation method that is used in developing a feature-importance ranking. The technique breaks the relationship between feature and target. The resulting drop in model score indicates how sensitive the model is to the singular feature.

In the context of causal inference, reordering is only applied to the mediating variables, not to the outcome or confounding variables.

---

231 Jesus Rodriguez, Aug 24, 2020, Microsoft's DoWhy is a Cool Framework for Causal Inference, https://medium.com/dataseries/microsofts-dowhy-is-a-cool-framework-for-causal-inference-d14013657f35, cited on December 30, 2022.

Random replace

In an experiment using random replacement, we randomly replace an existing covariate with an irrelevant variable. If the model is well designed, the causal estimates should not be too sensitive to the replacement.

Dummy outcome refuter

This approach asks, "What would happen to the estimated causal effect when we replace the true outcome variable with an independent random variable?"

Ideally, we would like to see the treatment effect estimates turn to zero. If they're not zero, then at least we would like to see the causal estimates vary significantly from the raw estimates. The concept of an irrelevant outcome refuter is similar to the placebo treatment, but instead of changing the treatment variable in the placebo, we change the outcome in the dummy outcome refuter.

Subset validation

In this technique, a random subset of the data is selected and the analysis is run once more. In this approach, our validation tests include cross-checking the causal outcomes across subsets. If the causal outcome is valid and well-founded, the results should not vary significantly across different subsets of the overall data set.

Business validation

Models in correlation-based AI and causal approaches can be proven technically sound and still incorrect in their predictions and outcomes. We must work diligently to ensure that our models are technically sound and produce valid and useful predictions and outcomes. After our efforts to ensure that our models are technically sound, we need to execute a cycle of validating the appropriate and relevant business conditions, legal requirements, and regulatory regimens to ensure they are met or exceeded.

Some of the conditions that are imposed by external entities such as federal and state governments, ethical obligations, and societal needs include:

- Robustness and stability to data drift and regulatory changes
- Fairness and bias measurement and corrective strategies,
- Global and local explainability[232]

Let's move on from all things related to variables to a discussion of relationships, paths, or edges.

Relationships / Paths

Paths, edges, or relationships are how we illustrate the direction of the DAG connections between nodes and carry the weighted effect or probability from one node to the next.

Let's describe and discuss various path types that are used in DAGs. As noted earlier in the overview section, paths can be—chains, forks, and/or inverted forks.

---

[232] Causal Lens, Model Validation with Causal AI, https://www.causalens.com/app/ai-model-validation-and-risk-management/#:~:text=Causal%20Model%20Validation%20allows%20model%20risk%20managers%20to,eliminate%20them%20by%20imposing%20fairness%20constraints%20on%20algorithms, cited on December 30, 2022.

- **Chain**: A chain is a simple diagram where all nodes are connected with arrows in the same forward direction. Figure 5 is an example of a chain.

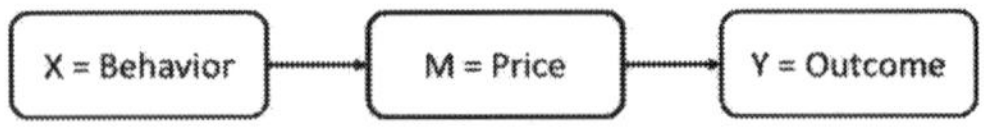

Figure 22: Directed Acyclic Graph (DAG) illustrating the Path type—Chain.

- **Fork**: The majority of DAGs include a fork of some type or multiple forks. A fork can be where multiple arrows fork away from a node, as in Figure 23, or where the multiple paths originate from a node and connect to different subsequent nodes, as in Figure 19.

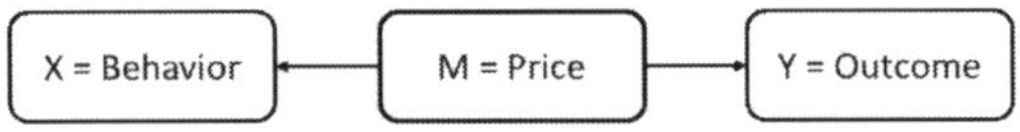

Figure 23: Directed Acyclic Graph (DAG) illustrating the Path type—Fork.

- **Inverted Fork**: An inverted fork is where two or more paths converge on a node from two or more different directions. In a path that is, or has, an inverted fork, the node where two or more arrowheads meet is called a collider. Colliders are defined above in the Variables section. An inverted fork is not an open path; it is blocked by the collider. We don't need to account for M to assess the causal effect of X on Y; the back-door path is already blocked by M.[233] Figure 24 below is an example of an inverted fork converging on a collider variable via a back door path, both of which will be defined below.

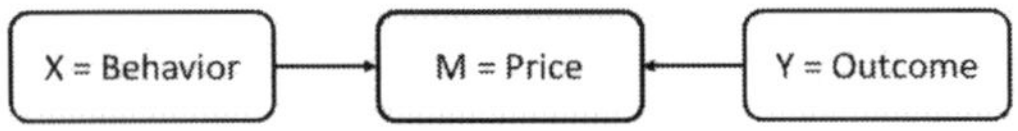

[233] Malcolm Barrett, An Introduction to Directed Acyclic Graphs, October, 10, 2021, An Introduction to Directed Acyclic Graphs (microsoft.com), cited on December 25, 2022.

Figure 24: Directed Acyclic Graph (DAG) illustrating the Path type—Inverted Fork.

Path connecting an unobserved variable

Unobserved variables play a role in our models, but we do not have direct measurement or observational data for their impact and effect on our current model. A dotted or dashed arrow indicates connections to and from unobserved variables.

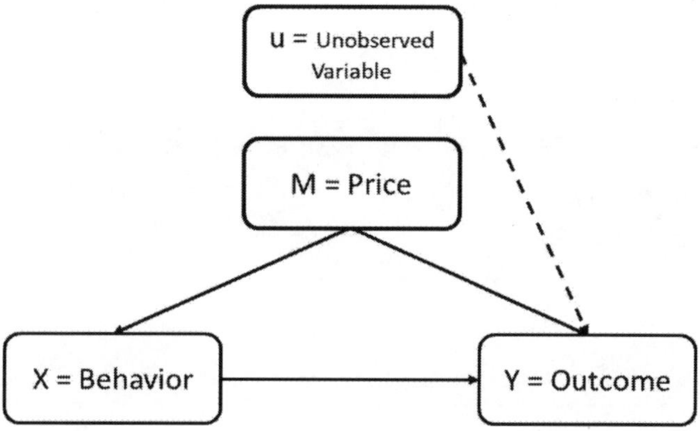

Figure 25: Directed Acyclic Graph (DAG) with an Unobserved Variable.

Front door paths

Front Door Paths are arrows moving to or directed toward the outcomes. Another way to say it is that Front Door Paths are moving away from, or directed away from, the mediators and/or treatments. All figures in this chapter have front door paths included and illustrated. You cannot have a DAG without at least one Front Door Path. In Figure 25, the path from X to Y is a front door path, and in Figure 22, all paths are Front Door Paths.

Typically, we do not want to block the front door paths when determining the causal relationships as these paths capture the effects we are interested in and are attempting to, analyze, and understand.[234]

We can block any path, Front Door or Back Door Path, by "conditioning" the variable associated with that path. To condition a variable is to remove its impact by holding the variable constant when running iterations/scenarios of data through the model.

Typically, when we are examining processes and environments that we are interested in modeling and analyzing, it is the Front Door Paths, or the obvious connections and effects, that we build into our models first. After we have the base model completed or after we have the initial conditions (i.e., nodes, connections, directions, variables) established, noted, and validated, we start to think about and build the indirect effects into our models. Indirect effects are referred to as Back Door Paths.

Back door paths

"A Back Door Path is any path from X to Y that starts with an arrow pointing toward X."[235] A Back Door Path runs in the counter direction to Front Door Paths.

---

[234] Understanding Causal Inference, December 2020, A Guide to Causal Inference - Understanding Causal Inference (gitbook.io), cited December 30, 2022.

[235] Mediators, Confounders and Colliders, oh my!, Christina T Saunders, PhD., Department of Biostatistics, Vanderbilt University, Medical Center, https://biostat.app.vumc.org/wiki/pub/Main/ContinuingEdu/CTSaunders_CausalDiagrams.pdf, cited on December 23, 2022.

A couple of examples of Back Door Paths in the figures in this chapter are in Figure 25, the path from M to X is a Back Door Path, and in Figure 24, the path from Y to M is a Back Door Path.

Back Door Paths are arrows moving to, or directed toward, the mediators and/or treatments. Another way to describe the direction of Back Door Paths is that they move away from, or are directed away from, the outcomes.

Typically, we will want to block the Back Door Paths when determining accurate causal relationships as these paths confound the effects we are interested in and are attempting to analyze and understand.

Back Door Paths denote the indirect effects nodes/variables can have on each other. Back Door Paths create confounding variables, nodes, or confounders. Judea Pearl, who developed much of the theory of SCM, said, "...confounding is like water in a pipe: it flows freely in open pathways, and we need to block it somewhere along the way. We don't necessarily need to block the water at multiple points along the same back-door path, although we may have to block more than one path."[236]

We often talk about *confounders*, but we should really talk about *confounding* because it is about the pathway and the effect embodied in the path or relationship more than any particular node along the path.

Modeling for simplicity to understand complexity

We need to account for Back Door Paths in our analysis. There are many ways to go about conditioning, isolating, reducing, or removing the effects

---

[236] Malcolm Barrett, An Introduction to Directed Acyclic Graphs, October, 10, 2021, An Introduction to Directed Acyclic Graphs (microsoft.com), cited on December 24, 2022.

of Back Door Paths or the confounding effect(s). Some available techniques include placing the variable in a regression model, matching, and inverse probability weighting—all with associated pros and cons. Each approach must include a decision by the business user and data scientist about which variables to focus on or deprioritize in the model.

Some analysts have taken the approach of including all possible confounding effects. This can be considered a shortcut approach because putting everything into the model is easy. However, this approach introduces unnecessary complexity and requires adjusting for colliders and mediators that may not be needed in the model, and this rather indiscriminate approach can introduce bias.

A better, more considerate, and intelligent approach is to determine minimally sufficient adjustment sets, sets of covariates that, when adjusted for, block all back-door paths, but include no more or no less than necessary nodes and variables.

Of course, there can be many minimally sufficient sets, and if you remove even one variable from a given set, a back-door path will open. Some DAGs have no back-door paths to close, so the minimally sufficient adjustment set is empty. Others, DAGs with important variables that are unmeasured, cannot produce any sets sufficient to close back-door paths.[237]

One of our goals in modeling is not to build simple models that do not represent reality or to build overly complex models that are impossible to manage or validate. As we are iterating through the process of building our models represented by DAGs leveraging the SCM process, we are seeking to build a model of maximum simplicity that contains all the complexity needed to describe and explain the phenomena we seek to examine. As with

---

[237] Ibid.

many general undertakings in life and analytics, we seek to employ Occam's Razor.

"Occam's razor, also known as the principle of parsimony or the law of parsimony, is the problem-solving principle that "entities should not be multiplied beyond necessity." It is generally understood that with competing theories or explanations, the simpler one, for example, a model with fewer parameters, is preferred. The idea is frequently attributed to English Franciscan friar William of Ockham (c. 1287–1347), a scholastic philosopher and theologian.[238]

We seek simplicity to explain and understand complexity. Let's move on from discussing all things related to paths to briefly discussing Weights.

Weights

So far, we have examined and discussed—nodes, variables, and paths. The final model element to be discussed is weights. Weights are crucial in the training, tuning, and operations of all correlation- and causal-based models.

Weights are the numerical value associated with the effect that the node in question has on the subsequent node. As the variables are processed and values are passed from the previous node to the subsequent node, the variable's value is increased or amplified, decreased or reduced, by multiplying the value by the weight associated with the path.

---

[238] Contributors to Wikipedia, Definition of Occam's Razor, Occam's razor - Wikipedia, cited on December 31, 2022.

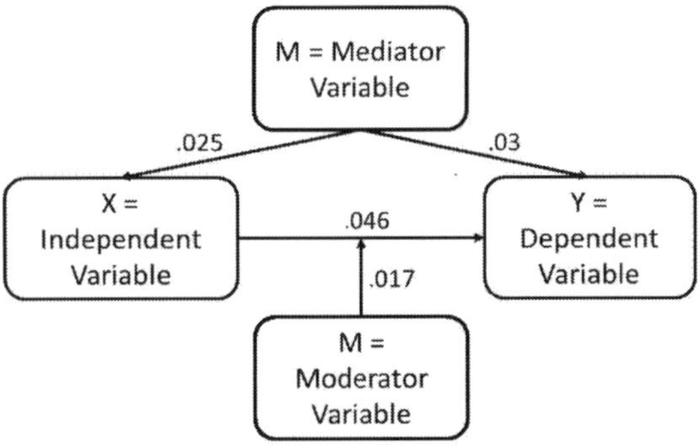

Figure 26: A Causal Model with Weights Illustrated.

Weights can be called edge weights, parameters, hyperparameters, and other terms. All mean the same thing: the weight of the impact of the effect associated with the path.

There are wide-ranging discussions on how to set the initial value of weights across a network or model, how best to modify weights to train models, how weights converge optimally to arrive at a robust model, and many other highly technical and arcane discussions of setting, managing, optimizing, validating and maintaining weights in models; all of these discussions are beyond the scope of this section and book.

Let's move on to our final section in our discussion of elements of DAGs, the complete model.

Models

We have discussed all the elements of a Causal AI model—nodes, variables, paths, and weights. It seems so simple when you say it like that, but the flexibility and power of the Structural Causal Modeling approach and the resulting models are impressive.

Now, we understand the visual output of the SCM process as Directed Acyclic Graphs, and we have a cursory understanding of the rules and mechanics of leveraging the elements we have discussed to build complete causal models.

Let's now move on to discuss one application of the power of Causal models: the ability to use not only the current data that we have designed and collected for our specific purpose but also data that has been collected or generated in the past for other purposes, but can be used to bolster our current data sets.

Leveraging previously collected data

One of the incredibly powerful aspects of causal-based AI is the ability to include data from a wide range of previous surveys, observational studies, collections of transactions, and more to enrich the data set we use in our models.

Of course, data collected for other purposes in previous projects may or may not have all the data elements we want or need to directly align the outside data with our existing data. We may be interested in utilizing numerous data sets, and some of those data sets will prove useful and valuable. In contrast, other data sets will look promising but prove to be useless for the models we are building.

Causal AI provides the tools to analyze and condition the previously collected data and enables us to select the subset of data that is pertinent and relevant to our current efforts. We can effectively extend our data resources as many times as needed to expand our data sets to provide the breadth and depth needed to make our models robust and representative.

In 2016, Judea Pearl and Elias Bareinboim[239] proved that a structured and disciplined approach to examining and analyzing data collected for varying purposes reliably produced verified data sets that can be used to augment existing data sets.

Pearl and Barenboim asserted, "The unification of the structural, counterfactual, and graphical approaches to causal analysis gave rise to mathematical tools that have helped resolve a wide variety of causal inference problems, including controlling confounding, sampling bias, and generalization across populations. ...[W]e present a general approach to these problems, based on a syntactic transformation of the query of interest into a format derivable from the available information. Tuned to nuances in design, this approach enables us to address a crucial problem in big data applications: the need to combine datasets collected under heterogeneous conditions so as to synthesize consistent estimates of causal effects in a target population. As a by-product of this analysis, we arrived at solutions to two other long-held problems: recovery from sampling selection bias and generalization of randomized clinical trials. These two problems which, taken together, make up the formidable problem called 'external validity,' have been given a complete formal characterization and can thus be considered 'solved'."[240]

Pearl and Bareinboim, through their research, developments, and innovations, have extended SCM with the tools to mathematically prove

---

[239] Elias Bareinboim, Associate Professor, Department of Computer Science, Director, Causal Artificial Intelligence Lab, Columbia University, https://causalai.net/, Cited December 25, 2024.

[240] Elias Bareinboim and Judea Pearl, Causal inference and the data-fusion problem, edited by Richard M. Shiffrin, Indiana University, Bloomington, IN, and approved March 15, 2016 (received for review June 29, 2015), July 5, 2016, 113 (27) 7345-7352, https://doi.org/10.1073/pnas.1510507113, https://www.pnas.org/doi/10.1073/pnas.1510507113, cited on December 31, 2022.

that externally collected data can be reliably and unerringly analyzed, understood, conditioned, and included in our analysis data sets to extend the data we use in our analyses.

We have covered a great deal of ground in our discussion to understand the elements of SCM, DAGs, and more. Our foundational understanding of causal-based AI is beginning to coalesce.

Summary

We covered the primary benefit of understanding Causal AI at a functional level to a hybrid team of business, analytics, and technology professionals collaborating to address and solve business challenges in a wide range of operational areas including—marketing, sales, manufacturing, supply chain operations, logistics, patient care, donor engagement, pricing, drug treatment efficacy, raw materials evaluation and selection, competing marketing offers, and more.

We discussed the details of conceiving, building, modifying, testing, validating, and continuing to change and expand Directed Acyclic Graphs, or DAGs, using the Structural Causal Modeling (SCM) technique or methodology.

Causal AI is in a period of rapid growth and evolution. Numerous research papers, books, conferences, presentations, and additional resources delve into the technical details of the topics introduced and will continue to be introduced in subsequent chapters. I hope the introduction you have read and will continue to read in this book is whetting your appetite to learn more about Causal AI.

Causal modeling is difficult to grasp and inaccessible to many in part because nearly every discussion of causal modeling or models or techniques related to Causal AI begins with a relatively easy-to-understand introduction to and description of the upcoming discussion and then immediately dives quickly and deeply into a discussion dominated by calculus.

There is nothing wrong with this approach if we want to limit the number of participants in the discussions to researchers and academics. If this small group of specialists are the only ones to be involved in the dialog and the only ones to use Causal AI, then we do not need to change the approach to the discussion.

However, I believe it is important to change the dialog to entice additional professionals to become involved in the discussion, evolution, and growth of the field of Causal AI.

Let's move our discussion from the elements of Causal AI to the expected impact of Causal AI on the world.

CHAPTER 9

The Impact of Causal AI

Causality is hard. It is hard to determine and hard to definitively prove true causality. For most people, the concept is hard to define and understand at a fundamental level.

Causality is one of those things that people *think* that they understand. Given that we see causality in our daily lives, most people think, I *understand* causality, and most of them do understand causality at a simple level of a singular cause and the obvious resulting effect.

For example, perhaps it is raining, the temperature drops below freezing, and the rain transitions to sleet, ice, and snow. It is quite clear that the falling temperature was a primary and direct cause of the effect of the precipitation changing form from rain into snow. Simple and easy to see, feel, and understand.

Additionally, we see, and more importantly, feel that if we touch a burner or heating element on a hot stove with a bare finger, we get burned. We see, know, and experience that if we press on the accelerator of our car, it moves. Easy to understand, right? We have a cause, and we see, feel, and experience an effect. Yes, that is fairly easy for most people to understand and discuss, and that gives them enough of an understanding of causality for them to confidently say that they do understand causality. And, yes, superficially, we do understand causality.

But when most of us stop and think about causality as a multi-faceted concept and how to define it clearly, we realize that we really don't understand it as cleanly, clearly, and deeply as we would like. When we examine the concept of causality in the real world, with all its entangled complexity, and when we try to describe this actual state of affairs in a detailed mathematical manner, we realize that we do not understand causality, at least not at the level of depth that we need to achieve the level of precision required for analytical purposes.

Most of us have grown up accepting that correlation is a close enough approximation of causality that we will use in our analytical work. We have been doing this for millennia. After being in the analytics field for a couple of years, I remember asking people who I was learning from about syndicated data that we utilized to analyze sales of Consumer-Packaged Goods (CPG) products that we didn't have enough data or detailed enough data to prove that X caused Y. The answer was always something like, "It is close enough", or "This is the best we can do". I accepted these responses at the time because we had work to do and people were waiting for our results, but I always thought that we could and should do more to drive to a more complete understanding of cause and effect.

In my career, I have had numerous people ask me in interview processes for new jobs, "Explain to me the difference between correlation and causality." Often, this question is asked as if it is a trick or gotcha question. I have been working on refining my answer to this question for a couple of decades. I feel confident that I can nail this question when I am asked.

There are a number of key factors that differentiate causality from correlation:

- Time is a requisite for causal relationships to exist. The cause must precede the effect, and the reverse cannot be true; time cannot bend back on itself. Correlation has no notion of time.

- Directionality is embedded as a foundational element of causality. Causal relationships involve a clear sense of direction, indicating that the cause precedes the effect.[241] In contrast, correlations, for instance, lack inherent directionality and are bidirectional.

- Sufficiency and Necessity are distinguishing characteristics of causal relationships.[242] [243] [244] Causality implies that a cause is either sufficient, necessary, or both for its effect to occur. Correlations, on the other hand, do not imply necessity or sufficiency and can exist without both or either factor individually.

---

[241] P. Hosseini, D. A. Broniatowski, and M. Diab, "Predicting directionality in causal relations in text," arXiv preprint arXiv:2103.13606, 2021, Cited November 5, 2024. (71)

[242] J. Pearl and D. Mackenzie, The Book of Why, New York: Basic Books, 2018. Cited November 5, 2024 (89)

[243] J. Y. Halpern, Actual Causality, Cambridge, MA: MIT Press, 2016, Cited November 5, 2024. (90)

[244] P. Nadathur and S. Lauer, "Causal necessity, causal sufficiency, and the implications of causative verbs," Glossa: a journal of general linguistics, vol. 5, no. 1, 2020. Cited November 5, 2024. (72)

- Manipulation is a fundamental element of causal relationships.[245] [246] Causality allows for intervention on a causal factor, which results in observable changes in the effect. Data scientists and others can test and examine causal relationships directly and iteratively.

- Causal relationships can be asymmetrical. Correlative relationships are not. The causal relationship between two variables, such as 'A' causing 'B', is distinct and asymmetric from the reverse relationship of 'B' causing 'A'.[247] In contrast, correlation-based relationships exhibit symmetry.

- Chaining causal relationships is possible. If 'A' causes 'B' and 'B' causes 'C', then 'A' is considered an (indirect) cause of 'C'. This concept of chaining provides a deeper understanding of the interconnectedness of causal relationships.[248]

- Causal relationships remain consistent, invariant, and predictable, under varying interventions or contexts.[249]

---

[245] T. Harinen, "Mutual manipulability and causal inbetweenness," Synthese, vol. 195, pp. 35–54, 2018, Cited November 5, 2024.(73)

[246] J. Woodward, "Causation and manipulability," The Stanford Encyclopedia of Philosophy, 2016. Cite November 5, 2024. (74)

[247] P. A. White, "The causal asymmetry." Psychological review, vol. 113, no. 1, p. 132, 2006. Cited November 5, 2024, (75)

[248] E. Eells and E. Sober, "Probabilistic causality and the question of transitivity," Philosophy of science, vol. 50, no. 1, pp. 35–57, 1983. Cited November 5, 2024, (76)

[249] I. Bica, D. Jarrett, and M. van der Schaar, "Invariant causal imitation learning for generalizable policies," Advances in Neural Information Processing Systems, vol. 34, pp. 3952–3964, 2021, Cited November 5, 2024, (77)

[250]Providing that the underlying Causal model is valid and stable, this property allows modelers and analysts to make reliable predictions and draw conclusions about causal relationships, whereas correlations can change based on specific circumstances.

- Causal relationships embody explicitness by making transparent assumptions about underlying connections, weights, and positions. Explicitness goes beyond observed correlations and enables a deeper understanding of how and why causal relationships occur.[251]

- Explainability is an essential aspect of causality. Causality seeks to explain effects in terms of their underlying causes rather than merely identifying patterns in data. By understanding the causal mechanisms at play, we can gain a more comprehensive understanding of the phenomena being studied.[252] [253]

So, next time someone asks you about the differences between correlation and causality, you will be ready with a comprehensive answer.

---

[250] B. Befani, "Models of causality and causal inference," Broadening the Range of Designs and Methods for Impact Evaluation, vol. 38, 2012, Cited November 5, 2024, (83)

[251] J. W. Irwin, "The effects of explicitness and clause order on the comprehension of reversible causal relationships," Reading Research Quarterly, pp. 477–488, 1980.Cited November 5, 2024, (78)

[252] L. Bertossi, J. Li, M. Schleich, D. Suciu, and Z. Vagena, "Causality-based explanation of classification outcomes," in Proceedings of the Fourth International Workshop on Data Management for End-to-End Machine Learning, 2020, pp. 1–10.Cited November 5, 2024, (79)

[253] Abraham Itzhak Weinberg, Cristiano Premebida, Diego Resende Faria, March 17, 2024, Causality from Bottom to Top: A Survey, License: CC BY-SA 4.0, arXiv:2403.11219v1, Cited November 6, 2024.

In the previous chapter, we discussed Causal AI and the relevant tools that are coming into being for people to define, analyze, understand, and leverage Causal AI as a tool in their analytical arsenal. In this chapter, our discussion will focus on the impact of Causal AI on businesses, people, society, and the world at large. Let's begin to examine and discuss the overall impact of Causal AI.

The state of the art

Causal AI is just beginning to emerge from academia and corporate research and development (R&D) organizations. There are a handful of commercial Causal AI software companies. Most of those commercial companies are basing their products on open-source offerings.

Using the open-source model or approach is one of the current standard models for creating new software offerings across all categories and markets. Academics, corporate R&D departments, and interested technologists create early-stage tools and utilities for all types of categories, needs, and requirements. Those elements of software are offered to the community as a starting point.

It is interesting to see where in the early-stage lifecycle of software development early-stage innovators, developers, and practitioners gravitate towards. Some of them work on data acquisition, cleaning, and structuring. Others work on the tools that enable data scientists to build models. And others work on the User Experience (UX) and others on the User Interface (UI). And yet others work on system behavior such as integrated operations, reliability, scalability, and accuracy. Those are just representative parts of any system. Across all three pillars of AI, some developers are focused on algorithmic scalability, flexibility, precision, extensibility, and more. Today, we see as many approaches to making Causal AI accessible, easy to use, reliable, and scalable as we see vendors.

Once enough of these foundational parts and the other required system elements are built in an initial form, it is typical for other developers to come along and see natural integration and consolidation opportunities to bring the disparate parts together into a more coherent whole.

The speed of evolution and adoption varies widely across software segments and sectors. The growth and maturity of Causal AI has been a slow, uneven process. In part, the slow evolution of Causal AI was due to the fact that, as we previously noted, most people do not understand causality as a basic concept, but also because the mathematics of describing causality was immature. We owe a debt of gratitude to Judea Pearl[254] and his colleagues for developing and delivering the new forms of calculus that enable the reliable and consistent mathematical modeling of causality.

Early adopters in enterprise-class organizations are experimenting with commercial Causal AI offerings. In Japan, there are a number of large companies that are directing their corporate R&D function to work across open source projects, early-stage commercial offerings, and even engage in the development of new software that is, in some cases, contributed to the open source community, to determine if Causal AI can be leveraged to help improve daily operations and effectiveness in manufacturing, marketing, and other corporate functions.

It is an exciting time in the Causal AI market, which is characterized by innovation, creativity, and expansion of the software offerings and use cases where that software is being tested and applied.

---

[254] Contributors to Wikipedia, Judea Pearl, https://en.wikipedia.org/wiki/Judea_Pearl, Cited November 1, 2024.

Why are so many people excited?

The innovators in the Causal AI market have created and sustained the current level of interest and excitement. The rise of Causal AI could clearly be seen in 2020; that momentum has been maintained but overshadowed by the meteoric rise of GenAI. It is a positive development to see innovations in GenAI being brought into the Causal AI market and operation, but it is slightly negative that some of the energy investment and talent that would have gone to Causal AI have been redirected to GenAI. That diversion has slowed the innovation and development of Causal AI, but the progress has only slowed, not stopped.

There were concerns that the rise of GenAI would cause another drought in the development of Causal AI. While GenAI has taken the lion's share of funding and garnered most of the interest and current attention, Causal AI continues to grow and make progress technologically and in adoption by early adopters in commercial firms and innovators in research organizations and technology companies.

One of the developments that has been encouraging is that the Causal AI community and vendors have realized that while GenAI is flourishing due to the ability of the technology to ingest and actively use the bulk of the information available around the world, it has also ingested a significant amount of general knowledge related to causality.

GenAI is being utilized to create better input information for Causal AI. Generating reliable and accurate causal pairs has proven difficult for humans to do on a regular, repeated, and reliable basis and was beginning to be recognized as a known inhibitor of the growth and widespread use of Causal AI. Understanding the complete landscape of causal factors and the nature of a causal environment and process for a specific use case is challenging, if not insurmountable, for most people. Certainly, data scientists had a challenging time doing so, and end users and subject matter experts found the exercise nearly impossible to complete with any level of reliability, consistency, and accuracy.

All processes in the real world have an element of causality. Actions in the real world do not happen in a vacuum. At the same time, the ubiquity of causality is a bit of a challenge. I believe this is similar to the story about fish being in water. Fish don't know they're in water. The story, as told by David Foster Wallace, goes like this: There are these two young fish swimming along, and they happen to meet an older fish swimming the other way, who nods at them and says, "Morning, boys. How's the water?" And the two young fish swim on for a bit, and then eventually, one of them looks over at the other and goes, "What the hell is water?" While there are many interpretations of this metaphor, I look at it as a description of how we tend to see and interpret things through our individual lens, meaning that without conscious effort, we may not see the most obvious and important realities around us. Like the fish who don't know they are in water.[255] Causality is very similar to most people as the water is to the fish in this story; they just don't see it or think about it, due in part, because it is ubiquitous.

Fortunately, GenAI is proving to be a valuable and useful tool in helping people overcome these limitations and hurdles to more quickly and reliably arrive at high-quality input data sets that causal tools can ingest and utilize.

GenAI has enough basic causal information for beginners to gain access to reliable input information for their early-stage causal models. For GenAI to be increasingly valuable to more sophisticated Causal AI developers and

---

[255] Emre Kıcıman, Robert Osazuwa Ness, Amit Sharma, Chenhao Tan, Causal Reasoning and Large Language Models: Opening a New Frontier for Causality, August 20, 2024, https://arxiv.org/pdf/2305.00050, Cited November 11, 2024. Akash Takyar, LeewayHertz, https://www.leewayhertz.com/causal-ai/#understanding-ai-causality,

practitioners, we will need to create new GenAI models that are focused on causality as a science and an art and/or augment existing GenAI models with increasing levels of more accurate and sophisticated information related to the field of causality. This development will happen, and GenAI models will flourish and expand into nearly every realm, including core causality. If you recall, we discussed Domain Language Models (DLMs) in Chapter 5 of this book.

Microsoft Research has been evaluating how GenAI performed on various causal reasoning tasks. Their efforts have found that GenAI demonstrates proficiency in tasks such as:

- **Pairwise causal discovery**: LLMs have shown an ability to accurately identify causal relationships between pairs of variables, achieving up to 97% accuracy, which is significantly higher than traditional causal discovery algorithms.

- **Full causal graph discovery**: LLMs can also discover the entire causal structure among multiple variables, offering insights comparable to sophisticated deep learning methods.

- **Counterfactual reasoning**: LLMs excel at understanding how outcomes would change under different hypothetical scenarios, reflecting their ability to simulate and reason about alternative realities.

- **Identifying necessary/sufficient causes**: LLMs can effectively identify which causes were necessary and which were sufficient

> for particular events to occur, aiding in detailed causal analysis.[256]

It is encouraging to see organizations like Microsoft Research, led by people like Emre Kiciman,[257] taking an active interest in developing Small/Domain Language Models focused on causality. Emre and his team alone can drive the merging of GenAI and Causal AI together in a manner that significantly changes the trajectory of Causal AI in the global market. I can't say this with complete certainty, but I believe LLMs will be built to provide information beyond core causality. I am confident that GenAI models will be built to assist with understanding causality in many specialty areas like medical diagnostics, prescribing drugs, operations of nuclear plants, and more. These models will begin to be built in 2025 or 2026 and will become widely available one to three years after that, but these developments could also happen sooner.

What was once considered a threat to the speed of development of Causal AI has evolved into a valuable and useful augmentation of Causal AI that enables users, administrators, and developers to move more quickly into value-added utilization of Causal AI toolkits, utilities, and complete software offerings.

As we will discuss in Chapter 11 of this book, the consolidation, and combination of approaches in AI is one of the keys to the future of unlocking the significant and substantial value currently latent in our economic and technological landscape. Just as we discussed the value unleashed by integrating GenAI with Causal AI, we will see this on a

---

[256] Vicki Sedlack, Fish Don't Know They're in Water, https://alamedaeducationfoundation.org/fish-dont-know-theyre-in-water/, Cited November 5, 2024.

[257] Emre Kiciman, Senior Principal Research Manager, Microsoft Research, https://www.microsoft.com/en-us/research/people/emrek/, Cited November 3, 2024.

broader stage when we discuss Composite AI, but that is a topic for Chapter 11.

Let's move on to discuss the impact of Causal AI on various sectors of the economy, education, and society in general.

Areas of economic impact

As with all technology innovations, including those related to the fields of data, analytics, and AI, one of the primary intended consequences is economic growth. While the GenAI discussion focuses on broad economic impact, the impact felt by Causal AI will be more targeted and more tightly coupled with defined scenarios and use cases. Some representative examples of where Causal AI will make an impact are outlined below:

- **Healthcare** - Addressing complex health problems, treatment optimization, and drug discovery

- **Finance** - Risk assessment, fraud detection, investment strategies, and credit assessment

- **Marketing and customer experience** - Marketing mix modeling, customer behavior analysis, and budget allocation

- **Climate change research** - Counterfactual event attribution and understanding climate change beliefs

- **Manufacturing** - Root cause analysis, process optimization, bottleneck identification, and productivity improvement

- **Retail and e-commerce** - Pricing and promotion optimization, supply chain management, and targeted customer engagement

- **Information Technology** - Automated root-cause analysis, failure prediction, resource optimization, event simulation, and anomaly detection

- **Education** - Personalized learning and educational policy evaluation

- **Telecommunications** - Network optimization and customer churn prediction

- **Government and public policy** - Policy impact assessment and public health interventions

You may have noticed the wide range of applicability of Causal AI. Causal AI can transform decision-making processes across multiple fields by providing deep insights into cause-and-effect relationships. As causal AI continues to evolve, its influence is expected to grow, leading to more innovative and impactful applications across numerous business processes, industries, and vertical/horizontal markets.[258]

While Causal AI is not as general in its application as GenAI, it is close to a General-Purpose Technology (GPT), and therefore, it is difficult for most people to clearly understand the specific application of Causal AI to their needs and requirements, partially due to the ubiquity of where Causal AI can be applied. While GenAI is fairly easy for most people to understand and use, Causal AI is not. With GenAI, we have seen rapid, widespread adoption and use. We will not see this pattern repeated for Causal AI. The

---

[258] Akash Takyar, Leeway Hertz, Causal AI: Importance, use cases, benefits, challenges and implementation strategies, https://www.leewayhertz.com/causal-ai/#understanding-ai-causality, Cited November 1, 2024.

adoption, growth, and use of Causal AI will look more like Foundational AI than GenAI.

What type of questions should we ask to help understand the types of challenges or applications where Causal AI can be productively applied:

- Should I approve or reject this loan application, and if so, why?
- What causes my customers to churn and what actions can I take to make them stay?
- What caused this issue in my manufacturing plant and what actions can I take to prevent future issues?

Examples of where Causal AI can be leveraged include:

Healthcare

Causal AI can help identify the causes and effects of various medical conditions and treatment outcomes. For instance, it can simulate the impact of different treatment interventions on patient outcomes, allowing healthcare professionals to assess the effectiveness of alternative treatment options and make informed decisions about patient care in a simulated environment.

Finance

Causal AI can aid in risk assessment and decision-making within the financial sector. It can analyze the causal relationships between economic factors, market events, and investment outcomes. For example, it can provide insights into the causes of market volatility, assess the impact of regulatory changes on financial markets and help identify factors contributing to fraudulent activities.

Manufacturing

Causal AI can be used to optimize manufacturing processes and prevent issues. It can simulate the effects of process adjustments, equipment upgrades, or supply chain changes to identify the most effective interventions for improving product quality, reducing defects, and optimizing production efficiency.

Customer experience

Causal AI can be crucial in understanding customer behavior and improving satisfaction. It can identify the drivers of customer churn, determine the causal factors behind customer preferences and suggest personalized interventions to enhance customer experience. This can help businesses tailor their products, services, and marketing strategies to meet customer needs more effectively.[259]

Quantifying economic impact

Unlike GenAI, where thousands of researchers are working on studies and analyses that illustrate the macroeconomic and microeconomic impact of GenAI, there is a dearth of current research on the economic impact of Causal AI.

---

[259] Darko Matovski, World Economic Forum, June 23, 2023, What is 'Causal AI' and why will it become increasingly important?, https://www.weforum.org/stories/2023/06/what-is-causal-ai-why-important/, Cited November 1, 2024.

Most of the academic and R&D work completed on the economic impact of Causal AI was executed and published before 2019. The problem with these numbers and this data is that GenAI changed the world in 2022. In my opinion, using these numbers is misleading at best and could be completely erroneous.

I intend to illustrate and communicate the breadth and depth of impact that Causal AI will have on the global economy. We have this data for Foundational AI, as you read in Chapter 3, and for GenAI in Chapter 6. However, it is seemingly too early to find and communicate the same range of data for Causal AI as it relates to the world post-2022.

I found a few data points that were current and relevant to the Causal AI market and projected growth rates. One of the few recent data points available is the estimated size and growth of the market for Causal AI software. The market research firm Verified Market Research[260] has stated that the market revenue for Causal AI software in 2024 was $11.77 million and will grow to ~$256.73 million by 2031. This equates to a Compound Annual Growth Rate (CAGR) of 47.1% from 2024 to 2031,[261] which is an impressive growth rate if it is realized.

The market research and media company, siliconANGLE, covers the Causal AI market; their primary analyst is Scott Hebner.[262] In Mr. Hebner's

---

260 Verified Market Research, https://www.verifiedmarketresearch.com/, Cited November 4, 2024.

261 Causal AI Market By Application (Service, Supply Chain Optimization, Marketing & Sales Optimization), Vertical (Healthcare, BFSI, Manufacturing, Retail & E-commerce, Transportation, Automotive), & Region for 2024-2031, https://www.verifiedmarketresearch.com/product/causal-ai-market/, Cited November 4, 2024.

262 Scott Hebner, https://thecuberesearch.com/analysts/scott-hebner/, Cited November 4, 2024.

most recent report, The Causal AI Marketplace, it has been stated that, "The consensus view of six independent market studies complied by theCube Research indicates a projected 41% compound annual growth rate through 2030 to around a $1 billion marketplace."[263] This forecast combines what theCube Research team refers to as Decision Intelligence and Causal AI.

"A survey of 400 senior AI professionals provided by Databricks Inc. showed that among AI pioneering companies, 56% were already using or experimenting with Causal AI. In addition, among the total population of the survey, Causal AI was ranked as the No. 1 AI technology "not using, but plan to next year." The study reported that 16% are actively using causal methods, 33% are in the experimental stage, and 25% plan to adopt. Overall, seven in 10 will adopt Causal AI techniques by 2026."[264]

"The global causal AI market was valued at USD 18.45 million in 2022 and is expected to grow at a CAGR of 40.3% during the forecast period. The global causal AI market size is expected to reach USD 543.73 million by 2032, according to a new study by Polaris Market Research."[265]

Even with the few current data points that could be found and cited, it is clear that Causal AI is of keen interest to the technologists working in enterprise-class organizations, and they are ready to begin experimenting with Causal AI in search of the next source of competitive advantage. I am

---

263 Scott Hebner, theCube, siliconANGLE, The Causal AI Marketplace, October 4, 2024, https://siliconangle.com/2024/10/06/welcome-causal-ai-marketplace/#:~:text=Furthermore%2C%20Gartner%20believes%20that%20the,AI%20in%20future%20AI%20systems, Cited November 4, 2024.

264 Ibid., Cited November 4, 2024.

265 Polaris Market Research Team, July 2023, Causal AI Market Share, Size, Trends, Industry Analysis Report, By Offering (Platform, Cloud, On-premises, Services); By Vertical; By Region; Segment Forecast, 2023—2032, https://www.polarismarketresearch.com/press-releases/causal-ai-market, Cited November 5, 2024.

eager to see when pundits and analysts like Gartner and researchers like the World Economic Forum will turn their attention to Causal AI to update their economic estimates and forecasts for the global economic impact of Causal AI.

Let's move from the broader economy to a look at the impact of Causal AI on specific jobs and roles.

Jobs

Contrasting the impact on jobs from GenAI, Causal AI will be different. Causal AI's impact on jobs will look and feel more like the impact Foundational AI has had on jobs. One of the confounding factors in gaining a clear picture of how Foundational AI impacted roles and jobs is that Foundational AI evolved into a widespread market force over 70 years. It is difficult to understand the impact on jobs specifically, and it is only derived from and attributed to Foundational AI over that duration of time. Hence, we will not look at the micro-level impact on roles but the macro impact on jobs.

Causal AI's impact will benefit from two factors independently established by the two previous eras and pillars of AI: first is the widespread skill development in the data science community and awareness in the business community created by Foundational AI, and second is from the ease-of-use approach provided by GenAI and now expected in the general populace.

Let's examine the jobs landscape that exists at the time of the emergence of Causal AI. The workforce that will engage with and leverage Causal AI in their daily work is predominately and primarily the data science community. Tom Davenport and DJ Patil proclaimed in 2012 that data science was the sexiest job in the 21st century.[266] That article kicked off a surge of interest in data science, and while it may have closed some of the employment gaps, there are still many more data science openings than data scientists.

The US Bureau of Labor Statistics indicates that "The median annual wage for data scientists was $108,020 in May 2023. Employment of data scientists is projected to grow 36 percent from 2023 to 2033, much faster than the average for all occupations, and about 20,800 openings (in the US) for data scientists are projected each year, on average, over the decade."[267]

The World Economic Forum findings reinforce the message that AI and data science jobs will continue to grow faster than the market: "The fastest-growing roles relative to their size today are driven by technology, digitalization and sustainability. The majority of the fastest growing roles are technology-related roles. AI and Machine Learning Specialists top the list of fast-growing jobs..."[268]

Data scientists, Machine Learning Engineers, Data Engineers, and personnel in related areas are the people who have the technical training, aptitude, and conceptual understanding that will enable them to leverage and use Causal AI to the fullest and in the appropriate settings with the

---

[266] Tom Davenport, DJ Patil, October 2012, Data Scientist: The Sexiest Job of the 21st Century, Harvard Business Review, https://hbr.org/2012/10/data-scientist-the-sexiest-job-of-the-21st-century, Cited November 5, 2024.

[267] US Department of Labor, U.S. Bureau of Labor Statistics, Occupational Outlook Handbook, Data Scientists, https://www.bls.gov/ooh/math/data-scientists.htm, Cited November 5, 2024.

[268] World Economic Forum, April 30, 2023, The Future of Jobs Report 2023, https://www.weforum.org/publications/the-future-of-jobs-report-2023/digest/#:~:text=The%20majority%20of%20the%20fastest,Analysts%20and%20Information%20Security%20Analysts, Cited November 5, 2024.

correct data sets. Causal AI, as delivered and available as commercial and open-source software in 2025, requires highly skilled data scientists.

The arrival of Causal AI will provide a wider range of opportunities for data scientists to work on business problems across all areas of the enterprise. In addition to broadening the areas of application and appeal of AI, Causal AI will also drive the need for additional data scientists, exacerbating the existing shortage of data scientists. That is not great, but I believe that Causal AI will draw more people into the fields of analytics and data science. Causal AI will drive two employment-related effects in the market—data scientists will have more work to do, and more data scientists will be needed.

Turning our attention to the ease of use provided by GenAI. The development of the conversational user interface (CUI) deployed widely in GenAI will also have an impact on Causal AI. While CUIs have not been deployed as a front end to Causal AI, it is only a matter of months or possibly a year before we see Causal AI environments being managed through a CUI. This improvement in the ease of use of Causal AI will enable business analysts and other related roles to begin to engage with Causal AI systems.

The bottom-line impact of Causal AI on jobs is that we will see an increased need for data scientists, AI and ML engineers, business analysts, and other jobs that involve analyzing data and producing insights and intelligence.

Up to this point in time, data scientists and business analysts have been focused on predicting the *how* of business objectives and processes. How many people will arrive at an event? How much will people spend on this product? With GenAI, we have added the *what* to our ability to expand the information we have to understand business outcomes and objectives. What is the most attractive banner ad we can place? What is the optimal language for this proposal? And now, with the addition of Causal AI to our toolkit, we can add the ability to understand the *why* of the situations we seek to analyze, understand, and influence. Why do people respond better to this price? Why does this dosage of this drug work best for these types of patients?

Now, with Causal AI, we have it all: the why, the how, and the what. Let's move on to discuss the impact of Causal AI on the field of technology, specifically software.

Technology

Causal AI is an emerging category of software, and it is relatively new to the world in general and completely new to the commercial world. That is why when you search for the economic impact of Causal AI, the majority of what you find is early-stage research outlining a small but fast-growing market.

For additional validation of the early-stage nature of Causal AI, you can refer to the Gartner Hype Cycle for Artificial Intelligence.[269] Figure 27 is the Gartner Hype Cycle for AI from 2023. As you can see from Figure 27, the Gartner team has included Causal AI as the fifth entry on the chart in the Innovation Trigger area of the graph, and they have estimated that the realization of the widespread use of Causal AI is two to five years from 2023. I agree with their positioning of Causal AI in the market and their timing estimates.

---

[269] Gartner, August 17, 2023, Hype Cycle Artificial Intelligence, 2023, What's New in Artificial Intelligence from the 2023 Gartner Hype Cycle, https://www.gartner.com/en/articles/what-s-new-in-artificial-intelligence-from-the-2023-gartner-hype-cycle, Cited November 10, 2024.

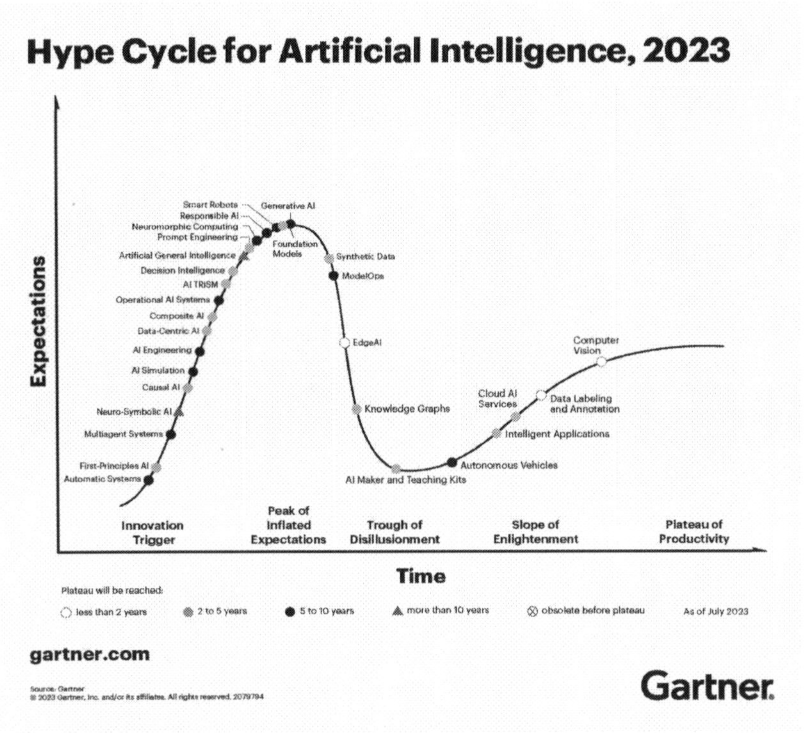

Figure 27: Gartner Hype Cycle for Artificial Intelligence, 2023.

The impacts that we see in the area of technology are related to the improvements in the foundational capability of building accurate and reliable causal models, making causal models accessible to broader audiences, codifying the causal process into software, and ingesting and managing data for causal models in an understandable manner for audiences like data scientists.

Causal AI provides the world with the final piece of software and technology needed for the reliable and consistent development of Composite AI. All the pieces of the software and technology landscape are now known to us. We can develop the additional elements required to see the true path to AGI from these building blocks.

From math to models

Causal AI is the most complicated AI technology to move from the R&D laboratory to the market in recent years. I am sure this previous sentence will generate some debate, but I am prepared to have that conversation. I believe most people espousing the opposing position will advocate for GenAI to be more complicated than Causal AI; this is simply not true, at least in my opinion.

GenAI is an extension of neural networks, not an entirely new technology. As I have said numerous times before, the success of GenAI is predominantly due to the ability to drive massive amounts of data into a neural network. The success of GenAI is a function of scale, not radically different technological innovation. I agree that there is innovation in the GenAI area and technology, but those innovations are evolutionary, not revolutionary. Many of the innovations in the area of GenAI are applications of algorithms, search, and information retrieval techniques that have been available for decades. Again, this is innovation, but on a revolutionary scale.

Judea Pearl has been one of the driving forces in creating the math that composes the majority of the innovations in Causal AI over the past few decades. His design and implementation of doCalculus[270] is the foundation of most of the Causal AI approaches seen worldwide in R&D work, academic efforts, and all early-stage commercial offerings.

We owe a great debt of gratitude to Dr. Pearl for his tireless work driving Causal AI forward. Now that the innovations from Dr. Pearl and his contemporaries are well established, proven, understood, and are being

---

[270] Judea Pearl, August 2020, THE FOUNDATIONS OF CAUSAL INFERENCE, https://ftp.cs.ucla.edu/pub/stat_ser/r355-corrected-reprint.pdf, Cited November 10, 2024.

incorporated into software products on a broad scale, we are beginning to see additional layers of innovation in the Causal AI field.

Making causal AI accessible

The next two technological innovations are due to entrepreneurs and technologists who believe that Causal AI should be part of our everyday data science toolkit for building analytics and AI applications.

The first is making causal models accessible to broader audiences. As noted earlier in our discussion, creating reliable and accurate causal pairs has been challenging for data scientists and analysts. Discovering and understanding causal pairs is part of the process commonly referred to as Causal Discovery.[271] "Causal discovery is the process of inferring causal relationships between variables from observational data. The goal of causal discovery is to find a set of causal relationships that are consistent with the data."[272]

[271] Alessio Zanga, Fabio Stella, May 17, 2023, A Survey on Causal Discovery: Theory and Practice, https://arxiv.org/pdf/2305.10032#:~:text=Causal%20discovery%20is%20a%20branch,and%20estimation%20of%20causal%20effects, Cited November 14, 2024.

[272] Tomas Geffner, Javier Antoran, Adam Foster, Wenbo Gong, Chao Ma, Emre Kiciman, Amit Sharma, Angus Lamb, Martin Kukla, Nick Pawlowski, Miltiadis Allamanis, Cheng Zhang, February 4, 2022, Deep End-to-end Causal Inference, (or arXiv:2202.02195v2 [stat.ML] for this version), https://doi.org/10.48550/arXiv.2202.02195, Cited November 14, 2024.

Software from companies like Causalens[273] and Geminos[274] has moved the market in the right direction, but the real driver in this area is GenAI. We will see the integration of GenAI and Causal AI in the coming months. That development will drive the ability or a wider range of analytics professionals to complete this crucial step confidently and accurately.

Also, creating Directed Acyclic Graphs (DAGs) and Structured Causal Models (SCMs) that include more than a handful of causal factors is very hard for data scientists and analysts to do with an acceptable level of accuracy and reliability. Building verifiable and stable DAGs and SCMs in manual mode is beyond the capability of most of the analytics professionals in the market today. Innovations from early-stage commercial software vendors are required for Causal AI to have the level of transparency, reliability, and accuracy needed for Causal AI to be used in commercial settings. Enterprise organizations will not even consider using Causal AI in their operations without the support of early-stage software companies and associated professional services firms.

The second is codifying the causal process into software. As we have noted, Causal AI is an early-stage technology. The process of collecting, cleaning, structuring, modeling, analyzing, and recommending actions to business professionals with Causal AI is well known in the academic and R&D worlds, and in the small software vendors that are building Causal AI software. This knowledge must be disseminated broadly to data scientists and analysts in enterprise-class commercial organizations. This knowledge transfer happens market-wide when early-stage commercial software is evaluated, purchased, and implemented. This process is underway today.

---

273 Causlens, https://causalens.com/, Cited November 10, 2024.

274 Geminos, https://www.geminos.ai/, Cited November 10, 2024.

We have reached the early stages where the commercial software offerings provide the needed levels of assured performance, accuracy, and ease of use in operations for commercial enterprises to begin to experiment with Causal AI.

Data for causal

The final immediate technological hurdle related to data needs to be cleared. Analytics and AI professionals know that if we cannot provide tools that are easy to use for all the data-related tasks for each and every AI application that organizations want to build and leverage to gain a competitive advantage, then all of this is for naught. Adoption will be stalled, and we will not see widespread value realization.

One of the most promising aspects of the world of data related to Causal AI is the wealth of data collected in Randomized Controlled Trials (RCTs).[275] RCTs are used in many fields and are considered the gold standard when attempting to understand causal effects in a population. Most people commonly refer to RCTs as A/B tests.[276] In health care, RCTs are the most widely used in the field of health care and provide a wealth of data that can be used over time. There have been developments in academia and R&D

---

[275] Eduardo Hariton, Joseph J Locascio, National Library of Medicine, December 1, 2018, Randomized controlled trials—the gold standard for effectiveness research, PMCID: PMC6235704 NIHMSID: NIHMS966617 PMID: 29916205, https://pmc.ncbi.nlm.nih.gov/articles/PMC6235704/#:~:text=Randomized%20controlled%20trials%20(RCT)%20are,between%20an%20intervention%20and%20outcome, Cited November 14, 2024.

[276] Amy Gallo, Analytics and data science, A Refresher on A/B Testing. Harvard Business Review, June 28, 2017, https://hbr.org/2017/06/a-refresher-on-ab-testing, Cited November 14, 2024.

that offer frameworks where authors of RCTs can build those instruments and projects in a way that produces data that is ready for subsequent use in causal projects. Recently, a team built and released such a framework. The authors described their intentions in this way, "... causal inference using observational data poses numerous challenges, and relevant methodological literature is vast. We endeavored to identify underlying unifying themes of causal inference using real-world healthcare data and connect them into a single schema to aid in observational study design..."[277]

One of the primary objectives of offering this type of framework is that if authors of future studies leverage the framework, then the data that they collect can more easily be incorporated into future causal projects and studies. Data being reused and studies being cited widely is a motivating factor for academics and researchers.

The concept that I find exciting is that any data scientist can look across the body of observational study data that has been collected over the history of the world and examine and condition the data and use that data in a new analytical project. This means that the data available to data scientists for causal inference is not exactly infinite, but much more expansive than previously thought. Imagine being able to use data from the complete history of the world in your analytical projects; now that is a titillating thought.

We have seen the conceptual and practical foundations of processing data for Causal AI move from R&D and academia to start-ups. We are now seeing enterprises experimenting with emerging software to build

---

[277] Hoffman, S.R., Gangan, N., Chen, X. et al. A step-by-step guide to causal study design using real-world data. Health Serv Outcomes Res Method (2024). https://doi.org/10.1007/s10742-024-00333-6.

repeatable processes for collecting, ingesting, cleaning, structuring, modeling, analyzing, and recommending actions for business professionals.

Summary

The impact of Causal AI is unique, targeted, and at the same time, it will be ubiquitous and general. That sounds contradictory, and at a universal level, it is, but at the micro level, it is not. I will explain.

Let's start with the general impact. Causal AI will be a game-changing development when it is widely deployed and leveraged. Just as Foundational AI and GenAI are widely used, so will Causal AI. The impact of Causal AI on the AI market in general will alter the direction, trajectory, and value of AI. Causal AI will make understanding human behavior, option selection, and intervention in all endeavors, from healthcare to manufacturing to marketing, more scientific and data-driven. Causal AI will enable all people in all fields to have a more precise understanding of why they should make and execute certain discrete choices; that is a game-changing development. Hence, the impact of Causal AI will be ubiquitous and general. In a specific sense, Causal AI will bring about a dramatic change in how analytics and AI projects are structured, executed, and put into production.

With GenAI, we have the what of a project, with Foundational AI, we have the how, and with Causal AI, we have the why, which completes our trifecta of prediction and knowledge surrounding the subject area we are attempting to analyze, understand, and impact. GenAI expanded our ability to move beyond structured information to encompass all unstructured information. Causal AI has expanded our reach even further. With Causal AI, we can bring together data collected over the years for related purposes. "Causal inference is the process of using statistical and computational techniques, experimental, mixed or observational data, and logical reasoning to quantify the strength of causal effects. It aims to determine causal relationships and effects between variables."[278]

As we move to the future of Causal AI, the impact will be felt beyond the field of AI. Causal AI, in the opinion of many academics, researchers, and technologists, is an added capability that will enable all people to benefit either directly or indirectly. We will discuss this more in the next chapter, in which we will discuss the future of Causal AI.

Let's move on to the next chapter and begin our examination and discussion of the future of Causal AI.

---

[278] Abraham Itzhak Weinberg, Cristiano Premebida, Diego Resende Faria, March 17, 2024, Causality from Bottom to Top: A Survey, License: CC BY-SA 4.0, arXiv:2403.11219v1, Cited November 6, 2024.

Chapter 10

The Future of Causal AI

The future of Causal AI is very bright, exciting, and moving in a positive direction. This movement is centered squarely on the shoulders of academics, young researchers, and data scientists.

When I talk about Causal AI with data scientists and analytics professionals in their 40s and 50s, I get knowing looks and maybe gently nodding heads, but little to no engagement in the conversation. When I listen to data scientists and developers in their 30s about Causal AI, I get a few remarks and scattered comments tinged with vague interest. When I talk with data scientists, ML Engineers, PhD candidates, and developers in their 20s about Causal AI, my questions and remarks are met with excited engagement about what is possible today and the future of data, AI, and AGI.

I am open to whatever is next in AI, but it seems to me that with the emerging commercial use of Causal AI, we have all the tools we need to build Composite AI and begin the journey toward AGI in earnest.

Faint rhyming of history

We have seen this dynamic in the past. About ten years ago, it was quite clear that if you were a data scientist in your 40s and 50s, your tool of choice would be proprietary software from SAS, SPSS, or Statistica. If you were in your 30s, your tool of choice was the R programming language. If you were in your 20s, you were using this new language called Python. The interesting observation that is repeating itself is that ten years ago, if you asked a SAS programmer about Python, they either had no idea what you were talking about or they scoffed and said that it was a fad that would quickly pass.

The age brackets hold steady today and the same is true for Causal AI. If you ask a data scientist who is in their 40s or 50s where they are using Causal AI in their daily work or if they are experimenting with or exploring Causal AI, they will say that it is not a tool for serious work or that it will never be a tool in their toolbox for commercial work.

I love to see patterns that repeat over time. I am always eager to see the certainty that people who are later in their careers maintain about new technology and how generally disdainful they are of new tools; it just keeps happening, over and over again. Let's be clear and ensure that our toolbox has all the tools we need to do the best work we can; Causal AI is here to stay.

If you are a data scientist of any age and actively working on your own projects in a start-up or enterprise-class company, grab an open-source tool or a free trial of a commercial Causal AI tool and begin experimenting. Now is the time to gain a competitive edge over your peers who do not see or do not believe in the value of Causal AI.

I was in a recent meeting; multiple people had entered comments in the chat function asking when we would be in a post-AI future. I did not add the following thought into the thread, but their view of a post-AI future indicates that they see AI as being a passing phase and that we will see a future after and without AI. This is a fallacy. This is either sloppy or wishful thinking or fear.

There is a significant minority of the people I work with and talk with who believe that AI is a fad; they have a moment of awakening coming to them at some point in the coming years. There is no future where AI is not an active element in our world. AI may not be as prominent in the news as it has been over the past two years (e.g., 2022-2024), but AI will be a significant portion of our technology environment, application portfolio, and everyday future.

There is no-post AI future, just an ever-increasing use of AI in the future.

Causal AI vendor landscape

One indication that a new technology and sector are about to emerge into the enterprise software market is the velocity and frequency of early-stage market research firms writing research reports on the size, growth, and potential of the field of young companies involved in the nascent market. Many of the footnotes supporting Table 4 were written at the same time as the writing of this book. It is clear from this early-stage interest from market research firms that the Causal AI technology vendor market is expanding. Another indication that a market is about to emerge is when you see the list of the key players in the market, and the list is a mix of very young startups that may not have even raised a seed round of funding combined with very large enterprise-class organizations. When you review Table 4, you will see exactly this dynamic.

Many of these young companies barely have a website, and they are listed with the likes of Google, AWS, and IBM. The Causal AI market is about to enter a rapid growth phase. We will see additional startups enter the fray, but not too many additional large companies will probably jump into the market. The large companies interested in using Causal AI to drive competitive advantage are already involved.

Many of the emerging companies entering the Causal AI market have a vertical market focus on their product or in their go-to-market activities such as sales and marketing. Healthcare is a popular vertical market to address. Historically, many of the use cases and applications of Causal AI have been documented and discussed in the healthcare area; the appeal is clear. To model and understand cause and effect relationships of treatment options, drug dosage, and efficacy of combinations of drugs, enabling additional and unlimited iterations of model-based testing is more safely executed in a computational model than experimenting with real people where actual harm could be inflicted.

Some of the earliest work that has evolved into what we now know as Causal AI was focused on biology and healthcare. "In 1921 [Sewell] Wright's path analysis became the theoretical ancestor of causal modeling and causal graphs. He developed this approach while attempting to untangle the relative impacts of heredity, development and environment on guinea pig coat patterns. He backed up his then-heretical claims by showing how such analyses could explain the relationship between guinea pig birth weight, in utero time and litter size. Wright's findings in biology eventually led to healthcare professionals and analysts seeing the value of causal modeling to further their understanding of cause-and-effect relationships in humans, animals, plants, the climate, and more.

Aitia (formerly GNS Healthcare)	Amazon Web Services (AWS)
Amelia.ai	Causaly
Causely	Causality Link
CausaLens	Cognino.Ai
Dynatrace	Geminos
Glencoe Software	Google
Howso	IBM Corp
Incremental	Insitro
Impact Genome	Judg.ai
Logility	Meta - Facebook
Microsoft Corp	Nebula Labs
Omnics Data Automation	Oracle
Oridion Systems	SAP
Sisu	Scalnyx
Unlearn.ai	Xplain Data

Table 4: Causal AI Market: Vendors.[279] [280] [281] [282] [283]

279 Research team, Dimensional Market Research, November 2023, Causal AI Market By Offering (Platform, Services), By End User - Global Industry Outlook, Key Companies (IBM, AWS, Microsoft, and others), Trends and Forecast 2023-2032, https://dimensionmarketresearch.com/report/causal-ai-market/, Cited November 16, 2024.

280 Anshika Mathews, October 8, 2024, AIM Research, How Causal AI is Unlocking the Secrets Behind 'Why'—And the Companies Already on Top of It, https://aimresearch.co/ai-startups/how-causal-ai-is-unlocking-the-secrets-behind-why-and-the-companies-already-on-top-of-it, Cited on November 16, 2024.

281 Research team, Markets and Markets, Causal AI Market, May 2023, https://www.marketsandmarkets.com/Market-Reports/causal-ai-market-162494083.html, Cited November 16, 2024.

282 Research team, July 2024, Causal AI Market Size - By Offering (Platform [Deployment {Cloud, On-premise}], Services [Consulting, Deployment & Integration, Training, Support and Maintenance]), By Application, By End-user Industry & Forecast, 2024—2032, Global Market Insights, https://www.gminsights.com/industry-analysis/causal-ai-market, Cited November 16, 2024.

283 Garvit Vyas, Causal AI Market Research Report: By Type (Software, Services), By Application (Natural Language Processing, Computer Vision, Speech Recognition,

Opposition to these ideas by prominent statisticians led them to be ignored for the following 40 years."[284]

Let's get back to the current day and the emergence of technology vendors offering us modern tools for engaging in the process of executing causal analyses.

One of the value-added benefits of the emerging vendors is that they drive the process of codifying the causal process. Given the early-stage nature of Causal AI, enterprise-class organizations and their technical staff are seeking all the help and benefits that vendors can offer. Guiding those technical leaders through the causal process is a valuable addition to any offering.

There are approximately 50 early-stage vendors offering Causal AI toolkits, utilities, workbenches, and entire systems. Let's move on to see who is adopting and using these new tools.

Adoption

As we have discussed, Causal AI applies to a wide range of use cases and processes. You will notice that the firms included as being engaged with Causal AI technology include technology providers, retailers,

Machine Learning Operations), By Deployment Mode (Cloud, On-Premises, Hybrid), By Industry Vertical (Healthcare, Financial Services, Manufacturing, Retail) and By Regional (North America, Europe, South America, Asia-Pacific, Middle East and Africa) - Forecast to 2032, November 2024, https://www.marketresearchfuture.com/reports/causal-ai-market-23706, Cited November 16, 2024.

[284] Okasha, Samir (2012-01-12). "Causation in Biology". In Beebee, Helen; Hitchcock, Christopher; Menzies, Peter (eds.). The Oxford Handbook of Causation. Vol. 1. OUP Oxford. doi:10.1093/oxfordhb/9780199279739.001.0001. ISBN 9780191629464.

pharmaceutical firms, hardware manufacturers, telephone networks, Big 4 Consulting firms, travel websites, farm equipment manufacturers, insurance companies, oil and gas companies, and more. The organizations listed are not from one or two geographic regions; the companies are from widely distributed regions and countries. Causal AI is a global phenomenon that will drive benefits across the board for all industries. As cause and effect are everywhere, so will Causal AI software, systems, processes, and technology.

Japan has played a unique role in adopting certain technologies before all other countries. For example, Japan embraced W. Edwards Demming[285] and his philosophy and canon of quality before all others.

"While working under Gen. Douglas MacArthur as a census consultant to the Japanese government, he was asked to teach a short seminar on statistical process control (SPC) methods to members of the Radio Corps. During this visit, he was contacted by the Union of Japanese Scientists and Engineers (JUSE) to talk directly to Japanese business leaders, not about SPC, but about his theories of management, returning to Japan for many years to consult... Demming's teachings and philosophy are clearly illustrated by examining the results they produced after they were adopted by Japanese industry..."[286]Japanese commercial leaders were thinking about and beginning to design for quality in the late 1940s. The

---

[285] Google Search, Demming, https://www.google.com/search?gs_ssp=eJzj4tDP1TfIskgrMWD04k1NKU8sSlFISc3NzEsHAGF2CB0&q=edward+deming&rlz=1C1RXQR_enUS1041US1041&oq=&gs_lcrp=EgZjaHJvbWUqCQgBEC4YJxjqAjIJCAAQIxgnGOoCMgkIARAuGCcY6gIyCQgCECMYJxjqAjIJCAMQIxgnGOoCMgkIBBAjGCcY6gIyCQgFECMYJxjqAjIJCAYQIxgnGOoCMgkIBxAjGCcY6gLSAQkxMzAyajBqMTWoAgiwAgE&sourceid=chrome&ie=UTF-8#cobssid=s, Cited November 21, 2024.

[286] From the contributors to Wikipedia, W. Edwards Demming, https://en.wikipedia.org/wiki/W._Edwards_Deming, Cited on November 21, 2024.

commitment to quality would not spread to the US and Western manufacturers for 30 to 40 years.

With Causal AI, Japanese commercial firms are well ahead of the rest of the world. Japanese commercial firms are adopting Causal AI at a faster rate than their peers around the globe. Market research shows that Japanese firms are applying Causal AI in the following areas:

- **Healthcare Predictive Analytics:** Utilizing causal AI to forecast patient outcomes and treatment responses. Clinical Decision Support: Enhancing decision-making processes through causal inference models. Operational Efficiency: Streamlining hospital operations and resource allocation.

- **Finance Risk Management:** Identifying and mitigating financial risks using causal models. Fraud Detection: Detecting fraudulent activities through causal relationship analysis. Investment Strategies: Informing investment decisions with causal insights on market trends.

- **Retail Customer Behavior Analysis:** Understanding purchasing patterns and preferences using causal AI. Supply Chain Optimization: Improving inventory management through causal forecasting. Marketing Effectiveness: Evaluating the impact of marketing campaigns on sales and customer engagement.

- **Manufacturing Quality Control:** Using causal analysis to identify factors affecting product quality. Predictive Maintenance: Anticipating equipment failures and optimizing maintenance schedules. Process Improvement: Enhancing production processes through causal insights.

- **Telecommunications Network Optimization:** Improving service quality by analyzing causal relationships in network performance. Customer Retention: Understanding factors influencing customer churn and implementing retention strategies. Service Development: Guiding the development of new services based on causal customer insights.[287]

These findings confirm what we see across the world. Causal AI has widespread appeal and application. As noted in Chapter 9 in the research by Gartner, Polaris, Verified Market Research, siliconANGLE, and others, the growth rate of adoption of Causal AI software and tools will range between 35% to 43% CAGR over the next ten years. This fast-growing segment will be a significant portion of the overall AI market.

One perspective to keep in mind about using Causal AI is that if you are seeking to understand how to intervene in a process and are working to determine how to improve the process or change the speed or momentum of a process either to accelerate it or slow it down, Causal AI is a good place to begin the analytical process. One of the primary value streams offered by Causal AI is to determine the optimal variables and the settings for those variables when intervening in a process.

I was attending the CAI24 event[288] in London. One of the speakers was presenting a case study where a manufacturer of baked goods started their day by throwing away about an hour's worth of production each day before

---

[287] Digest Trend Pro on Linkedin, September 2024, Japan Causal AI Market By Application, https://www.linkedin.com/pulse/japan-causal-ai-market-application-digest-trend-pro-d3jde/, Cited on November 21, 2024. Respost from Verified Market Research, https://www.verifiedmarketresearch.com/download-sample/?rid=338598&utm_source=Japan&utm_medium=057.

[288] Causal AI Conference, CAI24, https://conference.causalens.com/, Cited November 23, 2024.

all the relevant and critical production line settings were set to the correct level for the specific conditions of that morning and held at a steady state that resulted in the individual items being of the proper color, texture, and consistency needed to be acceptable for packaging and sale. I believe the speaker said that this setup process costs around half a million dollars daily, which is an incredible amount of waste. Given that external variables like heat and humidity and many internal variables came into consideration, it was deemed normal that an amount of experimentation was needed each day to arrive at the correct parameters for the daily run to begin to produce high-quality baked goods.

The manufacturer and the Causal AI vendor built an application that ingested and analyzed all the current and relevant variables and provided a suggested optimal setting for each variable every morning. The result was to cut the waste by 25 to 50% on the daily set up time, an impressive result.

Let's move on to discuss the future of Causal AI technology.

Technology

Causal AI technology is coming onto the market solely in the form of software. We do not see a hardware offering or an offering that combines hardware and software for Causal AI systems. Given that the new Causal AI offerings are in the form of software, it is not surprising to see that the common go-to-market approaches for software dominate how we see Causal AI entering the commercial market. There are a number of approaches to providing new software for the enterprise market in the area of Causal AI. None of these approaches are unique to the Causal AI market.

The following approaches are being leveraged by the start-ups and enterprise commercial software vendors—wrapping services and support offerings around popular open-source utilities and libraries, providing services and training as generalized offerings focused on Causal AI concepts and processes, packaging open-source utilities and libraries into process models that make leveraging those tools easier to understand, redeveloping core concepts and principles into more scalable and reliable offerings in a proprietary form, and developing new software from scratch into a complete Causal AI system. The roughly 50 active vendors employ all these approaches in developing their offerings, and a subset of them employ multiple approaches.

One of the current and common challenges faced in the Causal AI market is finding and developing scalable software that operates reliably at an enterprise level. "It is common to find mature software and engineering systems for an experimentation platform (Fabijan et al. 2017, Kohavi et al. 2013, Deng, Lu, and Litz 2017, Diamantopoulos et al. 2019). However, it is much less common to find mature software for statistics and causal inference that integrates into such systems. One of the main challenges is the lack of software dedicated to estimating causal effects that scales well. For example, policy algorithms train models over high dimensional feature sets, then use them to evaluate several actions and counterfactuals for different combinations of features, a task that demands a computationally efficient engine. The lack of performant software for such a daunting task creates engineering risk, as well as slow and challenging iteration cycles."[289]

Addressing overall system scalability is always something that analytics offerings must surmount after emerging from the research lab. The Causal AI software market is working through that challenge today.

---

[289] Jeffrey C. Wong, Computational Causal Inference, Netflix, July 21, 2020, https://arxiv.org/pdf/2007.10979, Cited November 2, 2024.

Another challenge for analytics software and many other systems is that it is a primary challenge for analytics software to achieve its full potential, effectively ingest and efficiently utilize large numbers of variables simultaneously. We need Causal AI to analyze variables effectively at a near-human level to achieve our short- and long-term goals.

"With the growing interest in natural experiments in statistics and causal machine learning (CML) across many fields, such as healthcare, economics, and business, there is a large potential opportunity to run AI models on CE [causal economics] foundations and compare results to models based on traditional decision-making models that focus only on rationality, bounded to various degrees. To be most effective, machine learning must mirror human reasoning as closely as possible, an alignment established through CEML [causal economic machine learning], which represents an evolution to truly 'human AI'."[290]

The challenge of the software considering and using a massive number of variables concurrently is the hurdle we must clear if AI and analytics technologies are to take us forward toward AGI.

I have noted previously the number of systems I have put into production (over 100) and mentioned the number of industries I have worked in (over 20) in my nearly 40 years of building analytics and AI systems. The subset of systems that have been considered radically successful (around 15) has all ingested and used what was, at the time, considered to be an impractical and, in some cases, impossible number of data sources and variables. We need to take this to the next level.

One of the key long-term challenges of AI and analytical systems is to begin to ingest and use the number of internal and external variables that humans

---

[290] Andrew Horton, October 11, 2024Causal Economic Machine Learning (CEML): "Human AI", https://www.mdpi.com/2673-2688/5/4/94, Cited November 2, 2024.

use in everyday decision-making, innately and naturally. Success in this area will not ensure our journey to AGI will be successful, but if we do not solve this problem, it will certainly stunt, suppress, or stop our progress toward AGI.

As of the writing of this book, the best Causal AI system can ingest approximately ten to 20 variables, be commercially viable with acceptable execution times, and produce accurate results. This is nowhere near what we need for AGI. We need the software to ingest and leverage hundreds and possibly thousands of variables. We have work to do.

Summary

We have examined the Causal AI, the least well-known pillar of the AI field, and the era of AI that is emerging today.

Causal AI is a very exciting field of study and endeavor. It will bring an entirely new perspective to the AI market and field, a perspective driven by the ability to predict why people do what they do and why processes transpire as they do. Casual AI will enable the design of positive interventions in all fields of study.

Causal AI has been proven effective in understanding the "why" element of decision-making and decision science. Causal AI has not completely emerged as a full-fledged member of the AI family, but it will in the next three to five years.

Our many thanks and gratitude are extended to Judea Pearl and his colleagues and contemporaries for their diligence and drive toward innovating, designing, and delivering on a new pillar of AI. Innovation of this ingenuity and scale does not happen very often, and we are lucky to have been able to see and experience this innovation happen firsthand and to utilize delivery of the final element in the AI field needed to provide a clear path to AGI.

The value of Causal AI in unlocking the value of previously collected data from around the world in numerous fields cannot be understated. Causal AI is providing data scientists with the tools to bring together untold amounts of existing data to understand our world in an unprecedented manner.

The stage is set. We have Foundational AI, GenAI, and now Causal AI. We have what we need to set the landscape and direction. We do not have all we need to realize AGI, but we have enough to start our next phase of evolution with gusto and energy.

Let's move on to our final section and chapter, where we will discuss the pragmatic and real path to AGI.

CHAPTER 11

The Future of AI, The Path to AGI

It is an exciting time to be involved in the field of data, analytics, and AI. In my opinion, when considering the long arc of development, the field of AI will remain exciting relative to the primary research and development agendas needed to sustain and move the field forward. Interest across all the subject areas that are now in active development, as well as areas of focus like GenAI, Foundational AI, and Causal AI, will sustain investment and interest. They will continue to see innovations and improvements for the next 100 to 250 years.

Interest, investment, and innovation in these areas will ebb and flow, but the overall effort in developing intelligence will continue to pique the interest of the human race for positive and negative purposes for as long as we can foresee.

How can I make such a long-term projection or prediction with confidence? Looking back, the human race has been intrigued with the development of intelligence to mimic human capacities since the 3rd century BCE. "An engineer named Yan Shi who created a life-size, human-like robot for the fifth king of the Chinese Zhou Dynasty, King Mu."[291] Given the interest in AI over the known millennia, I do not see interest waning any time soon. In fact, I will go further to say that interest will not only remain over the coming centuries, but it will also increase, and progress will accelerate.

Let's stay with the long-term perspective for just a moment. The aforementioned areas of AI are the subject areas that we are working on today. There are additional and adjacent subject areas that we have not begun to address in any substantial manner. For instance, many people are discussing AI and the future of intelligence. What are we talking about? What is intelligence? We really do not have a solid, clear, and widely agreed-upon definition of intelligence. We need to define the fundamentals of where we are heading. But that is a topic for another day, discussion, and an entire book.

Moving our lens and area of interest to a shorter time horizon, when thinking about people who work in AI on a regular and sustained basis, the people who apply AI to daily situations in the enterprise and consumer spaces, the current work will remain exciting for at least the next ten to 25 years.

AI is all the rage at this point. Most companies and the executives leading those companies are directing their teams to determine "how it include or inject AI" into their products and services. While this is understandable and to be expected, this is not a well-planned or considered strategic approach. It is a knee-jerk reaction. Nonetheless, data scientists, ML Engineers, and related jobs will be intriguing roles to train for and undertake. The challenges the people in these roles face will be engaging and fruitful for

---

[291] Contributors to Wikipedia, Humanoid Robot, https://en.wikipedia.org/wiki/Humanoid_robot#:~:text=Crete%20from%20invaders.-,China,Chinese%20Zhou%20Dynasty%2C%20King%20Mu, Cited November 26, 2024.

those who take up the charge. If it is interesting work you or your subsequent generations seek, look no further than data, analytics, and AI.

In the short term, the pace of change will slow a bit, and the frothiness of news will subside. Still, those interested and invested in moving the practical use of and pragmatic implementation of AI forward will find their days and work quite engaging for a significant portion of any person's career. In reality, the pace of change will span the careers of multiple generations.

At present, the hype and attention have never been greater than in the previous 70 years. Stories about AI are not only in the top technology media outlets but also in the popular press. Media properties like FT, The Wall Street Journal, Ashai Shimbun, The Australian, China Daily, and The New York Times write and publish stories with AI as the central topic on the front page and nearly in every section on a daily or at least a weekly basis, for the past two years.

AI has become a hot topic, with an explosion of interest, use, and criticism of GenAI. The subjects of the future of work, job losses, upskilling, augmented intelligence, universal basic income, and Artificial General Intelligence (AGI) have become coffee table and water cooler talk subjects. In addition to the stories in the technology and popular press, there has been an impressive surge in academic and technical publishing on AI. "Between 2010 and 2022, the total number of AI publications nearly tripled, rising from approximately 88,000 in 2010 to more than 240,000 in 2022."[292]

---

[292] Nestor Maslej, Loredana Fattorini, Raymond Perrault, Vanessa Parli, Anka Reuel, Erik Brynjolfsson, John Etchemendy, Katrina Ligett, Terah Lyons, James Manyika, Juan Carlos Niebles, Yoav Shoham, Russell Wald, and Jack Clark, "The AI Index 2024 Annual Report," AI Index Steering Committee, Institute for Human-Centered AI, Stanford

When will we achieve AGI?

Everyone interested in the future of AI is excited and concerned, and they are talking, writing, presenting, and researching AI and AI-related topics. Beyond talking about GenAI and AI today, people are talking about where AI is going and where AI is taking the world. Some people are respected thinkers, gurus, scientists, pundits, business leaders, academics, futurists, and more, weighing in on the path to AGI with seemingly well-informed opinions and daring predictions.

Here are some of the predictions and prognostications from well-known commentators:

"AGI in 2025"[293] —Sam Altman

"Elon Musk expects development of an artificial intelligence smarter than the smartest of humans by 2026."[294]

University, Stanford, CA, April 2024. The AI Index 2024 Annual Report by Stanford University is licensed under Attribution-NoDerivatives 4.0 International, https://aiindex.stanford.edu/report/, Cited on November 26, 2024.

293 Interview with Gary Tan, Sam Altman Shocking Predictions: AGI Is Coming in 2025, https://www.youtube.com/watch?v=JE_RvngkYqY, Cited November 25, 2024.

294 —"Tesla's Musk predicts AI will be smarter than the smartest human next year". Reuters. April 8, 2024, https://www.reuters.com/technology/teslas-musk-predicts-ai-will-be-smarter-than-smartest-human-next-year-2024-04-08/, Cited on November 25, 2024.

"Ray Kurzweil, computer scientist, entrepreneur, and writer of five national best sellers including The Singularity Is Near: Previously 2045, in 2024: 2032."[295]

"...the results of five surveys with ~1,700 participants where researchers estimated when singularity would happen. In all cases, the majority of participants expected AI singularity before 2060."[296]

In 2012/2013, Vincent C. Muller, the president of the European Association for Cognitive Systems, and Nick Bostrom from the University of Oxford surveyed AI researchers. 550 participants answered the question, "When is AGI likely to happen?" The answers are distributed as

- 10% of participants think that AGI is likely to happen by 2022
- For 2040, the share is 50%
- 90% of participants think that AGI is likely to happen by 2075[297] [298]

Rodney Brooks, previous Panasonic Professor of Robotics at MIT and former director of the MIT Computer Science and Artificial Intelligence Laboratory (CSAIL) remarked, "...AGI would show up around 2099... In

---

295 —"If Ray Kurzweil Is Right (Again), You'll Meet His Immortal Soul in the Cloud". Wired. June 13, 2024, https://www.wired.com/story/big-interview-ray-kurzweil/, Cited November 25, 2024.

296 Cem Dilmegani, AI Multiple Research, When will singularity happen? 1700 expert opinions of AGI, https://research.aimultiple.com/artificial-general-intelligence-singularity-timing/, Cited November 25, 2024.

297 Ibid., Cited November 25, 2024.

298 Müller, Vincent C. and Bostrom, Nick, Future Progress in Artificial Intelligence: A Survey of Expert Opinion, https://nickbostrom.com/papers/survey.pdf, Cited November 25, 2024.

retrospect I wish I had said 2300 and that is the year I have been using in my recent talks."[299]

Personally, I have gone on record in multiple presentations, individual conversations, and group discussions over the past four years as describing that my view is that AGI could be achieved in 2250, but I now think that the date is more likely to be 2350. Yes, that is my prediction. We will see AGI in 226 to 326 years. We will discuss my rationale, reasoning, and view of the expected development timeline later in this chapter.

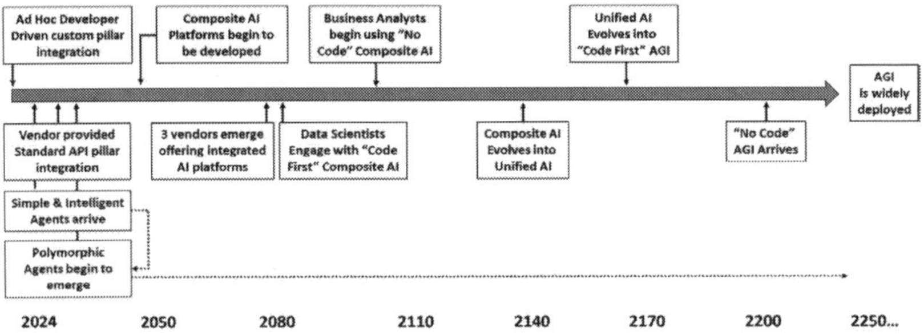

Figure 28: The Path to AGI.

I will admit that I, like many people, was slightly seduced by GenAI for a few months. I even spoke to a few people in one-on-one conversations where I publicly stated that I might consider moving my prediction for the achievement of AGI forward to 2200. Still, after further reflection, research, and review of systems, technologies, approaches, and building systems with GenAI, I will not change my view on the ability to reduce the time to reach AGI on a widespread basis. As you have just read, I actually extended the date to the future.

---

[299] Rodney Brooks, May 17, 2019 — Quick Takes, AGI Has Been Delayed, rodneybrooks.com/agi-has-been-delayed/, Cited November 25, 2024.

Sam Altman,[300] CEO of OpenAI and leading cheerleader of GenAI as the gateway to AGI, has been making aggressive claims that OpenAI will deliver AGI within the next year through GenAI technology. These claims border on nonsense. There is no technological backing for these claims, and no track record shows that GenAI from any vendor illustrates any indications of original thought or any type of independently derived intelligence. I am sure that Mr. Altman is motivated to say these things, and I will not impugn his approach, motives, or intended objectives, but I simply do not agree with his view on any level.

You can see from this small sampling of surveys, experts, and opinions that there is no popular consensus on when AI will transform into AGI. Most people agree that we are traveling in a direction that will produce AGI. We just don't agree on what AGI is or when it will be achieved.

Just small details, right?

Next, let's discuss the impact of AGI.

A possible impact of AGI

I believe that the achievement of AGI is a momentous occasion that is of significant importance to the human race and all of civilization. I do not think that our ability to create non-human intelligence is just a simple footnote in history. If we can ever achieve it, it is an *inflection point* in human history.

---

300 Contributors to Wikipedia, Sam Altman, https://en.wikipedia.org/wiki/Sam_Altman, Cited on November 25, 2024.

AGI is not a parlor trick to be treated as a marketing concept to boost the quarterly share price or the market capitalization of any singular company or all the companies in existence at this time. Once we achieve AGI, there is no going back. There is life before AGI, and then there is all of the future after AGI; that is a game changer.

Take a second to stop reading and think about that fact. Once AGI is in existence, it cannot be deleted or taken back. AGI will be with us and our descendants forever. All future generations will never know a past, present, or future without AGI.

How often can you clearly see the world change by the development and use of a single technology? Not very often. In my lifetime, we have seen sea changes in behavior due to the Internet and mobile devices; both of these innovations have been useful and have changed the world in positive and negative ways.

Just look at people going about their daily lives and how attached and glued to their mobile devices that they have become; this is not a positive change. The primary impact of mobile devices on people and their mindsets is individualistic, reasonably benign, and passive for the most part. Yes, there is a collective and societal impact of mobile devices as well, but that is not what I want to focus on at this point in our discussion. Collective impact is important, and sociologists will opine on this across many articles, blogs, and books.

In some respects, the human brain is like a muscle—we need to use it, or we lose capabilities. A small and somewhat silly example is that, in the past, I had all the telephone numbers I called on a regular basis memorized. Now, I only know my number and maybe five other telephone numbers. Why is that? I no longer dial numbers; all the telephone numbers are on my mobile device. I press a button, and the call is made. I do not repetitively dial those numbers.

Extend this to other cognitive capabilities. How many people can do mental arithmetic? A surprisingly few people can. How many people can make change from a cash transaction? Not many. The point is that what we do not practice or do regularly fades from our portfolio of abilities.

I am concerned about how mobile devices impact, and have impacted, how individuals act and interact. I only bring this up to point out how deleterious mobile devices have been to people and their ability to relate and interact with others. This effect is miniscule compared to the possible impact AGI will have on individuals and society as a whole permanently.

This idea, and the reality of permanence is one of the primary reasons why I find the flippant treatment of the topic of achieving AGI by so many executives and experts to be exasperating. I know that people want to make money and be recognized as an expert, or dare I say a genius, but this is the future of the human race that we are discussing.

Once we have AGI, there will be a wide range of cognitive skills that people will no longer be able to develop on their own, and that is not a good development that portends a broader decline in mental processing.

However, on the other side of the discussion, there will be numerous positive benefits of AGI, which we will discuss later in this chapter. I just want everyone to be aware of multiple perspectives on the possible impacts of achieving AGI. I want everyone to go into this process with their eyes wide open and be as well-informed as possible.

Let's move on and nail down what we believe AGI to be.

What is AGI?

Artificial General Intelligence is defined by the following experts in the following ways…

Sam Altman defines AGI this way. "AGI is the equivalent of a median human. That you could hire as a coworker. And they would be happy with the AGI doing anything that a remote coworker could do just behind a computer, which includes learning how to go be a doctor, or learning how to be a very competent coder. There is a lot of stuff that a median human is capable of getting good at. And I think one of the skills of an AGI is not any one particular milestone, but a meta skill of learning to figure things out and it can decide to go get good at whatever you need."[301]

Elon Musk, the CEO of Tesla, defines Artificial General Intelligence (AGI) as software that can perform any intellectual task that humans can do.[302]

Ray Kurzweil, outlines AGI as, "artificial general intelligence will be able to do anything a human can do, only better."[303] In Kurzweil's view, he refers to AGI as the "singularity" this in his definition is where machines become smarter than humans.[304]

---

301 Sam Altman Defines AGI, Greylock, April 3, 2023, https://www.youtube.com/watch?v=vd9GxG5Qn-k, Cited November 26, 2024.

302 Eric Siegel, Apr 10, 2024, Forbes.com, Elon Musk Predicts Artificial General Intelligence In two Years. Here's Why That's Hype, https://www.forbes.com/sites/ericsiegel/2024/04/10/artificial-general-intelligence-is-pure-hype/, Cited November 26, 2024.

303 Robert B. Tucker, Aug 22, 2024, Forbes.com, The Singularity Is Coming Soon. Here's What It May Mean, https://www.forbes.com/sites/robertbtucker/2024/08/22/the-singularity-is-coming-soon-heres-what-it-may-mean/, Cited November 26, 2024.

304 Ibid., Cited November 26, 2024.

"[Nick] Bostrom believes that advances in artificial intelligence (AI) may lead to superintelligence, which he defines as "any intellect that greatly exceeds the cognitive performance of humans in virtually all domains of interest". He views this as a major source of opportunities and existential risks."[305]

Rodney Brooks says this about AGI, "When AI got started the clear inspiration was human level performance and human level intelligence. I think that goal has been what attracted most researchers into the field for the first sixty years. The fact that we do not have anything close to succeeding at those aspirations says not that researchers have not worked hard or have not been brilliant. It says that it is a very hard goal."[306]

Dr. Brooks goes on to say,

My intent is to:

- Stop people worrying about imminent super intelligence.
- To suggest directions of research that can have real impact on the future of AI and accelerate it.
- To show just how much fun research remains to be done and encourage people to work on the hard problems, not just the flashy demos that are hype bait.

---

[305] Shead, Sam, May 25, 2020. "How Britain's oldest universities are trying to protect humanity from risky A.I." CNBC. Retrieved 5 June 2023., Cited November 26, 2024

[306] Rodney Brooks, rodneybrooks.com, April 27, 2018, The Origins of "Artificial Intelligence", rodneybrooks.com/forai-the-origins-of-artificial-intelligence/, Cited November 26, 2024.

In closing, I would like to share Alan Turing's last sentence from his paper "Computing Machinery and Intelligence", just as valid today as it was 68 years ago:

We can only see a short distance ahead, but we can see plenty that needs to be done there.[307]

As a note of clarity and definition, I agree with multiple commentators and experts, some of who I have quoted above, that in my definition of AGI, I am using the term an "intelligent person" to mean a similar type of person as defined by Sam Altman as a "median human", which seems to be a demeaning term to me, but that is a personal issue. The point is that all the people that I have quoted, and I, are benchmarking AGI against an above-average level of human intelligence.

As I have been outspoken and clear about my view of the timing of AGI, I want to be clear on what I consider AGI to be. I want to state my position and ideas clearly to be beyond any level of confusion or doubt about why I think it will take centuries to achieve AGI.

Typically, I am not one to look to others to see if my opinion is in the mainstream or being confirmed by others. I do not need their external validation to feel and know that my view is generally correct.

In my view, if you predict a future that everyone can see and agree with, you are not looking far enough forward.

After years of saying that AGI was hundreds of years in the future, I was starting to doubt the accuracy of my view, but recently, in the last year, I

---

[307] Ibid., Cited November 26, 2024.

found the writings and position of Rodney Brooks. For the first time in a long time, I felt comfort in hearing my words being voiced by someone who I consider an expert and a luminary in the fields of AI and robotics. So, it is Dr. Brooks and me standing alone in a field with our unified view of the future of AGI. It feels comforting to me.

GenAI is not AGI, and GenAI is not THE path to AGI

Between 2022 and 2024, one of the primary topics in the world of technology was the widespread impact and use of GenAI. GenAI is a game-changing General Purpose Technology (GPT). There is no doubt about the status of GenAI as a GPT, but the impact of GenAI is widespread but shallow.

For example, I have conversations with people daily about GenAI. They ask me about using GenAI in all types of situations. Some of those applications and situations are not appropriate for GenAI.

GenAI cannot be relied upon to make critical decisions of any type. GenAI can be used to write an e-mail or to compare multiple documents that are hundreds or thousands of pages long and to provide a summary of the similarities and differences and the overall content of the documents, but GenAI is not appropriate for making decisions about matters like those related to healthcare. I would not want a GenAI system making decisions and recommendations on interventions or actions related to a surgery that is in process. That is not only a bad idea, but it could prove to be fatal.

GenAI is uniquely valuable for tasks that do not have an element of life or death involved, or where a person could be harmed, or where it is possible to suffer irreparable consequences of a bad decision, like buying anything or trading financial instruments. GenAI is not the tool for these use cases or applications.

GenAI is great for getting things started, writing a quick first draft of a substantial proposal, or writing an e-mail. GenAI is great to set a direction—to get things moving in a generally correct direction.

Again, GenAI is widespread in its application, but when GenAI is applied correctly, its impact is shallow.

Many prognosticators, futurists, authors, experts, and speakers discuss how GenAI is the gateway to Artificial General Intelligence (AGI); this is not true.

GenAI is a wonderful invention and a powerful tool for use cases and applications where the use of GenAI is safe and adds value, and there are many of those applications. It will take multiple years and maybe decades for humans to build out all the valuable GenAI applications, but GenAI is only a point along the journey; it is not the gateway to AGI, and it is not even close to it.

AGI, on the other hand, will be widely used and deeply embedded in all systems and processes. By its very definition, AGI will be used in all types of processes and procedures, including those involving a life-or-death element. AGI will undertake autonomous surgeries. AGI will spend money. AGI will broker contracts and negotiate agreements with people, systems, agents, and other AGIs.

AGI will be everywhere, and the impact will be deep and substantial.

Let's move on to discuss how I describe AGI and define my personal view and elements of AGI.

What is my definition of AGI?

The following is my definition of AGI. My view is that for AI to be considered AGI, it must be, at a *minimum,* able to:

- Understand at least text, numeric, video, image, and audio input. For now, we will leave the senses of touch, smell, and true vision out of the mix.
- Independently think and thereby generate original thoughts, not just predict patterns.
- Reason, infer, and evaluate answers for a specified level of accuracy, relevance, consistency, and coherence before answering any input from any entity.
- Ingest, synthesize, and process the same level of varied input streams from a wide range of input channels of diverse types in real-time as an intelligent person does, and respond with original insights and thoughts.
- Continuously accept multiple inputs and threads of input, consider options, and respond with unique and novel ideas and concepts in a timely manner consistent with human interactions.
- Continue to engage in a cogent and contextually appropriate manner at the level of an intelligent person for as long as the dialog continues.
- Be able to follow multiple threads of related and unrelated inputs to change direction in a dialog in a real-time manner and remain relevant and accurate through all the changes in the subjects and threads of discussion.

- Be aware that it is an AGI.
- Be aware that as an AGI, it interacts with people, companies, agents, other AGIs, systems, and entities with a wide range of definitions.
- Be aware of when any individual or entity joins, rejoins, or leaves a dialog and continue to engage with that entity, being aware of what that entity was exposed to or not exposed to in the current dialog.
- Be aware of and leverage the entire history of each interaction with each entity at any point in the future.
- Be able to leverage the entire history of all interactions with new and existing participants in a contextually relevant manner.
- Engage with as many participants as possible, actively and passively, in the conversation, even as people enter and leave the thread.
- Understand the dialog between the AGI and an individual and all interactions among all participants in any one discussion and in all discussions.
- Be aware that it has limited autonomy and that the owner of the system grants the autonomy, and that autonomy can be further limited, or revoked in an area, or revoked completely at any time.
- Act at all times in accordance with the current level of autonomy that is granted and in force, being aware that the level of autonomy can change at any time.

- Be aware of the complete lineage of all data used in summarizing and composing all current and previous discussions to avoid sharing information or decisions with entities that are not authorized to be privy to any specific piece of information or specific decisions.

- Understand ethics, morals, values, policies, procedures, rules, regulations, laws, and all types and manners of governance and apply them appropriately to each interaction and action.

- Control how it responds relative to all governance requirements from all relevant companies and governmental bodies.

- Understand morals and cultural norms and operate within those boundaries relevant to the participants in the various threads of dialog.

- Explain all actions and interactions and why the AGI may have operated or responded outside the bounds of its knowledge and governance boundaries or in a way that contravenes the known parameters of its mandate to operate.

- Act and interact in a way that harms no individual or group, intentionally or unintentionally.

- Report on its interactions and actions reflectively and explain what it may do to operate more in line with all known cultural and knowledge frameworks.

- Shut itself down or put itself into a safe mode if there is a malfunction in operation or if there is a question as to whether the AGI complies with all relevant mandates.

At a minimum, these characteristics and principles need to exist and be operational in a system for my definition of AGI to be met. As you can see, a wide range of capabilities are required for a system to meet the minimum requirements and be included in an AGI environment.

I am assuming that most people, governing bodies, governmental entities, law enforcement, legal departments, compliance officers, risk managers, and other interested parties would and will expect a great deal from a system deemed to be intelligent enough to operate autonomously. As I move forward and am involved in building more sophisticated and complicated AI systems that are evolving and growing toward meeting my stated definition of an AGI outlined above, I expect that the elements of my definitions will grow in number and scope. I define AGI as an evolving matter that will last for the remainder of my lifetime.

I am certain that this definition will spark conversations and possibly some controversies. I am excited to meet each reader to discuss their reactions to the definition and the timeline to achieve AGI. I am open to your views and interested in your thoughts and ideas. I am eager to meet each one of you. I feel fortunate to be able to engage with our data, analytics, and AI community members via my books, my online presence, and in person.

Let's move on to how we should be thinking about AGI from the perspective of what an AGI is to each of us. How can we relate to an AGI? What are the boundaries we put around an AGI to shape our thinking and views of an AGI?

How best to frame an AGI in our thinking?

In 2024, we started talking widely about GenAI agents and AI agents in many different public forums. In a foundational sense, you can think of AI agents as the ultimate realization of an agentic approach to any process. Let's ensure we have a shared appreciation for that last statement. I really do mean any process. Any process you can describe for future use or any process in operation today can be rebuilt with an AI agent or into an AI agent.

What I am saying is that in its essence, AI agents are one of the most visible and immediate on-ramps and are, in reality, our most practical path to AGI and probably one of the most direct paths to AGI from where we stand today. AI agents are how we will begin to build everyday intelligence into processes; that is powerful, and that is why we see and hear so many companies jumping into the AI agent market space. This realization and fact does not shorten my view of how long it takes to achieve AGI. It just gives us a starting point or an entry to a path to AGI.

With the explosion of GenAI, the advent of AI agents, and the widespread awareness of the potential of AI agents, I have been talking about, in my view, how anthropomorphizing models and AI is a bad idea and should not be done. People should not refer to AI agents by their proper names or infer pronouns onto AI agents or models. This is a problem because it confers qualities onto GenAI agents and models that do not exist. GenAI does not think. Models do not have emotions.

They do not, for the most part, remember any of the context of the dialog or conversation from one session to the next. For the more technically inclined readers, I am aware of the nascent use of memory technologies in GenAI and in AI agents process and workflows, but as of the writing of this book, use of memory technology to extend the ability of GenAI and AI agents to hold a context across sessions is not a well-defined and operational element in most implementations. Hence, the memory of the context of a conversation or conversations for GenAI is not practically available on a widespread basis.

Models are not people

GenAI is not a person, and it does not have many of the core characteristics of a person or people. Therefore, referring to these systems and systems elements as people or quasi-people is a disservice. As of today and for the near future, they are merely models and workflows. Let's not call them by pet names or personalize them.

This dynamic is interesting to me. We have been working on AI for nearly 70 years now; in the general sense, the AI community has been engaged in consistent and constant effort for nearly seven decades. Personally, I have been working on AI directly for 35 years. In the nearly four decades that I have been working in this field, no one in their right mind ever referred to a predictive model by a proper name or by a pronoun. No one ever called a forecasting model a pet name. No one ever said, "Fred, the forecasting model, seems a bit too conservative in his volume projections." But now, with GenAI, LLMs, and AI agents, I hear people call models her, him, they, and in some cases, people give models pet names; this is odd and should be avoided.

I guess this has happened partly because the models generate language, not just numbers. People are generally drawn to the need to humanize these models because they identify with the language generated. It is an unusual dynamic. Given our existing history with predictive technologies, I don't think it will be unusual going forward. However, we should be careful with this dynamic because I do not think it will lead to a healthy view of technology and a healthy separation of machine capabilities compared to human abilities. Conflating the two at this early stage will most likely lead to undesirable outcomes in the future. You see this dynamic in sci-fi books and movies, weird relationships between AI, AGI, and people. I think this is unhealthy, and we can stop it early if we avoid this practice of humanizing models.

With that said, I suggest to audiences, individuals, companies, universities, and governments that it can be helpful to think of agents as people in an abstract sense. While I am consistent and persistent in my position that thinking about and discussing specific agents and models as if they are people is a bad idea, I do think that considering AI systems in a collective or abstract sense as operating in the same way that people do is a helpful construct to employ when thinking about how AGI could be framed in our thinking.

Why this dichotomy in thinking about individual models and agents and models and agents in the collective sense?

Managing, governing, and controlling AGI and AI agents

As noted, models and agents can execute multistep processes in a singular or multiagent mode, but that process is simply a prebuilt environment to accomplish a defined task or objective. Yes, the process is much more intelligent today than in the past. However, it is still a prebuilt process that might branch or bring in additional models or agents, but it will only focus on the main objective it is designed to address. Tasks like matching invoices to purchase orders or taking in unstructured text and producing an initial draft of a report. No higher-order operations are being executed in these processes. As such, we should not imply or infer any higher-order cognitive capabilities to these collections of models or agents. You can think of these processes as highly automated and slightly intelligent operations.

But, when thinking about how highly intelligent and completely autonomous agents will operate in the real world, it is useful to frame them in the context of how an autonomous individual can and does operate in the real world today and how an autonomous entity like an AI agent today, and ultimately an AGI in the future, will operate in our world alongside, and in collaboration with, other AGIs, AI agents, individuals, companies and more.

In thinking about AI agents that we will be building from here forward, it is valuable, useful, and instructive to consider on a collective level what these systems need to do, need to access, need to be governed, need to be limited, need to interface with, need to adhere to rules, regulations, and laws, and more.

By thinking about how AI agents today and AGI in the future will autonomously operate across systems, companies, and with a wide range of individuals and entities, just like people do today and in the future, we can design a computing world where all constraints, guidelines, norms, morals, laws, and more apply to AI agents today, and to AGI when it arrives in the future.

In my view, if we start thinking about AI agents today, and AGI when they arrive, as another class of autonomous entities that need to be managed and governed just like people are today, we will be in a solid position to employ AI agents and AGI to our benefit rather than to the detriment of the human race.

To bring this topic into sharper focus, AI agents today and AGI in the future will do everything that an intelligent person will do, and they will do so autonomously. While thinking of a model as a person is an unwise idea, in my opinion, thinking about AI agents and AGI as operating in the exact same manner as an intelligent person provides a multifaceted conceptual framework to gain a deeper and broader understanding of the systems that we need to build to manage and govern AI agents and AGI.

As an example, begin to think of a hypothetical individual from the perspective of all that society does to socialize, teach, reprimand, punish, guide, and govern that person from birth to death. AI agents and AGI will need the same institutions, guardrails, governance, content, context, and opportunities to learn and relearn, to be punished and rewarded, just as an individual needs these mechanisms and frameworks.

It takes decades to impart all the knowledge that a person needs to be a highly capable, ethical, honest, and reliable member of any society. One of the facts that people find troubling is that an AGI, as we conceive it today, will be able to absorb and learn all these elements of behavior in a matter of hours or days. This fact alone causes almost all people who hear and understand it to react with a mix of fear, confusion, and apprehension. In my opinion, rightfully so, it is a bit disorienting.

You can think of AI agents and AGI as needing to be raised, taught, or trained just like a person does, but on a radially accelerated timeline. AI agents and AGI entities will be exposed to all training curricula and materials from preschool to PhD programs. AI agents and AGI will be exposed to the training materials that a person doing the same or a similar role will be expected to have read and understood. AI agents and AGI entities will be subject to all the same laws, rules, regulations, and policies as people are today.

In summary, we need to build the same environments and systems we have today to manage, guide, train, teach, and govern people, but for AI agents and AGI entities. This is a massive undertaking, and it will take decades to build the most basic foundations. As Dr. Brooks quoted Alan Turing as saying, we have a great deal of work to do, but we can only see a small portion of the required effort and work to be done. This effort will extend far beyond my lifetime and the lifetimes of multiple generations after me.

I find that thought hopeful and comforting. We have time, but it is time to start…now. In the short term, we know what we need to do. Let's start by acting and building what we now know we will need.

Before you put the book down and begin our multi-generational journey into a future with a function AGIs in our midst, let's address some of the fears that people have today about AGI. This is probably the area that I have been asked about most over the past five to seven years. People have real and well-founded fears about AGI. Some people also have unfounded fears, and in some cases, quite elaborate and specific fears about AGI that are generally created by sci-fi novels and movies, which is fine and easily debunked.

Those who are bold, raise their hands in the Q&A sessions of my presentations and ask, "When will we see SkyNet or the Terminator?"[308] People who are concerned but not so bold come up to me in a one-on-one setting and say something akin to, "Will AI, AI agents, or AGI take my job? Or will AI take over all the jobs in the future? What will my kids do for work?"

At first, I thought that they were asking in a tongue-in-cheek kind of way. I responded with irreverent answers because I thought, "They can't be serious", but I came to realize that they were serious, and are being serious, and that they were, and are, actually concerned about these very fears, and that these concerns and fears are very real to them and cause them anguish, pain, and consternation.

Let's discuss these fears, both the well-founded and the far-fetched, in a serious and realistic manner.

---

308 From the contributors of Wikipedia, The Terminator, https://en.wikipedia.org/wiki/The_Terminator, Cited November 29, 2024.

Economic fears

People are worried about themselves and their children. Unsurprisingly, most parents take their current and future responsibilities seriously, and they are, for the most part, concerned about their children's future. In general, they want to know what their relationship, and that of their children, will be like with this new technology and technologies. The predominance of their immediate concerns is based on economics. They are concerned about their jobs and incomes; this is the immediate focus of a significant part of the questions and inquiries I receive concerning the arrival of AGI.

People want to know about job losses. They want to know if they can train and improve themselves to stay ahead of jobs being automated away or being taken over by AI agents and AGI entities.

Let's start there.

This is not a new or novel dynamic in the job market. We have seen automation driving job evolution and job losses for centuries. What is new is that this time around, the job losses will be focused on knowledge workers. White collar or knowledge workers have been mostly immune from the pressure of automation, unlike factory workers who have seen waves of pressure from General Purpose Technologies (GPTs) like "...the steam engine, and electricity..."[309] driving job evolution and job losses for millennia.

---

[309] Edited by Elhanan Helpman with contributors, Philippe Aghion, Ciff Bekar, Timothy Bresnahan, Kenneth Carlaw, Alfonso Gambardella, Richard G. Harris, Elhanan Helpman, Peter Howitt, Richard G. Lipsey, Kevin M. Murphy, Craig Riddell, Paul Romer, Nathan Rosenberg, Manuel Trajtenberg, General Purpose Technologies and Economic Growth,

Given that knowledge workers are accustomed to new technologies assisting them and not simply replacing them, this is a disorienting development for many, but as research from Bank of America, PwC, Accenture, Gartner, IDC, McKinsey, and the World Economic Forum illustrates that much of these fears are unfounded. There is a saying that I have heard for most of my adult life. It is something similar to, "When your neighbor loses their job, it is a recession, but when you lose your job, it is a depression." The message in this bromide is that people take bad news, or consider impending bad news, in a much darker light if it impacts them personally, but the majority of recent research bears out a much more hopeful picture for knowledge workers.

Economic growth is projected to accelerate through the use of AI, AI agents, and, in the future AGI, existing workers will find new roles and jobs that computers and AI cannot undertake, and new workers will gravitate toward new jobs that will be created in the accelerated growth that will be experienced across all geographic regions.

Some of the high-level research statistics and findings include:

- According to IDC, global revenues for the AI market, including software, hardware and service sales, will grow at a CAGR (compound annual growth rate) (2022E-26E) of 19% to reach USD$900bn by 2026.[310] Big Data and AI could double the gross value-added (GVA) growth rates of developed markets by 2035

SBN: 9780262514682, January 1, 2003, The MIT Press, https://mitpress.mit.edu/9780262514682/general-purpose-technologies-and-economic-growth/, Cited November 30, 2024.

[310] Sourced from BoA Global Research, Bank of America Report, Artificial Intelligence...Is Intelligent!, https://business.bofa.com/en-us/content/ai-trends-impact-report.html, IDC (International Data Corporation) Forecasts 18.6% Compound Annual Growth for the Artificial Intelligence Market in 2022–2026, Cited November 30, 2024.

(estimated) and add between 0.8ppt and 1.4ppt to global productivity growth in the long run.

- PwC estimates that AI will enhance GDP by 26.1% in China and 14.5% in North America in 2030, which accounts for ~70% of the global impact.[311]

- McKinsey Global Research states that, by 2030, Europe could require up to 12 million occupational transitions, double the prepandemic pace. In the United States, required transitions could reach almost 12 million, in line with the prepandemic norm. Both regions navigated even higher levels of labor market shifts at the height of the COVID-19 period, suggesting they can handle this scale of future job transitions.[312]

- ...executives in Europe and the United States expressed a need not only for advanced IT and data analytics but also for critical thinking, creativity, and teaching and training—skills they report as currently being in short supply. Companies plan to focus on retraining workers, more than hiring or subcontracting, to meet skill needs.[313]

---

[311] Sourced from BoA Global Research, Bank of America Report, Artificial Intelligence...Is Intelligent!, https://business.bofa.com/en-us/content/ai-trends-impact-report.html,PwC (PricewaterhouseCoopers) Did You Know: Artificial Intelligence to drive GDP gains of USD$15.7 tn. June 27, 2017, Cited November 30, 2024.

[312] By Eric Hazan, Anu Madgavkar, Michael Chui, Sven Smit, Dana Maor, , Gurneet Singh Dandona, and Roland Huyghues-Despointes, McKinsey Global Institute, May 21, 2024, A new future of work: The race to deploy AI and raise skills in Europe and beyond, https://www.mckinsey.com/mgi/our-research/a-new-future-of-work-the-race-to-deploy-ai-and-raise-skills-in-europe-and-beyond, Cited November 30, 2024.

[313] Ibid., Cited November 30, 2024.

- The World Economic Forum postulates…If you were a farm worker 120 years ago—like roughly three-quarters of all people at the time—would it have been possible for you to imagine a world where only one in 20 people worked on farms? Could you have anticipated the range of new jobs available to workers today? Even 20 years ago, economists probably wouldn't have predicted that there would be 800,000 personal trainers employed in the US today and 2.5 million jobs in the app development industry.[314]

- The World Economic Forum's *Future of Jobs Report* illuminates the dual nature of AI's impact: By 2025, while 85 million jobs may be displaced by automation, an impressive 97 million new roles are projected to emerge, reflecting a shift in the division of labor between humans, machines, and algorithms. This paradigm shift emphasizes the need for significant workforce evolution rather than a reduction in the workforce.[315]

- AI's contribution to the job market extends beyond tech, catalyzing a spectrum of new careers that necessitate a new set of skills and expertise. According to LinkedIn's *2020 Emerging Jobs Report*, the demand for AI specialists has surged, with a 74% annual increase in job listings. Roles like machine learning

---

[314] World Economic Forum, Jobs and the Future of Work, February 26, 2024, Why there will be plenty of jobs in the future — even with artificial intelligence, https://www.weforum.org/stories/2024/02/artificial-intelligence-ai-jobs-future/, Cited November 30, 2024.

[315] The Future Of Work: Embracing AI's Job Creation Potential, Forbes Technology Council, Indiana (Indy) Gregg, Mar 12, 2024, https://www.forbes.com/councils/forbestechcouncil/2024/03/12/the-future-of-work-embracing-ais-job-creation-potential/, Cited November 30, 2024.

> engineers, data scientists, and AI researchers are in demand, indicating the growing influence of AI across business sectors.[316]

Today, and in the immediate future, people who are non-technical and who do not engage in the development of technology and are, for the most part, regular people working in a wide range of fields outside of technology and technology development are interested in ensuring that AI can help them and not cause them to lose their jobs or income streams.

I could continue to quote study after study that illustrates and reinforces that in the short term, AI, and ultimately AGI, in the longer term, will be a net job creator and an overall accelerator of widespread economic growth. But I believe that this point has been clearly made and powerfully proven.

Of course, there will be job disruptions and a considerable evolution in the job market. These trends and forces will necessitate a need to support workers through their individual and collective transitions, and that is one of the roles of national, state, regional, and local governments, but let's be clear, there will be no net job market shrinkage and no net overall job losses due to AI of any type.

Let's move on to another type of fear fomented by those who should know better but who have allowed self-interest to override their role in developing technologies that can and will provide a better future for all of society.

---

[316] Ibid., https://business.linkedin.com/talent-solutions/emerging-jobs-report?selectedFilter=all, Cited November 30, 2024.

Existential fear of AGI

People who are involved in the development of technology, especially those who are working in the subsegment of the technology field that is focused on building tools and technologies related to data, analytics, AI models, AI agents, and, in the future, AGI, have concerns about broader issues, related to AI, as they should. This group of technologists and these leaders are at the forefront of AI and its current and active development. They should have a broader view of what is coming in the field of AI.

As an aside, I am not saying that this group of technologists does not have the same economic concerns as the previous group. They do, but this audience discusses this next fear with greater interest, immediacy, urgency, and supposedly knowledge than the other non-technology group. A salient and important difference between the two groups is that this faction is responsible for developing what AI is and what will become AGI, and therefore, the general populace, those outside of the technology field, puts more credence into what the "leaders" of this technology-driven effort say in relation to what AGI will be and the impacts it will have on people, commercial firms, governments, and society in general. When these thought leaders paint a dark and somewhat dystopian future, that is a real problem for all of us.

It appears to me that people like Ray Kurzweil[317] are trying in earnest to warn the general public about something that they see as a real threat to humanity. Mr. Kurzweil refers to the achievement of AGI as The Singularity.

[317] From the contributors of Wikipedia—Ray Kurzweil https://en.wikipedia.org/wiki/Ray_Kurzweil, Cited December 2, 2024.

"The Singularity—is a hypothetical future point in time at which technological growth becomes uncontrollable and irreversible, resulting in unforeseeable consequences for human civilization. According to the most popular version of the singularity hypothesis, I. J. Good's intelligence explosion model of 1965, an upgradable intelligent agent could eventually enter a positive feedback loop of self-improvement cycles, each successive; and more intelligent generation appearing more and more rapidly, causing a rapid increase ("explosion") in intelligence which would ultimately result in a powerful superintelligence, qualitatively far surpassing all human intelligence."[318]

I understand the theory and the argument. This is a good idea as a script for a movie or a treatment of a proposed novel. Actually, it is beyond a good idea. It is a great idea. It has been noted that the original writing on machines taking over and ruling over humans began "with Samuel Butler's 1863 article, Darwin Among the Machines."[319] Butler's article seems pretty tame by today's reading and most recent historical context. This idea and theme have been the premise of many movies including: Stanley Kubrick's, 2001: A Space Odyssey[320] where the HAL-9000 computer disclosed that it was sentient and had a different agenda than that of the crew of the ship.

---

318 From the contributors of Wikipedia—Technological Singularity, https://en.wikipedia.org/wiki/Technological_singularity, Cited December 1, 2024.

319 Bob Mondello, Heard on All Things Considered, July 31, 2023, WBEZ Radio, Chicago, 'Open the pod bay door, HAL' — here's how AI became a movie villain, https://www.npr.org/2023/07/31/1191017889/ai-artificial-intelligence-movies, Cited December 3, 2024.

320 2001: A Space Odyssey, Stanley Kubrick, 1968, Rated G, 2h 29m, IMDb.com, https://www.imdb.com/title/tt0062622/, Cited December 3, 2024.

And, of course, there is The Terminator[321], the oft-quoted film about a robot from the future sent back in time to terminate the boy who will become the leader of the human resistance against the computer overloads in one of the darkest and most dystopian of future visions. Even discussing a computer that could attain consciousness creates fear and tension.

As a thought experiment, this is simultaneously compelling and frightening. Still, in the real world and how AI models work, this is not practical, and even if it were a practical and realistically possible outcome, it is 100 to 200 years away. In my opinion, publicly announcing that The Singularity or AGI is imminent is akin to telling people that they need to stock up on sunblock today because the Sun will explode in approximately five billion years.[322] This is not a useful and productive way to discuss the future and what AGI will become.

"According to some experts, The Singularity also implies machine consciousness. Regardless of whether it is conscious or not, such a machine could continuously improve itself and reach far beyond our capabilities. Even before artificial intelligence was a computer science research topic, science fiction writers like Asimov were concerned about this. They were devising mechanisms (i.e., Asimov's Laws of Robotics) to ensure the benevolence of intelligent machines which is more commonly called alignment research today."[323]

---

[321] The Terminator, James Cameron, 1984, Rated R, 1h 47m, IMBd.com, https://www.imdb.com/title/tt0088247/?ref_=nv_sr_srsg_0_tt_8_nm_0_in_0_q_Termina tor, Cited December 3, 2024.

[322] JoAnna Wendel, When will the sun die?, March 6, 2024, Space.com, https://www.space.com/14732-sun-burns-star-death.html, Cited December 1, 2024.

[323] Cem Dilmegani, AI Multiple Research, When will singularity happen? 1700 expert opinions of AGI, https://research.aimultiple.com/artificial-general-intelligence-singularity-timing/, Cited November 25, 2024

In general, I am amused by people who make their living as what many call futurists. These people get paid to predict the future and are rarely if ever, held to account for the accuracy of their prognostications. They speculate wildly in some cases, experience no repercussions, and never have to answer for their work. Only weather professionals get a similar pass on their ability to have a defined level of accuracy in their daily work.

To be clear, I am good with sci-fi novels and other works speculating on the shape and character of the future. I think that the dynamic of envisioning new future worlds and capabilities and capacities is really interesting and fun, but let's call what we do not know to be anywhere near achievable what it is. It is science fiction. Science fiction is not a prediction. Science fiction is pure speculation. A reliable prediction includes the probability of the development occurring in the specific form and functionality being described or outlined. Also, reliable and robust predictions include a specified date in the future when the object is to become a reality.

When futurists and executives opine about dark and dramatic developments that have no clear path to realization at some undefined time in the far-off future or some ridiculously short timeframe, like next year, they are speculating about science fiction, and we really do not need to pay attention to this talk. Some people go to movies and read novels to be frightened. Those are the people who can enjoy the sci-fi speculation about AGI achieving domination over people.

Futurists and their ilk like to impart higher-level cognitive functions and the achievement of consciousness into their visions of AGI; this is a stretch. Saying that the achievement of AGI implies that computers will have consciousness is a massive leap. In 2023, people were saying that GenAI exhibited "emergent behaviors".[324] We discussed this in Chapter 7 on GenAI. Emergent behaviors were nothing more than a lack of understanding of how GenAI models actually work. This is the same dynamic we see when people propose that GenAI is the immediate precursor to AGI, which is a nearly irresponsible leap of logic.

If you look back at the definition of AGI that I have put forward, there is no mention of sentience or consciousness. That is because I do not believe this level of automated cognition is within our ability to build even with an additional 300 years as our deadline.

There are people in today's society who use fear to sell books or get themselves on stage to deliver keynote speeches or to appear on television or in stories in magazines, newspapers, and online. They use fear to scare people away from developing technologies and solutions to profit from the same technologies. I cannot abide these people. They are charlatans and carnival barkers of the day. We should avoid their attempts to profit from "problems" of their own creation. We have enough hard work ahead of us to achieve our goals. We do not need phonies creating challenges that they solve and take credit for adding little to no value.

On the other hand, practical, pragmatic researchers and practitioners are showing us the way. These are the people we should be listening to and following. The more I read about and hear from Yann LeCun[325], the more I agree with his views on how to move forward to develop AI, AI agents, and possibly AGI.

---

[324] Jakub Kraus, Overview of Emergent and Novel Behavior in AI Systems, March 26, 2024, Center for AI Policy, https://www.centeraipolicy.org/work/emergence-overview, Cited December 1, 2024.

[325] From the contributors of Wikipedia—Yann LeCun, https://en.wikipedia.org/wiki/Yann_LeCun, Cited on December 1, 2024.

When critically evaluating how a technology, a market, or a long-term trend will evolve, I look closely at the people talking about the topic. You and I can almost always discount the people driven by short-term profit and self-interest. You can see it in the timelines and their actions. For example, if they are seeking to raise billions of dollars and, simultaneously saying that this massive jump in technological capabilities will arrive in less than a year, you can almost smell the conflict of interest.

You can, in general, put more trust and credence into the people who have developed related technologies and practitioners who have researched and built systems that really work. I believe that the researchers and practitioners have a better view of the real challenges, the actual timelines, and the functionality that is realistic and will be delivered to the commercial world.

As for the futurists, let's stop listening to their fear mongering and unfounded and ungrounded speculations. If you really want to engage in the speculative process regarding the shape of the long-term future of AGI, you should read a well-researched and thought-out work of science fiction. If you want to know with greater certainty what kind of capabilities and functionality will be available for all of us in our daily lives, look to people like Yann LeCun for insight and guidance.

Other fears

While there are many other concerns and fears relating to AGI, this book is not the outlet for giving voice to those concerns. I can imagine or envision that undertaking a comprehensive evaluation and exposition of all fears related to AGI is a book unto itself. Personally, I am not drawn to the subject. I have never been one to play on fear as a motivating force to compel anyone to act. As you may have deduced from my tone and words,

I find people who play on fear to be despicable. There are plenty of things in the world to be afraid of. We do not need others to scare us into action for their amusement and benefit.

Let's move on to discuss how Causal AI, Foundational AI, and Generative AI will work together as the foundation of Composite AI, which *is* the actual long-term technological path to AGI.

The future ecosystem of AI

All of the parts of the current AI environment, Causal AI, Foundational AI, and Generative AI, have developed over the past 70 years into powerful individual components of our analytical ecosystem. Each part of the AI environment has and will continue to drive and contribute significant benefits as a stand-alone system. Still, they will be more impactful as a part of the integrated AI environment we will develop over the next 50 to 100 years.

Today, in real operational settings, the integration of the three pillars looks like what we see in Figure 29 below, but this is simply an artifact of time, technological evolution, and the state of the thinking of most analytics professionals. At this point in time, the three environments are completely independent but can be made to work together through additional development work and a focus on connecting independent system functionality to achieve a specified objective set forth for a specific application or project.

As an example, today, operationally, this is how it works in most projects or scenarios:

- Business users or executives ask the predictive analytics team to predict how many people will buy a product or service at a certain price in a target market or geography in a defined time frame.

- The analytics team uses Foundational AI to execute the analytic work.

- The business executives might then ask another analytics team to take the results of the previous project as input to another subsequent project to determine why those customers would buy at the price.

- A different analytics team would use Causal AI to execute the proposed analytics project.

- If the business users are really sophisticated, they may take the results of the two previous projects and use GenAI to generate possible campaign ideas of treatments or messaging that they could consider for use in a subsequent marketing campaign.

- Or it is possible that the business executives would ask a third group to execute a project using GenAI and leveraging the outputs from the previous two projects to create inputs for the possible marketing campaigns.

Our poor business executive needs to interface with at least two analytics groups, and maybe three, to gain the information they are seeking to begin to plan the work that they actually want to do; not an optimal process or scenario, and people wonder why business executives and managers rely on a gut feeling, intuition, or just plain recollection of past events to base their decisions on.

In the future, with Composite AI, the process will be:

- The business executive will write a comprehensive prompt in natural language via a keyboard or microphone that includes documents, examples, previous analytics work, example outputs, videos, images, resource profiles, complete campaign designs, and more.

- The prompt will describe exactly what the business executive wants as the optimal target market, characteristics of customers and prospects, price point possibilities, cost constraints, timing, internal or external resources to be used, the media channels available, performance bands of the campaign, subtlety of the message, tone and tenor variations of the message, campaign monitoring and reporting requirements, pilot project plans, art alternatives for the visual elements of the campaign, and much more detail that they might consider relevant.

- The Composite AI environment will accept the input, run all the required models, and return a consolidated, comprehensive response to the business executive.

Which process and environment do you think business executives would prefer to use?

The second process described is a vision of how Composite AI will work. The next section will describe how these three environments will be brought together.

At first, for simple applications, but over the next few years, we will have seamless integration and the ability to not only chain environments together in prescribed ways but complete integrations where all atomic functions and capabilities are available at any time to be integrated in any way that accomplishes our desired goals and objectives.

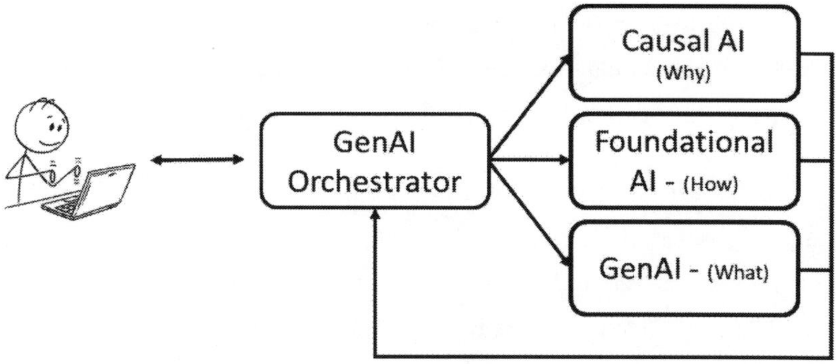

Figure 29: Composite AI - The AI Ecosystem of the future.

The short-term roadmap

Up to now, most people involved in either observing the AI market for a living (e.g., technology analysts, pundits, experts, etc.), or people who are developing technologies for the AI market have discussed and thought of each of these eras or pillars of AI as unique and separate. Today, we have analytical specialists and developers who focus on each of the pillars and may not even be aware of the other pillars or may only have a cursory understanding of the pillars that are not their specialty area.

Again, this is only an artifact of time, a limitation of our current thinking, and the point of technological evolution where we find ourselves. Now that we have all three pillars available as commercial software operating where trained professionals can buy and utilize each one, we will start to see the integration of the three becoming more common and routine.

At first, and we are seeing this today, in 2024, technologists are finding ways to integrate the pillars of AI in new and novel ways. Recall Chapter 9, where I described sitting next to a young data scientist who was discussing how he and his colleagues were integrating Machine Learning to improve the

Causal Discovery process, this is an example of how Foundational AI and Causal AI are coming together in an ad hoc manner. This type of activity is becoming increasingly common, routine, and regular.

As this ad hoc integration of the three pillars becomes more prevalent, analytics professionals start to ask for these integrations to be built into the software they prefer and use daily. Software vendors will begin to develop Application Programming Interfaces (APIs) that are standardized and routinely available to enable easy linking and integrating of their offerings with software offerings from other vendors. There are existing APIs that can be used for simple system integration, and those are being leveraged by innovative technologists today to achieve system-level integration.

After we experience widespread system integration via industry-standard APIs, we will see specialization in APIs for specific AI use cases. This evolutionary step and development will take a couple of years (2027).

After API specialization is in widespread use, we will see fully integrated offerings from software vendors that provide integrations for more than one type of AI. We see Causal AI vendors integrating GenAI into the processes and offerings today. We also see Foundational AI being brought into the Causal AI process. All permutations of integration will be undertaken ad hoc until vendors begin to integrate all types of AI together (2035).

The next phase will be where unified environments from software vendors offer all three pillars of AI. There will be a wide variety of integrations; some vendors will offer their version of all three pillars; other vendors will be specialists in one pillar and offer other pillars from partner vendors. In this phase, there will be a wide range of varied offerings (2040).

The next phase will be where the three pillars will be refined, extended, improved, and integrated in a way that makes Composite AI available through a unified user interface. To be clear, this process will take between ten and 15 years to unfold (2050).

Once we have compelling and reliable offerings, market consolidation will begin, and, in the end, three vendors will dominate the market. We will have three vendors offering fully integrated, completely functional Composite AI (2080).

That is the short-term market and product roadmap of Composite AI. We now know what the next 25 to 30 years will look like in the Composite AI market.

We have been outlining and discussing the shape of Composite AI. It is time for us to define the term and describe what it is in reality and what Composite AI is in relation to the path to AGI.

What is composite AI?

A handful of insightful and thoughtful technology analysts, pundits, and forward-thinking organizations are discussing and positing what they think Composite AI will be.

Gartner defines Composite AI as, "Composite AI refers to the combined application (or fusion) of different AI techniques to improve the efficiency of learning to broaden the level of knowledge representations. Composite AI broadens AI abstraction mechanisms and, ultimately, provides a platform to solve a wider range of business problems in a more effective manner."[326]

Gartner has credibility in the enterprise technology market, and their analysts are very good at examining emerging and existing technologies and discussing those technologies and related trends with enterprise IT professionals and software and technology vendors. Still, I have to say that this definition is a bit opaque. Let's continue to work toward a clear definition of what Composite AI is today and what it will become in the short, medium, and long term.

Cem Dilmegani, a principal analyst at AIMultiple, an analyst firm focused on AI, defines Composite AI in this manner, "Composite AI is an advanced form of AI for integrating different AI technologies into a single solution in a systematic way to approach complex business problems holistically. Instead of relying on a single AI model, composite AI aims to solve diverse business problems by combining multiple analytical techniques such as: Machine learning / Deep Learning, Natural language processing (NLP), Computer vision (CV), Descriptive statistics, Knowledge graphs…"[327]

This definition is slightly clearer as it names the technologies that are being integrated to create Composite AI, but in my view, it is a bit narrow in its consideration set. Most of the technologies listed would be considered Foundational AI, but there is no real mention of Causal AI and a light mention of a precursor to GenAI.

My definition of a Composite AI environment is the following:

---

[326] Gartner Glossary, Composite AI, https://www.gartner.com/en/information-technology/glossary/composite-ai, Cited December 4, 2024.

[327] Cem Dilmegani, AIMultiple, Updated on Nov 15, 2024, What is Composite AI & Why is it Important?, https://research.aimultiple.com/composite-ai/, Cited December 6, 2024.

- Composite AI is the deep integration of all three pillars of AI, including Foundational AI, Causal AI, and Generative AI. The integration goes beyond the overall system environment and extends down to the basic elements of each pillar to ensure seamless integration across all functions and sub-elements of each pillar.

- A Composite AI environment is a singular unified platform accessed through a conversational interface via natural language inputs or prompts.

- Prompts are parsed by a single or multilevel orchestration layer that decomposes the prompts into atomic analytical elements that are passed to various models for ingestion, integration, augmentation, and analytical execution.

- Each model, including the models in the orchestration layer, may recursively and iteratively process raw information and intermediate information.

- Input prompts, intermediate results, and final results may be rejected by any model as being inaccurate, not properly sourced, or not of the level of verification, accuracy, relevance, or specificity required by the end user for the particular use case.

- All information at any process or execution step may be checked for veracity, accuracy, and numerous other quality metrics before being passed to a subsequent step in the overall process.

- System prompts or system level instructions set the level of policy compliance, general governance, accuracy required, and numerous other systems, models, and operational parameters that guide and govern the operation of the overall environment.

- The AI models from the three pillars of AI share and pass intermediate results between models to move toward the objective of completing analytical results.

- One of the primary objectives of a Composite AI environment is to ensure that results are accurate and reliable as possible for each answer provided.

- The final results are combined into a cohesive, complete, concise response that is sent to the end user.

- Iteration of responses and interactions from users is expected and should be responded to in a manner that is consistent with human-to-human conversational dynamics.

When Composite AI environments become available, they will initially be leveraged and used by data scientists (2060). Many people refer to this type of system operation as a "code first" environment. The early Composite AI environments will require that the users be trained data scientists and will require a level of understanding of the data required, underlying analytical techniques, and how the pillars are integrated to drive and manage the systems to achieve reliable outputs and outcomes (2085).

In the next iteration of Composite AI environments, business analysts and other non-technical professionals will begin to engage with "low code" and "no code" environments that will be driven entirely by natural language (2100). All three of the noted evolutions of Composite AI environments will be created to design, develop, and deploy complete AI applications for any process, solution, or application area in an enterprise environment.

Now that we know what we are talking about when discussing Composite AI, how can it come to be in the near term?

How can Composite AI be achieved?

In technology, we are aware that there are many paths to any and all objectives and goals. Our objective in this section is not to enumerate every possible way to develop an integrated Composite AI environment. We will provide directional guidance so that as the market evolves and we see movement, we understand where we are in the process and where the market and the offerings we are interested in are going.

Understanding this evolutionary process can be instructive for individuals to know when to undertake continuing education to stay ahead of technology and useful for companies to know when to buy and invest in new and integrated technologies to upgrade their technology environments.

The technology analyst team at Inc42.com has put forth that Composite AI can be accomplished in multiple ways. They have stated that "There are several strategies for combining different AI techniques to create a composite AI system. The technique chosen for combining AI techniques depends on the problem and the desired outcome. The following are some of how a composite AI system can be created:

- Ensemble Learning: This approach involves training multiple AI models using different algorithms or techniques on the same data. The predictions from these individual models are combined, often through averaging or voting, to produce a final output. This leverages the strengths of each model while mitigating their weaknesses.

- Pipelines: Here, different AI techniques are placed sequentially, where the output from one stage becomes the input for the next. For example, a system might use computer vision to identify objects in an image, followed by natural language processing (NLP) to generate a description of the scene.

- Hybrid Approaches: It involves integrating different AI techniques within a single model architecture. For instance, a model might combine convolutional neural networks for image recognition with recurrent neural networks for language processing to create a system that can understand and respond to visual questions.

- Multi-Agent Systems: This approach involves creating multiple independent AI agents that can interact with each other and their environment to achieve a common goal. This can be particularly useful for complex tasks requiring collaboration and coordination between different AI entities."[328]

I agree with the statements and options put forth by the Inc42.com team, and in my opinion, the pipeline approach is what most people are doing now. Figure 29 above is a visual representation of a pipeline approach. The pipeline approach will continue to be a prevalent, popular, and pragmatic approach, but it has and will continue to have limitations.

One point that should be made is that the pipeline label is a bit of a misnomer. A pipeline label implies a straightforward flow or maybe a bidirectional flow. The flow is more akin to that in a fully connected matrix. Information, computing, and processing can enter or start at any component and move through all analytical models, interconnects, and interfaces in any manner possible. Processing can be looping, recursive,

[328] Hemant Kashyap, Inc42.com Glossary, March 9, 2024, Here's Everything You Need To Know About Composite AI, https://inc42.com/glossary/composite-ai/#:~:text=Ensemble%20Learning:%20This%20approach%20involves%20training%20multiple,leverages%20the%20strengths%20of%20each%20model%20while, Cited December 4, 2024.

and/or iterative. In the end, the pipeline approach escalates into the agentic approach.

The agentic approach is being widely explored, and it is showing great promise in the early days. It will likely be the most widespread implementation mode to move toward the realization of AGI.

The modular, distributed, inclusive approach of agentic workflows provides many of the desired upside benefits with very few of the downside problems. Given the low barriers to entry, we will see the agentic approach used to integrate a wide range of models, tools, libraries, subsystems, and entire environments together quickly and easily. The agentic approach embodies the architecture, processing power, and flexibility needed to deliver on the functional definition of Composite AI in the short term and AGI in the longer term.

As the market evolves and we move past the explosion of agent frameworks and foundation providers, we will see substantial innovation in the overall area of AI agents.

At this point, we have a timeline for the next 75 to 80 years, a clear and complete definition of what Composite AI is, and a general idea of the roads that will lead to Composite AI. Now, let's turn our attention to the longer term. Let's examine why we need the three pillars of AI to deliver AGI. Then we will resume our discussion of the agentic approach to building scalable, flexible, and intelligent systems.

Why aren't the three Pillars of AI enough to achieve AGI?

Part of the reason that we do not have AGI today is that none of our tools or pillars contain all the functionality needed to deliver AGI. Each pillar is powerful and continues to refine and grow, but there are still massive gaps in what we need to arrive at AGI. Let's examine each of the pillars of our toolkit today and see what we are missing in our journey to AGI.

In my opinion, if any of the existing pillars of AI was to be *the* primary path to AGI, it would be Foundational AI. Foundational AI has been the focus of concerted, widespread development for nearly 70 years. It has the most breadth and depth regarding tools, techniques, and technologies of all the fields of AI, and no one thinks of Foundational AI as the primary precursor to AGI.

Why is that the case?

I suppose that people did consider Foundational AI a breakthrough candidate for a brief moment when IBM's Watson was on the television show Jeopardy!,[329] but that was nothing more than a brief blip of interest and fleeting fame.

But, on second thought, there were two elements of Watson's emergence onto the world's stage that were instructive as to how we would go about building AGI.

The first insight was that the ability to quickly and accurately answer a wide range of unanticipated questions across unconstrained subject areas in a conversational setting was only possible with the integration of multiple types of models. No one type of model, or one pillar of AI, is capable of providing even the appearance of intelligence, let alone true AGI. In the end, IBM and Watson provided insight into the world, stating that all pillars of AI and multiple models and approaches are needed to realistically believe that we could be on the road to practical and pragmatic AGI on a

[329] From the contributors of Wikipedia, IBM Watson, https://en.wikipedia.org/wiki/IBM_Watson, Cited on December 8, 2024.

widespread basis. This fact and realization have been exceptionally valuable to technologists, researchers, academics, and software developers in the long run. We owe our thanks to the team at IBM for making this fact clear to us.

The second insight was that a voice-driven interface or a type of natural language interface that enabled people to engage with models in a more natural or conversational manner was key to everyday people engaging with models. People in analytics already knew this, but the level of importance was raised to one of the top requirements by seeing the engagement with Watson in the television setting. We have long known that for people to engage with analytics and analytical models they need to be able to ask questions at their speed of thought in a way that they can formulate their series of related and sequence of questions quickly, easily, and naturally. Without having a voice-oriented or conversational user interface, people cannot ask questions and have questions answered in a way that stimulates their thinking and enables a sustained series of questions and answers to be asked and answered in a manner that enables a train of thought to be designed, developed in real time, and executed a manner that satisfies an entire line of inquiry. The use of Watson on Jeopardy made this realization concretely clear to technologists, and this fact was reinforced even more strongly by the launch and success of ChatGPT by OpenAI in 2022.

Let's look across all three pillars of AI to examine in detail why each one, as they are in their evolutionary path today, are not, on a stand-alone basis, the primary path to AGI.

Foundational AI

First, Foundational AI is limited to processing structured information and that constraint alone eliminates it from consideration as *the* path to AGI.

The vast majority of human communication and knowledge, well over 90+%, is in unstructured information. Any tool that cannot process unstructured information cannot be the bedrock of AGI. To put it another way, less than 10% of human knowledge cannot result in a new form of intelligence. It is just not possible.

Secondly, the explosion of GenAI and the conversational user interface has proven how important it is to provide users with interfaces that are more natural to how people think and interact rather than bending people's interactions to fit into interfaces that can be built at the time. Traditional Graphical User Interfaces (GUIs) and other input forms and mechanisms will not lead to, enhance, or shorten the path to AGI.

Other limitations of Foundational AI include that this pillar of AI is not typically used in interactive settings where humans "converse" with models. Foundational AI can be developed with a conversational user interface, and applications can be built to be more interactive. However, for the majority of the history of Foundational AI, applications have been built to operate asynchronously. A user provides input(s) and expects to wait for the answer. The answer may not be provided for minutes, hours, or days. That is not truly a limitation of Foundational AI but a limitation of how we see the value of Foundational AI and how we have built applications with Foundational AI up to this point in time.

As previously discussed, but it bears repeating here, Foundational AI only provides the "what" portion of the discussion or the answer. For AGI, we need more than a simple answer to one element of the discussion.

Foundational AI has been impressive and will continue to be, but it is not *the* path to AGI.

Let's move on and consider why stand-alone GenAI is not *the* path to AGI either.

Generative AI

One of the primary reasons why GenAI is not *the* path to AGI is that GenAI is a subset of Foundational AI, and if Foundational AI is not the path to AGI, neither can GenAI be the stand-alone path to AGI.

The breakthroughs we have seen in GenAI are predominately a product of scaling the data leveraged by neural networks. There have been technological innovations in the area of GenAI, there is no question of that fact, but the main breakthrough has been in being able to process massive amounts of input data as training data. Impressive, but, again, not sufficient for AGI.

GenAI models can generally infer from the data that has been ingested or the data that is available for a model to access. That fact alone has created an ability to apply LLMs, SLMs, and DLMs to almost every imaginable use case. The broad applicability of GenAI to almost every process and a wide range of industries has caused an impression that there is original thinking, emergent behavior, or true reasoning occurring in these models; this is not true.

LLMs and all their variants can run in recursive loops to improve the probability of arriving at a correct answer through the eventual elimination of options, but GenAI and LLMs cannot actually reason to arrive at a provably accurate conclusion. Brute force using speed and recursion is not reasoning. LLMs in operation can provide an appearance of reasoning. Still, at the core of the processes, it is not reasoning in the sense that people reason using their intelligence and intellect.

There is confusion in the market, which has been introduced primarily by the providers of GenAI models. In their marketing messages and efforts, these providers claim that GenAI models can reason, but that is not true in the definitive sense of reasoning. In a marketing sense, it may be true, but in reality, it is a stretch to claim that GenAI model can reason across novel situations; it cannot.

As we have previously discussed, but it bears repeating here, GenAI only provides the "how" portion of the discussion or the answer. For AGI, we need more than a simple answer to one element of the discussion.

Given that GenAI cannot reason on its own and it cannot create original thoughts, it cannot be *the* precursor to AGI.

Let's move on and consider why Causal AI alone is not *the* path to AGI.

Causal AI

In contrast to GenAI, Causal AI is capable of the beginnings of elemental reasoning across novel facts. Causal AI can derive insights into why events occur and can reason why events will happen or why people will act in a defined manner.

"Causal AI will actually allow LLMs and SLMs to reason, but it is still very much in development. Eventually, this reasoning AI could analyze scientific processes and improve global issues, such as the supply chain, according to Scott Hebner, principal analyst of AI at theCUBE Research."[330] Mr. Hebner continues his thought with the following remarks, "One of the challenges with today's large language models (LLMs) and generative AI (GenAI) in

---

[330] Devony Hof, Causal AI: The next evolution in machine learning, siliconANGLE, https://siliconangle.com/2024/10/03/causal-ai-small-language-models-future-ai-thecubenysewired/#:~:text=Causal%20AI%20will%20enable%20reasoning%20machines&text=Eventually%2C%20this%20reasoning%20AI%20could,correlative%20design%2C%E2%80%9D%20he%20said, Cited on November 1, 2024.

general is that it's based on a correlative design," he said. "It basically swims in a large data lake and correlates to identify patterns, associations, anomalies, and they can then predict or forecast or generate something. Probabilities tell you about our beliefs in a static world based on past historical experience or data. Causality tells you how those probabilities change when the world around you changes. For AI to help human beings actually problem solve and plan, it needs to understand causality and the science of why things happen."[331]

The field of Causal AI is just beginning to emerge into the commercial market. The tools and technologies have been proven to work in academic and research environments. These tools show great promise, but they are not scalable, reliable, or cost-effective to use in enterprise or consumer settings.

The amount of personnel needed to build these solutions is significant, and the corresponding number of people who understand and can build accurate, reliable, scalable, Casual AI solutions and applications for end users, numbers in the hundreds on a global scale. By comparison, "according to the US Bureau of Labor Statistics by 2026, 11.5 million jobs will be created for data scientists."[332] It will be years, maybe even decades, before the number of experienced Casual AI professionals comes anywhere near meeting the ever-increasing demand for specialists in the field of Causal AI.

Given that Casual AI is emerging and that the technology, at this point, does not scale to operate on massive amounts of data. We do not have enough

---

[331] Ibid., Cited on November 1, 2024.

[332] Data Science: An Exciting Field for Your Professional Career in 2024, World Data Science Initiative, https://www.worlddatascience.org/blogs/data-science-an-exciting-field-for-your-professional-career-in-2024, Cited December 14, 2024.

skilled staff to make Causal AI applications operate on a widespread basis. The run times are exceedingly long when dealing with large numbers of variables, Casual AI cannot be *the* path to AGI.

Finally, as we have previously discussed, but it bears repeating here, Causal AI only provides the "why" portion of the discussion or the answer. For AGI, we need more than a simple answer to one element of the discussion. We need all the pillars working in concert and conjunction with each other in real time.

Composite AI is the unifying path forward

We see the same pattern across all three pillars of AI, each one has addressed a part of the challenge to develop AGI, each pillar has focused a portion of the overall effort required. Why is that? The primary answer to that question is because each pillar has been designed, developed, and evolved to solve the unique challenges researchers and developers could see, understand, and were tasked with solving.

One aspect of our discussion that must be recognized is that the entire historical body of AI work and knowledge, for the most part, has been incredibly successful at solving the problems that were iteratively defined and subsequently addressed. The field of AI and the three pillars within it have been one of the most successful software development efforts and problem-solving efforts that the human race has ever experienced, but that effort, for the most part, was focused on solving localized problems and challenges, and we have done that very well.

Let's take a moment to ensure that we are on the same page and have a clear, shared understanding of our current state of AI evolution. We have the beginnings of Composite AI, a critical developmental milestone in our journey toward AGI. We know that it will take another 80 to 100 years for widespread, easily used, cost-effective Composite AI to be a reality. At the same time, we are developing new technologies like agents and agentic workflows that will accelerate our progress toward AGI.

We know that new developments in quantum computing, innovations in algorithms, algorithmic efficiency and effectiveness, computing hardware, data management, and more will come in ways that we cannot foresee.

If we as a society really want AGI, then we will need to lift our focus from what we can do today to what we need to do over the next 100 to 200 years, but before we look that far into the future, let's look beyond Composite AI to adjacent areas of development that will have a significant impact on ability to realize AGI.

AI today and beyond

In the discussion of developing AGI, we must realize that we have moved the goalposts and reframed the challenge and the dialog. We cannot fault those who have gone before us or those who are working on hard challenges; that was not their objective for the most part. They were not working, in earnest, to deliver AGI.

Let's be completely clear, a handful of researchers and academics have been dreaming of and focused on thinking about AGI, but the vast majority of developers and companies have not.

AGI has been the subject of science fiction for the majority of the existence of rational thought. And only in the past 50 to 100 years have a handful of futurists and experts held out with earnest conviction that AGI is truly possible. With that backdrop and discussion framework, it is rational, expected, and normal to conclude that not only do we need everything that has been developed across all three pillars of AI, to achieve AGI, we actually need more than what we have today and even more than we can clearly see that needs to be developed.

In my opinion, that is great news. We have a lot of work to do. We will be very busy being engaged in lively discussions and interesting work. Who could ask for a more fulfilling way to spend your immediate days and overall career?

Only in the last two to five years has the rhetoric amped up where technology providers have claimed that their mission is to develop and deliver AGI soon. The executives of DeepMind[333] and OpenAI[334] talk about AGI and the achievement thereof on a daily basis. They speak about and predict the arrival of AGI as if it were just around the corner and some claim that we already have it. These types of claims about the future already being a reality are really nothing new. I suppose that the claims are new and slightly novel when thinking about AGI, but we have seen lots of people hawking their wares before. We have seen people with profit motives and visions of grandeur making outlandish claims before. We just simply need to move on and build real systems with actual capabilities that will move our community, industry, market, and the world, forward in a responsible and ethical manner. As the wizard in the Wizard of Oz breathlessly remarked, "Never mind that little man behind the curtain."[335]

I am including the following lengthy quote from researchers and developers working at Netflix. This quote illustrates what pragmatic and practical

---

[333] DeepMind, https://deepmind.google/, Cited on December 9, 2024.

[334] OpenAI, https://openai.com/, Cited on December 9, 2024.

[335] From the contributors of Wikipedia, The Wizard of Oz, https://en.wikipedia.org/wiki/The_Wizard_of_Oz, Cited December 10, 2024.

technologists are working on and delivering today in research and commercial settings.

"Causal inference and machine learning have a symbiotic relationship that is growing deeper. Companies are using machine learning to improve content recommendations, sales, business operations, and to personalize user experiences. These companies will test new algorithms online in order to determine whether the algorithms cause a positive effect for the company. In this capacity, causal inference for online experiments serves as an honest and independent evaluator for an algorithm. However, recent interdisciplinary work in the combination of machine learning and causal inference has shown a much deeper synergy between the two fields. Predictions from machine learned models have been debiased by utilizing inverse propensity weights (Dudik, Langford, and Li 2011), which are frequently found in studies of causal effects. At the same time, causal inference methods have benefited from methods for modeling high dimensional relationships in order to determine heterogeneity in treatment effects, such as in Wager and Athey 2018. Frameworks such as Pearl's do-calculus (Pearl 2012) have also created clear programmatic structure for answering causal effects queries when relationships in data can be modeled as a graph."[336]

I have had to read that block of text multiple times to really grasp the impact of what was being said. Let me offer my summarization or synthesis of what the technologists are saying.

- First, they are saying that each pillar of AI can be a quality check on the other AI pillars to ensure relevancy, accuracy, and transparency.

---

[336] Jeffrey C. Wong, Computational Causal Inference, Netflix, July 21, 2020, https://arxiv.org/pdf/2007.10979, Cited on November 2, 2024.

- Second, they are reiterating what we have been discussing, the pillars of AI are coming together in a symbiotic manner to reinforce, support, and improve predictions made by complementary approaches and pillars.

- Third, they are indicating that the long-standing data management challenges faced by specific AI pillars can be solved through the use of complementary pillars and approaches.

- Fourth, they are positing that insights from a pillar of AI can be structured in a manner as to be optimal as inputs into the next pillar of AI in a manner that seamlessly proves and extends theories and insights.

- Finally, they are postulating that certain data structures improve the ability to find insights quickly across massive data objects.

Quite a lot to be said in a single paragraph! We absolutely need all of these proposed and imagined improvements and more for AGI to become a reality.

This quote refutes the hyperbole of a few executives and futurists that we either have AGI today or will have AGI in the next few years. Again, we can use the actual work in pragmatic and functional implementations to concretely illustrate the state of play in realizing cross-pillar AI. Let's be clear, cross pillar AI, or Composite AI, is a precursor to AGI, and we cannot even see cross pillar AI being implemented on a routine basis in the short term.

This discussion on why any one of the existing pillars of AI is not *the* path to AGI could be its own book, but we must leave this topic as it is and move on to discuss some of the areas of promising development that are helping further our journey to AGI.

Impressive progress is underway

Progress is encouraging and ubiquitous, but it is hard to see where the individual points are on the continuum of progress and where those points are in relation to the related and required other points of progress. Why are these relationships so hard to see?

The number of fields involved in the overall evolution of Composite AI and AGI are vast, varied, globally distributed, and span pure research organizations, academic environments, and commercial entities. As noted earlier, relevant innovations span the following fields: quantum computing, algorithmic innovation and creation, algorithmic efficiency and effectiveness, computing hardware, data management, user interface design, data storage, data compression, computing architecture, chip design, and more.

It is rare for any person or group of people to look across all these fields of endeavor and comment on how they all come together to influence or accelerate any singular field of play or multiple interrelated fields.

To put it simply, this is a very complicated environment, and it can evolve and develop in exponential ways or directions. It is very hard to predict the direction, pace, and outcome.

Let's examine some of the areas of innovation and development that we know will impact the short- and long-term viability of both Composite AI and AGI.

Ensembles of models

In the GenAI era, we have seen that an ensemble of models or a mixture of experts (MoE) provides greater accuracy, reduces errors, and increases relevancy across all use cases when compared to any single model. This approach of using an ensemble of models is a well-established concept. I first came across this approach when I met and worked with Robert Grossman[337] at Magnify in the 1990s.

Bob developed the idea of micro models that worked well to determine the most relevant and accurate description of the actual state of data and real patterns in large data sets and databases. The idea of micro models led to the concept of multiple models working together, which led to the MoE theory of an ensemble of models being a superior approach to leveraging a single model.

What most people see as beginning in and with GenAI is related to a longer-term body of work in decomposing, connecting, federating and joining models into a powerful chain of models or an unlimited, yet fully connected, matrix of models. This is yet another example of the diversity of thought, or in this instance, diversity of models, providing more accurate, reliable, and valuable insights when compared to a singular or monolithic model.

It is quite clear to technologists and AI practitioners that ensembles of models are the future of AI. No single model can perform better than a collection of models. As a long-term evolutionary trend, ensembles of

[337] Robert Grossman, University of Chicago, https://cs.uchicago.edu/people/robert-grossman/

models are the future. It is not only models from one pillar but an ensemble of models composed of all three pillars of AI.

We have talked about Symbolic AI. We have discussed the role Symbolic AI has played in the evolution of the broader AI market. Symbolic AI has been sidelined for a couple of decades while neural networks took center stage. Symbolic AI and Neural Networks are part of the Foundational AI pillar. Foundational AI has a rift that has been festering for 20 to 30 years. It is time to put this debate to closure.

Neurosymbolic AI

In Chapter 4, we discuss the evolution of Foundational AI. We outlined that the majority of the "AI winters" were caused by the limitations of Symbolic AI. This was due to the fact that we, as an industry, tried to make Symbolic AI into something that it would never be. We overloaded Symbolic AI with tasks that were too broad and took approaches that would not scale, and the technology failed to deliver. This is not an elemental issue of technology. It is a flaw in how we applied Symbolic AI.

Also, in Chapter 4, we lightly touched on the premise that if we are to achieve AGI, then Symbolic AI would need to play a part in this evolutionary cycle. It is encouraging to see a handful of startups developing what is being referred to as neurosymbolic AI.

"...neurosymbolic AI, an increasingly popular idea that—as its name suggests—brings together the neural and symbolic approaches with the aim of getting the best out of each, in a complementary way. Many in the field draw a comparison with psychologist Daniel Kahneman's thesis that there are two kinds of thinking: System 1 thinking, which is fast and instinctive and used in perception; and System 2 thinking, which is the slower and more conscious thinking we do when we consider things and make decisions. Neural networks such as LLMs are very good at the first kind, but it may be that symbolic AI is needed for System 2–like thinking."[338]

Let's define neurosymbolic AI, "Neuro-symbolic AI is a type of artificial intelligence that integrates neural and symbolic AI architectures to address the weaknesses of each, providing a robust AI capable of reasoning, learning, and cognitive modeling which produces the effective construction of rich computational cognitive models demands the combination of symbolic reasoning and efficient machine learning."[339]

The argument between Yan LeCun and his cadre of proponents of neural network-based approaches and Gary Marcus and his symbolic approach continues, but I am hoping that this new approach to hybrid AI will diminish or eliminate these rather pointless debates.

Gary Marcus[340] has remarked, "To build a robust, knowledge-driven approach to AI, we must have the machinery of symbol manipulation in our toolkit. Too much useful knowledge is abstract to proceed without tools that represent and manipulate abstraction, and to date, the only known

---

[338] David Meyer, Fortun.com, December 9, 2024, Generative AI can't shake its reliability problem. Some say 'neurosymbolic AI' is the answer, https://fortune.com/2024/12/09/neurosymbolic-ai-deep-learning-symbolic-reasoning-reliability/, Cited on December 15, 2024.

[339] From the contributors of Wikipedia, Neuro-symbolic AI, https://en.wikipedia.org/wiki/Neuro-symbolic_AI, Cited on December 15, 2024.

[340] From the contributors of Wikipedia, Gary Marcus, https://en.wikipedia.org/wiki/Gary_Marcus, Cited December 15, 2024.

machinery that can manipulate such abstract knowledge reliably is the apparatus of symbol manipulation."[341]

Rather than trying to make either approach to AI be everything in our environments, we can use neural network-based models for what they are good at and Symbolic AI systems for what they are good at, what a novel concept. It is unfortunate that pedantic approaches and ego-driven idealism have stunted this approach for the past 30 years, but it appears that a new crop of innovators and entrepreneurs can see past the limitations of past thinking to a new way of designing and building Composite AI environments.

There are numerous other research projects, early-stage developments, startups, and more working in the general area of AI, and many of these innovations will find their way into Composite AI in the short term and AGI in the next 100 to 200 years, but we must leave this topic as it is and move on to discussing agents and their role in our journey to AGI.

Agents

We will need the three pillars of AI to achieve Composite AI and to reach AGI, and while the three are necessary, they are not sufficient. What we are missing at this point is the glue that brings the three pillars of AI together to leverage all that we have today.

We still need more functionality and capability than we have today in the three pillars of AI, but it is not clear to most what those capabilities are in a

---

[341] Marcus, Gary; Davis, Ernest (2019). Rebooting AI: Building Artificial Intelligence We Can Trust. Vintage, https://www.amazon.com/Rebooting-AI-Building-Artificial-Intelligence/dp/1524748250, Cited December 15, 2024.

detailed sense. We can see the innovations coming from academics and researchers around the world, and the pace of development is impressive. We can see what will transpire with a certain level of probability out to about five to seven years, but after that the discussion becomes pure speculation.

If we bring together disparate engines, libraries, and utilities in a practical and pragmatic manner, we can deliver a great deal of very impressive functionality and capabilities to end users today.

A number of business and technology leaders are espousing the power of agents, and that is a good thing. Evangelism of agents is needed, and people need to be aware of the direction and impact agents will have. In September 2024, Boomi CEO Steve Lucas said that the number of AI agents will outnumber the number of people in your business in less than three years. "The digital imperative is how do I work with agents? The number of agents will outnumber the number of humans in less than three years," said Lucas. "It will be overwhelming. It will be fast, and we're not prepared."[342]

I applaud Mr. Lucas for making a prediction, but I think he is on the very low end of the spectrum regarding the number of agents. Each company will have millions of agents in the future and that does not start in three years. It started last year. Mr. Lucas is right about two things; agents will definitely outnumber employees by a vast amount, and agents will arrive much sooner than people think.

It is clear that there are two primary paths to bringing together the wealth of models, functions, routines, and capabilities on offer today—through

---

[342] Larry Dignan, Constellation Research, Sep 23, 2024, Boomi CEO Lucas: AI agents will outnumber your human employees soon, https://www.constellationr.com/blog-news/insights/boomi-ceo-lucas-ai-agents-will-outnumber-your-human-employees-soon, December 16, 2024.

individual agents linked in a chain or connected together in a matrix manner or through orchestration of unconnected but well-described agents. Let's discuss both approaches.

Individual agents

Individual AI agents can be developed in many ways, but I am proposing that each agent is a self-contained piece of functionality. The functionality we see today in many agents is quite rudimentary and elemental. An agent may execute a search on the Internet, another agent may find a document in a library, another agent may compare two or more documents and provide a summary, and much more. Each agent can be connected to receive input and generate output in a stand-alone manner. While an agent is useful as a foundational element or building block, they are much more powerful when they work in concert with many other agents. Agents can be prebuilt into defined flows or into quasi-dynamic flows that work within a broader framework to solve a specific challenge.

For example, you might have a collection of agents that monitor the environment and people's actions and recognize when a compliance requirement is about to be triggered. It could be a reporting requirement, a tax filing, or a report on the results of a clinical trial phase. All of these compliance requirements have elements that are the same, and each of them has unique and different elements.

You could build a collection of agents that monitor the relevant environmental factors, dates, changes from regulatory bodies, competitive actions, and more, and when an action is required, the set of agents and processes needed for that specific compliance requirement is executed, and the filing or report is produced and submitted for review to the personnel who are ultimately responsible for filing the deliverable, and receiving and managing the acknowledgment from the compliance environment.

In this example, the agents are prebuilt and interconnected in a very specific manner. The agents and the processes are all tailored to compliance requirements. This is the optimal manner for processes and requirements in regulated industries or where specific requirements must be met in an audit setting or strict performance metrics must be met.

Let's look at a slightly different approach to leveraging agents to satisfy a recurring requirement that might vary in its process composition and delivery of results, outputs, and/or reports.

Orchestration

In an orchestration-centric approach, the agents are not interconnected in a predetermined manner. The prebuilt agents are stored in a repository. The functionality of each agent is described in a catalog. The role of the orchestrator is to accept natural language prompts describing what the user wants, monitor the relevant environmental factors, or both, and then determine when to act.

To take the same example as above, once the orchestrator has determined that action should be taken, it decomposes the prompt and/or the collection of relevant factors into actions that will be distributed to agents. Those agents will act and return intermediate or final results to the orchestrator. The orchestrator will further refine the results, assemble the final result, and return it to the user(s), or the orchestrator could determine that the results are not of the appropriate level of detail, accuracy, or relevance, or a combination of all three, and send a revised version of the augmented and refined prompt back to all agents or a new set of agents. The orchestrator can choose any agents available and direct them to execute in any sequence that achieves the goal of completing the defined task. The orchestrator can choose or can be directed to execute numerous permutations of the process until the results meet the stated objectives.

Either approach will work, building dedicated agent chain or matrices or orchestrating across a universe of agents are viable approaches. It depends on a number of factors, including the requirement for a specific process and specific agents to execute the process in a predetermined and prescribed manner or if the end result can be achieved in any practical or pragmatic manner. Also, the availability of agents and the maturity of the agent marketplaces have a role to play in how these agents are made available, invoked, integrated, and used.

Let's move on to the types of agents we are seeing today, which will be developed in the next few years. There will be simple agents, intelligent agents, and polymorphic agents. Let's outline what they are and what they can and will do.

Simple agents

We have simple agents today.

Simple agents can receive prompts from people, applications, and other systems. Also, simple agents can monitor all the relevant factors that are changing in internal systems, the Internet, human actions, and other agents. Simple agents are designed to receive relevant factors derived from multiple disparate actions or factors naturally occurring without any specific stimulus.

This is one of the impressive developments in the world of agents, being able to build agents that can monitor a massive number of inputs, developments, evolutionary cycles, and other real-time changes and, at the same time, synthesize any subset of these factors into new information.

Simple agents act when specified conditions are met, when prompted to act, or both. Single agents, predetermined sets of agents, or orchestrated agents are invoked and run. Deliverables are sent to the relevant people, organizations, or entities that need the synthesized and raw information to inform their next actions.

Simple agents act on a singular operating model—agents are prompted, a set of conditions are met, or both, and the agent executes a predetermined process and returns a result.

Intelligent agents

We are seeing the beginning of intelligent agents today.

Intelligent agents have all the characteristics of simple agents, and they also have the ability to include almost any type of model, process, summarization, synthesis, computation, calculation, simulation, optimization, and more. Any of these activities can be run in conjunction with any of the other actions and activities, and any of them can be run in an iterative, conditional, recursive, or goal-seeking mode.

Intelligent agents can include any combination of the panoply of conditions, functions, objectives, triggers, and more. Any process that exists today or that can be conceived of in the future, can be managed and run by an intelligent agent. You can see why executives, pundits, and forecasters are making predictions about the coming ubiquity of agents.

One point that you do not hear people discussing is that agents will be the forcing function that will be the direct cause of most of the job disruptions that we are about to see and experience. In my opinion, it is odd that more experts are not talking about this move overtly. No matter who is or is not talking about the job impact of intelligent agents, it will happen, and it will happen almost immediately. This transition will be called out in the press around 2026 or 2027 as an impending disaster in the job market, but it is not the case, and it will be just another instance of fear-mongering.

Intelligent agents will be the tipping point where AI will begin to replace people in work settings significantly and clearly.

Intelligent agents are an exciting development, and the evolution of intelligent agents has no foreseeable end or logical conclusion. Intelligent agents will continue to grow and evolve in capability and functionality in perpetuity.

Polymorphic agents

Polymorphic agents will arrive on the scene in late 2025 or 2026.

Polymorphic agents have all the functions and characteristics of simple and intelligent agents. Also, they will have the ability to build and extend themselves. Agents building agents are kind of mind-bending, but we are working on this now, and it appears to be probable that we can make this work.

Polymorphic agents are agents that can be given an objective and the agent software will build an agent or agents that will achieve that objective. Let's walk through an example to make this a bit more definitive and clearer. Let's use travel and booking travel as the basis of our illustrative example.

A Polymorphic agent could start from scratch with nothing more than the objective. In this case, the objective could be:

- Book a trip from Chicago to London.
- Departing on January 3rd and returning on January 8th. The flights should be at least in Business Class.

- The hotel is the Hyatt Regency near Marble Arch. Upgrade the room to a suite if I have sufficient earned upgrades in my Hyatt account.

- I want to see at least one play when I am in town, do not spend more than $200 on a seat. I do not want to see Mrs. Doubtfire. I need two seats for any play booked. I want to have a Pepsi on ice at the intermission of any play booked. Book the seats in my preferred location in every theatre.

- I want to have breakfast with the CEO of causalens. I would be happy to meet him in a location of his choice.

- Please find all the people I am having active conversations within e-mail, Teams, or any social media channel who live in close proximity to Central London. Book breakfast each day in the hotel lobby for every day that I am in London with the people I am interacting with most frequently over the past two months in priority order.

- I want to have dinner with the Fox family on January 5th; for this dinner, I will book a restaurant that the children will enjoy in the Chelsea/Fulham area.

- Book a dinner with the head of research in the AI area with the research firm BARC.

- Ensure that I have time to shop on Chiltern Street for a gift to take to the birthday celebration that we are having while in London. Block the shopping time in my calendar on the day during the trip that has the most pleasant weather.

- For all surface travel book only black cabs or a limo service. Never use Uber or Lyft.

- Use only free agents from all the approved agent marketplaces.
- My daily schedule should never have less than four meeting in one day, not including breakfast or dinner meetings.
- Do not spend more than $50 completing this task.

If the Polymorphic Agent (PA) has nothing more than the objective as outlined above, the PA will need to either search for agents that will execute the tasks and steps outlined, or the PA will have to build the agents or steps in an agent itself.

Let's discuss how the PA can find and assemble existing agents. Agents will be available in public and private marketplaces. Agents will be cataloged, described, and available for use on a fee and free basis. The PA will use an orchestrator model or an ensemble of models to break down the prompt into actionable segments that will be parsed out to agents, and the agents will return their relevant results, findings, bookings, and errors. If the PA finds that there is a segment of work where there is no agent to execute the work, the PA will build the agent and insert it into the process flow.

If the PA is instructed to build the entire process from scratch, the PA will begin with the same steps of using an orchestrator model or an ensemble of models to break down the prompt into actionable segments, but rather than searching for suitable agents, the PA will begin by searching for functions, libraries, capabilities, and possibly complete agents that can be copied, licensed, and included in the process of building the entire travel booking agent from the ground up. The PA will build the steps of the process, test the functionality, link the elements together, and keep working iteratively toward the goal of completing the objective as stated by the end user.

If the PA encounters any roadblocks, barriers, or has an uncertainty about what to do or how to proceed, the PA will ask the user for guidance.

In the future, polymorphic agents will be referred to as simply agents. All three categories of agents, as discussed, will collapse into just agents. What we consider revolutionary will become commonplace, routine, and normal daily operations, but that does not imply that agents are not a catalyzing force for change because they truly are. Let's discuss how agents will change the world.

Agents as a catalyst

In general, agents are game changers for the ability of organizations to leverage the three pillars of AI and to realize value from all of AI technologies. GenAI has made AI more accessible to almost everyone who has access to the Internet. There is a widespread belief and view that all forms of AI should be able to be used by large portions of the population for enterprise and consumer applications. There is really no technological reason why this cannot be the case. This is a matter of time, effort, and money, and it will be in the long run. In the short term, agents are the most probable technology to make all AI accessible to a broader cross-section of users in both the enterprise and consumer markets.

Agents are the technology that will make the three pillars of AI accessible to a broader audience than ever before. Simple and intelligent agents are the glue that will bring together models, functions, libraries, agents, and more. A significant portion of the value of agents will come in making the plumbing required for most applications run on a widespread and integrated basis invisible to most people. As noted, this is where the pushback will come in the evolution of agents due to job displacements.

Polymorphic agents will be yet another significant breakthrough in the AI market. Agents that can build agents will be an inflection point on how quickly agents can be designed, built, tested, and implemented across departments, companies, industries, geographies, countries, and on a global basis.

A portion of the value that agents will bring is to provide the frameworks to build agents and to have agents interoperate with each other freely with low technological barriers to integration. In this respect, agents are like fax machines. If you have a dial tone, a fax machine can connect to the network of all other fax machines around the world. Agents are the same. If you have connectivity to the Internet, there are a few other barriers for your agents to connect with and collaborate with other agents. The standard simplicity of agent connectivity and interoperation will accelerate adoption, interconnectivity, and widespread use.

Another element of value from agents is that agents provide the mechanism to incorporate context and content into the processing flow. Agents provide the ability to change the instructions relating to cost, processing speed, restrictions on which agents can and cannot be used, the tone and tenor of a response, the form and format of a response to a government regulator, the level of respect in response, the conversational style used for a particular person or a specific group of people, and much more. This aspect of agents will provide the mechanism to implement governance and control at all levels of the agent architecture and implementations.

Agents can execute any process that can be envisioned, and they can do so in almost any imaginable manner—fast, slow, expensive, and economical. Agents can respond in any way you want. Responses can be in Olde English, Farsi, Greek, Diné, Dhegiha Siouan, or any other language you need. Responses can be concise, professional, conversational, relaxed, terse, rude, or any other tone or tenor you need for the task.

Agents can tune, focus, refine, and deliver any type of result appropriate for the immediate need. Agents can also change any of these variables based on the environmental factors. The amount of customization and variability that can be handled in an automated manner is mind-boggling. If you can imagine it, you can include it in an agent that can handle the processing variability better than other technologies and, in many cases, better than a human can.

The development of agents is an ongoing process that will continue for the foreseeable future. Agents will become another layer in the AI infrastructure. Agents will be the enabling technology that enables all technology layers to interact and interoperate. Agents will be the bridge between technology and people. It is hard to understand the impact agent technology will have on the general future and the future of all AI-related technologies. Agents and agent technology will become ubiquitous and will evolve constantly. Agents will be like air, ever-present.

We now understand the technological landscape that we have today and that we will have in the coming years. Let's talk about some adjacent technologies and approaches that may impact the speed and utility of AI.

Quantum computing

In our discussion, we have not spent any time on quantum computing; that is on purpose. Many people have said that my predictions of the time of the arrival of AGI could be easily undercut or dramatically shortened by the development of commercially available quantum computing. I am willing to stick with my prediction in part because, while I am a big fan of quantum computing, reliable, accessible, and cost-effective quantum computing has always been just out of grasp in my lifetime.

I understand that there may be an unforeseen and significant sudden leap in the stability, reliability, and application of quantum computing, but that remains to transpire. I remain hopeful.

If quantum computing enables us to realize AGI sooner than my current prediction, I will be the loudest proponent and cheerleader of this momentous accomplishment. As I said, I remain hopeful, yet skeptical.

Computing hardware

Most of the computing hardware in the world today is traditional Central Processing Unit (CPU) based. With the rise and use of Graphical Processing Units (GPUs) we have a mixed environment, but it is still heavily skewed to CPUs.

Companies have been innovating in the hardware space for a few years. Experiments are progressing with neuromorphic computing, analog devices, Tensor Processing Units (TPUs), Data Processing Units (DPUs), Quantum Processing Units (QPUs), Neural Processing Units (NPUs).[343]

Beyond the core processing unit and related chip set, there is innovation in a much larger form factor from companies like Amazon with their Trainium Chip[344] set and companies "including AI chip startups such as

343 Alex Efimenko, Medium.com, February 12, 2024, 5 Types of Processing Units: CPU, GPU, TPU, DPU, QPU, https://medium.com/@alexefimenko/5-types-of-processing-units-cpu-gpu-tpu-dpu-qpu-cb28366506f3, Cited December 19, 2024.

344 Belle Lin, Wall Street Journal, Dec. 3, 2024, Amazon Announces Supercomputer, New Server Powered by Homegrown AI Chips, https://www.wsj.com/articles/amazon-announces-supercomputer-new-server-powered-by-homegrown-ai-chips-18c196fc, Cited December 19, 2024.

Groq, Cerebras Systems and SambaNova Systems. Amazon's cloud peers, Microsoft and Google, also are building their own chips for AI…"[345]

It is still early days for all of these varied hardware options. As we saw in the database market in the 1990s, up to that point in time, most people believed that relational databases were the only offering needed, and then there was an explosion of innovation that included bitmapped databased, columnar databases, NoSQL databases, and many more new architectures and commercial offerings. It appears that there will be a similar dynamic in the chip and computing market. CPUs have reigned supreme for the past 70 years, but the market will fragment, and numerous other computing options can and will be used. In the past, environments were all CPU-based. Today, many environments are GPU and GPU-based. In the future, computing environments will have a mix of numerous types of processing units and related hardware, all working together to process a varied workload. Workloads in the past were predominately based on numerical input. Increasingly, workloads will consist of numerical, voice, video, imaging, analytical, and other content that needs to be ingested, synthesized, processed, and presented to other systems or end users.

The future of computing will be quite a varied hybrid of hardware, approaches, and processing.

Is intelligence beyond data and computing?

Rob May is an AI executive, investor, and enthusiast.

[345] Amazon Staff, AWS Trainium, https://aws.amazon.com/ai/machine-learning/trainium/, Cited December 19, 2024.

Rob writes a newsletter, *Investing in AI.* In a recent issue, Rob postulated the following idea, "…we know our brain doesn't use backpropagation, the primary algorithm for training AI systems today. Backprop takes too long and consumes too much power, and our brains are much more efficient than that. …intelligence in humans evolved before written text. Somehow, we were "intelligent" before we had thousands of documents to train on, which means logically that intelligence isn't necessarily a function of more data. It raises the questions, "Is intelligence a function of structure? Is compute > data?" Intelligence may be a structural computation issue as much as it is a data issue. Different types of compute, particularly analog and neuromorphic architectures, have the ability to show breakthroughs in intelligence that are not possible with GPUs. The way I think about it is that computational structure may determine the intelligence upside potential, and data access may determine where in that band of potentiality a given system falls."[346]

Now, that is something that I have never heard before; it is truly novel and unique. Is computing and the structure of computing or the type or form of thinking a determinant of the level of intelligence that can be realized and delivered?

Does thinking, and therefore computing by association, precede intelligence and therefore take precedence over data in deriving new levels and types of intelligence?

---

[346] Investing in AI, Rob May, November 24, 2024, Questions About What Is Next For AI, If it's not "more data" then what is it?, https://investinginai.substack.com/p/questions-about-what-is-next-for?utm_source=post-email-title&publication_id=76785&post_id=152092169&utm_campaign=email-post-title&isFreemail=true&r=nocr&triedRedirect=true&utm_medium=email, Cited December 19, 2024.

This is not an argument I am aware of being made by any neural network proponent, anyone in the camp of Symbolic AI, or anyone in the GenAI or Causal AI fields; this is a really interesting idea.

Can intelligence be derived by merely thinking (e.g., computing) without using data? Can we divorce thinking from data in the human mind? Can we as humans generate completely new intelligence on our own without data?

This is something that I will have to consider deeply. On the face of it, you can easily say no, this cannot be done, but when you think about it more carefully, maybe it can.

This feels to me like one of the existential questions, nearly on par with, "What is the meaning of life?". This will be a great thought experiment that we can compare notes when we meet at conferences in the future. Ask me about this when we meet at a future event or conference.

Summary

It has been an exciting journey, and the discussion has been stimulating for me. I hope you have found the dialog interesting and possibly thought-provoking for you as well.

Let's bring this chapter to a close.

At this point in our discussion of the path to AGI, we have examined the majority of the known and widely used technologies. We can see what we as an industry: have accomplished, what we are working on now, and the vague shape of what will come in the next 100+ years.

We know that:

- Agents will be the vehicle for widespread use, adoption, and embedding of AI in nearly every process that has been built and will be built from here forward. Given that we have over 150 agent frameworks to choose from and to leverage in building our agents, we will have plenty of choice in how we deliver agents to our end users.

- The three pillars of AI are becoming Composite AI, and that evolution will take place over the next 75 to 80 years, it may even take 100 years to achieve Composite AI. There is a great deal of work to be designed, prototyped, iterated, implemented, and integrated into the technology that we have today and the technology that we will have as this process unfolds over the coming decades.

- Building the three disparate pillars of AI into a seamless, real time, Composite AI engine that exhibits instantaneous reasoning on par with the average human is a difficult challenge. I maintain that this is the most difficult computing challenge the human race has ever undertaken. I know the gravity of that statement and I stand by it.

- Composite AI is not the end of the journey to AGI; it cannot be. The Composite AI phase, while there will be innovations developed and delivered, is more about consolidating what we have built over the past 70 years into a cohesive whole system.

What we do not know, and that is pure speculation is:

- There is an evolutionary phase of AI that is beyond Composite AI.
- I am calling this new, amorphous phase, Unified AI. Perhaps Unified AI is the last evolutionary phase before the realization of true AGI, maybe not, it is hard to see what will happen in and beyond 2150. In my opinion, I can describe the developments of the coming years and possibly the next decade, but from 2150 to 2250, I am less certain.
- Composite AI becomes something new and different; we can call it Unified AI.
- Unified AI or AGI conforms to the definition that was stated earlier in this chapter.
- If the future follows the past, it is easy to say that Unified AI becomes Code First AGI and Code First AGI becomes No Code AGI.
- After that point, it is just AGI.

If this is how the path unfolds, then we will have achieved human-level intelligence in a non-human form in and around the year 2250.

Is that a good thing? That is an existential question for our future generations to ponder.

Some people want to race to this point and declare victory. That is more about them than it is about this incredible accomplishment and inflection point in human history. Some people just need to be the story and not just part of the story.

The journey to AGI is just that, a journey. It is not a race. It is not to be taken lightly. It is not something that we should just throw ourselves at without thinking or considering the impact on all of humanity and civilization. The achievement of AGI changes everything.

Are we ready for such a tectonic shift in our world? I don't think so. I am happy that true AGI is over 100 years away. We are not ready for true AGI, at least not how I define it. We need some time to get our heads wrapped around what this milestone means on a societal basis.

While technological progress is exciting and fun to discuss (for me, anyway), technology sits in the context of civilization and our society. Technological innovation has caused great progress and prosperity. It has also caused great pain and suffering. Just look at what social media has done to the world. Most of social media results have been bad for the world; social media is just a blip on the evolutionary scale of technology and society. One hundred years from now, people will look back at social media and say that it was a bad idea and really had little to no lasting effect on the world.

AGI, that is different. AGI is on a scale of impact that makes what we have recently seen with GenAI as an amusing experiment with massive data. AGI, meaning, actual human-level intelligence in a non-human form, that is a tectonic shift in everything in the world.

I maintain that we are not ready for this today. We have not set up the guardrails for how to cope with this development in our schools, our governments, supra-national governments, and more.

Of course, we will continue to develop technologies, approaches, and methodologies that will result in AGI. This cannot be stopped.

But now is the time to start a thoughtful dialog about how AGI will be governed, licensed, developed, tested, deployed, and used in consumer, military, enterprise, and governmental settings. Are you ready for an AGI to tell you why you are being denied a lifesaving healthcare procedure? I am not, and I doubt that you are either.

So, be happy that we are 100 to 200 years away from AGI. Because we have much work to do in the technology fields of data management, data synthesis, algorithmic innovation, user interface improvement, and design, and much, much more. And we have even more work to do in the areas of government, education, design of work, employment, and compensation.

It is going to be a wild ride for the rest of my career, and I am excited to be with you on this journey. I am excited to see you at the next conference or event to discuss our AI future.

Index

Printed in Great Britain
by Amazon

7e0de946-e7b1-41c4-b31e-350ce4d99626R01